As if by
Magic

The Story of Larry Bird's Indiana
High School Basketball Days

Randy Mills

Indianapolis, Indiana

As If By Magic, The Story of Larry Bird's Indiana High School Basketball Days
Copyright © 2024 by Randy Mills

Published by Blue River Press
Indianapolis, Indiana
www.brpressbooks.com

Distributed by Cardinal Publishers Group
A Tom Doherty Company, Inc.
www.cardinalpub.com

All rights reserved under International and Pan-American Copyright Conventions.

No part of this book may be reproduced, stored in a database or other retrieval system, or transmitted in any form, by any means, including mechanical, photocopy, recording or otherwise, without the prior written permission of the publisher.

ISBN: 978-1-68157-231-4

Book & Cover Design: Tessa Gunderman
Editor: Laurel Robinson

Cover photos:
Top Left - Springs Valley High School 1974 yearbook,
Top Right - *Jasper* (Indiana) *Herald*,
Bottom - Springs Valley High School 1974 Yearbook.
Back Cover - Louisville (Kentucky) *Courier-Journal*

Printed in the United States of America

10 9 8 7 6 5 4 3 2 1   23 24 25 26 27 28 29 30

As if by *Magic*

For Jerry Birge, sportswriter extraordinaire, and for all the other great sportswriters of that era who spun their tales and thus preserved the heart of the Indiana high school basketball story.

And for Tom Roach, a media artist with a big heart, who gave essential help and support at the very beginning of this writing journey.

TABLE OF CONTENTS

He loves the game of basketball
best when the game is over,
the scoreboard blank,
and he's the only soul left
up in the high-rise bleachers.
He is anything but lonely.
A janitor dry mops
the parquet floor
until it reflects ghosts.

- Ryan Mills, from his *Wonder Cabinet* poems

The sun had not yet set on Indiana highway 37 as my grandfather drove south. Our final destination was New Albany, his home. First stop: Heltonville. A sojourn of sorts. The year was 1991. I was fifteen years old and had spent the week in Bloomington at the Bob Knight Basketball School with a buddy from Atlanta. Fireflies dotted the Sunday evening lawns. Sprinklers sang out. A hoop on every dwelling.

We weren't sure where Damon Bailey lived. We'd already turned around at Stone City Mall. We passed and passed again a First Baptist Church, a Church of Restoration, and a Church of God. We had no phone. No GPS. By faith we moved. We knew who Damon Bailey was—Indiana high school Mr. Basketball, Naismith Prep Player of the Year, the all-time leading scorer in Indiana high school history—but so did the world. By the time he was in eighth grade, Damon Bailey had appeared in a *New York Times* bestseller and a cover story in *Sports Illustrated*.

Sidewinding through the hills of southern Indiana, we also drove in the shadow of another figure, Larry Joe Bird. From 1984 to 1986, Bird was the greatest basketball player on the planet. From nearby French Lick, his rise lifted a region, a state, and the banner of Indiana high school basketball. Nowhere in the world was basketball loved more. For the 1990 Indiana High School State Championship, 41,046 fans filled the Hoosier Dome. And no one player embodied this love more than Bird. By 1991 he was simply legend. To step on a court in Indiana was to step into Larry Bird's shadow.

Just when we were about to give up on finding Damon's home, an old-timer on a front porch swing pointed the way.

We grabbed our ball from the van and knocked on Bailey's front door. Wendell Bailey, Damon's late father, answered. Damon wasn't home. Like Bird before him, he was headed to Bloomington. We explained. Our request was not the first of its kind. "Sure," he said.

Standing on Damon Bailey's driveway, I took three dribbles, drew in a deep breath, and leaped to take a jump shot.

Hold a basketball. The laces give pleasure. The roundness too. We love the ball and the game for its symmetry. The clear lines and scoreboards of the game are a relief from real life that doesn't always track or traffic in such order. (The winding hills of southern Indiana do not.) But a good story, unlike a ball, should startle us. A good story, even a legend, will have bad bounces, broken ankles, wrong turns, breakthroughs, and surprises.

What you hold here is such a story.

Randy Mills tells a richly researched and reported tale with swift narration that allows a front row seat to the world of Indiana high school basketball of before. This is the world that made Larry Bird and the world he helped make. A world before consolidation. Before classification. Before online recruiting services started scouring every nook and AAU corner for kids to scout and silo. Before Damon Bailey's Bedford North Lawrence High School were the Stars, they were the Bedford Cutters. Named for the limestone quarries that sustained a people, they played a ferocious style of ball.

In their final season of 1974, the Stonecutters took on the Springs Valley Blackhawks led by Larry Bird for the regional championship.

You will find that game here in these pages. Mills brings back those players—that bruising double-team on number 33—and the crowd's roar. Mills gives us a ticket to the seasons, practices, and games that led to this moment. We have front row access to young Larry Bird's ascent. There is much to see here. A whole world.

You will hear the squeaks of the Biddy Ball courts. You will stand with a gutsy Mark Bird on the free-throw line against Milltown and watch the tears fall from his kid brother's eyes. You will see Marvin Wood, half the inspiration for Gene Hackman's character Norman Dale in *Hoosiers*, pass through French Lick. The other half of Coach Norman Dale's inspiration—Bobby Knight—stands in the back of packed gyms ever-watching too. You'll find that now extinct species, the local sports reporter, and sage Jerry Birge, who did see it all. You'll see the strategist Coach Jim Jones tighten the strings and the young Coach Gary

Holland cut them loose. You'll see the playground and stall ball. You'll see Bird given the green light. There are the drugstore coaches and the barbershop chair experts who've seen it all and would love nothing more than to tell you all they saw. Surprises live here too. A post-game telephone call to a defeated Jasper player and the head coach. But the game is the thing. A looming tilt with Loogootee awaits as the drums and the din of the Jasper gym beat louder and the fever and temperature in Corydon rises. It's all here. Mills conjures the beating heart of that now past era. All of it juices once again.

I'm biased toward the part of the state where Larry Bird played and Mills recasts here. The hoop stories from my family are here in southern Indiana. My daughter was born in New Albany, and for four years we lived there. Home, the writer Gregory Martin says, is the place we can't disappear from. For me, that's southern Indiana. We took in our share of games and Seymour Sectionals from 2009 to 2013. But that was afterward.

Now, on YouTube, you can likely find a kid in Floyd Knobs with a flinty jumper or a star in Gary going behind her back or a middle schooler with a killer crossover in Carmel. They're all a few clicks away. We're connected by technology, but more isolated, consolidated, and classified. The surprises are fewer. In the wider basketball universe, the surprise of Larry Bird was a supernova. Those universal surprises now will come from Serbia or Nigeria or a remote province in China. We'll see them on our phones.

But what was it like before, and to watch Bird first take flight? One of my favorite chapters here is "Glory," where we see the shock and wonder of the opposing coaches and players upon seeing Bird his senior season. One of the joys of that chapter, like each chapter here, is that Mills whips the ball around and gives us voices from then and now. These pages sing and are the ones I already return to. You'll have yours as well.

The jump shot in Damon Bailey's driveway? All net, I wish I could say. That might make a better story. A truer story is that the shot missed (long) and my granddad got the rebound and flipped it underhanded to my buddy Jason, who saw me raise my hand and cut to the basket and lobbed me a pass so I could hit a layup in the shadow of Damon Bailey's boyhood hoop. When the ball moves and everyone gets involved, basketball exerts its magic. A kid prodigy, Larry Bird knew this. Randy Mills, a historian with an eye toward the poetic, does too.

Jeremy Collins is a freelance writer and essayist and winner of the Pushcart Prize, with bylines in Sports Illustrated *and* Esquire. *His work has been anthologized in* Best American Sports Writing. *Collins' most recent sport essay, "When my Father Talked about Larry Bird," appears in a 2024 issue of* Esquire.

Part I:
Hoosier Hysteria

It's a trip to the moon, a ride across the heavens on a crazy thunderbolt, lightning bottled in a jug, a community gone mad.

- Tom Tuley, *Evansville Press* sportswriter

No One Saw It Coming

It seems impossible today to imagine a time when Larry Bird was known only in the small town of his birth, a skinny kid whose family was poor and Larry himself hardly noticed by the community. Sure, he stood out a bit from the time he picked up a basketball, but this was in southern Indiana, in a town where skilled young basketball players were the norm and high school basketball games were all but sacred religious events, Coke and popcorn replacing wine and holy wafers. I first laid eyes on Larry Bird before he was Larry Bird, when he was simply Mark Bird's younger brother. I attended Oakland City College in Indiana with Mark, who played there on a basketball scholarship, this at a time when younger brother Larry was on the cusp of beginning his amazing transition into basketball greatness. At that time Larry was probably a little over six feet tall and very thin. He came to the campus a few times, and Oakland City students who saw him often commented how much he and Mark looked alike. Other than that, Larry seemed like a typical shy high schooler, his eyes often cast down during those visits.

When I decided to write about Larry Bird's high school basketball days, an era I believe to be shortchanged in previous books about Larry, I started from the understanding that Bird's amazing performances were somehow unique and disconnected from what was going on around him. But writing is a journey, full of surprises. As I gathered research, found new sources of information, and put my findings into words, unexpected insights emerged.

Reading through the many articles and books on Indiana high school basketball, it became obvious that the primary emphasis of the game had always been on the communal—the love, adoration, and complete loyalty toward a particular school team by a deeply interconnected community, the stories of that school's basketball successes told and retold over the years like an ancient mythology that offered important life lessons. Bobby Plump may have scored the last-second shot in 1954 in what many consider the most famous Hoosier high school basketball game ever, but the legacy is remembered as the "Milan Miracle," and the movie *Hoosiers*, based on the event, stressed the team, the community, and the coach, items at the very heart of Indiana high school basketball. Yet there have been a few exceptions, a handful of players whose stories overwhelmed the communal aspect. Oscar Robertson, Damon Bailey, and especially Larry Bird are the best examples.

One could argue that many of the narratives of the Larry Bird story have become so fixed over time that they are all but impervious to change, locked in ice, the initial tales becoming ironclad truth guarded by a crowd of true believers. This seems particularly so when the books and articles touch upon Larry's high school basketball days, that period when Bird experienced a metamorphosis in his basketball skills and performances almost beyond belief. Previous biographers have noted, however, that part of the problem of getting down a rich and full narrative of this time revolved around Larry's concerns about his and his family's private life, leaving friends, players, and coaches who have been interviewed over the years to be extremely careful about the information they shared. It is not surprising either that Larry is so guarded even today about his story. Bird once told his brother Mark, "I really don't ever look back, and I never wonder."

Previous books about Larry Bird present little information concerning his high school basketball years. That Larry's early playing days have not been well covered is a great loss, especially when it comes to understanding what laid the foundations for his later greatness. No one appears out of a vacuum. But how to overcome a shortage of information and a "locked in ice" narrative? For me, what really broke open the narrative of Larry's early days and the communal nature of his story was my access to old newspapers, most of them unavailable to earlier writers.

I dug deeply into these sources, for I knew from personal experience how they could reset a historical understanding. When

I wrote my own high school basketball memoir a few years ago, I learned something astounding, if not disturbing from these now accessible narratives. I had been a member of a team that had experienced great success and the story was one I held close. Writing a memoir about that time and place would honor that extraordinary experience. But in going back and reading all the sports articles and box scores from that time, I realized that my recollections of those games were not always accurate. I was dumbfounded, realizing I was half right and half wrong about my memories of both goof-ups and accomplishments. Yet I would have staked my life on what I remembered.

With this realization, this new tool, I quickly went to the sports articles to validate the accounts that had been written about Larry Bird's high school games. I found, for example, that even a single newspaper box score could be a great help in understanding the dynamics of a particular game and Larry's part in it, some of these even challenging the old narratives. With new access, I had all the box scores. More importantly, studying newspaper articles allowed me to go back and talk to prior interviewees, such as Larry's coaches and fellow players, with more specific questions about particular games and incidents. These new conversations in turn led to more questions and more new insights, discoveries I was able to include in the book.

I became aware, too, while reading the newspaper accounts, of the valuable, rich, and wonderful narratives produced by the sportswriters of that day. Their work created an important framework for this book's story, their columns like time machines, offering a greater sense of the struggles and the wonders that were part of Larry's high school years, evoking the detailed textures of the sights, sounds, and smells of that era. Most of all, these newspaper accounts helped me break through the grip of the old Larry Bird narratives, revealing the powerful communal elements of family, community, competition, and coaches that helped shape and make Larry into what he would become.

I used other new and important sources in the writing of this book—high school yearbooks from the region, along with original scorebooks, shooting charts, and comprehensive team stats for Larry's Springs Valley varsity years. Another new and essential part of this book was the inclusion of many new voices, adding the contributions of other players, including those who played against him, of opposing coaches, and of the Indiana high school basketball culture that helped make Larry while Larry was making himself. These new voices add an exciting dimension and understanding to Larry Bird's story.

Finally, this book addresses the question of magic.

The colorful *Jasper* (Indiana) *Herald* sportswriter Jerry Birge may have been the first to cast Larry Bird as having magical powers, calling Bird "the Blackhawk magician on the basketball court" at the end of Larry's senior high school year. Mark Shaw, in his 1988 book, *Larry Legend*, noted that "Larry Bird appeared almost as if by magic. Somehow, he catapulted from being a decent player his junior year to being one of the finest high school seniors in Indiana history," and fellow Springs Valley Blackhawk player Tony Clark also suggested "magic" to describe Larry Bird's sudden out-of-nowhere freaky play. "I never saw him play like that before. It was like a magic wand had touched him."

Opposing coaches were just as dazzled by Larry's amazing transformation during his senior year. Larry remembered the sudden changes himself, how in games it suddenly seemed he could not miss. Of course, there were also his rising, unbelievable rebound and assist totals that glorious season and innovative basketball passes that made everyone shake their heads in wonderment. But as much as sports historians and basketball fans might wish to believe that a kind of magic caused Larry Bird to emerge from being just a solid high school basketball player in his junior year into an unbelievable superstar by his senior season, they might be wrong in doing so.

Magic suggests the instant, the supernatural, the unearned, leaving out aspects of hard work, dedication, and sometimes just plain luck that operate in real life. Thus, using magic to explain Larry Bird's extraordinary high school senior year excludes the more complex elements of detailed history, of key people, and of events that, if absent, would likely have left Larry living in rural Orange County today.

Perhaps the most significant aspect that created a sense of the supernatural was simple: no one saw Larry's greatness coming, not even after Bird's solid junior year. Take, for example, Jim Jones' leaving the Springs Valley coaching position before Bird's senior year, believing perhaps, like many local fans, that "the team would be lucky to win half their games."

Sportswriter Jeremy Collins, who read an early draft of this book, offered another take on my questioning of the magic aspect. "On the physical level, it is not so much that other observers are using 'magic' in the negative sense. It was like being hit by a wand. A gift." Collins went on to point out that the convergence of several elements that I used to frame the story is itself "a type of magic too in terms of the cultural and media pressures at work here. In many ways, the 'reframing' you are doing is in reality 'an excavation of the magic' of putting us back in that lived era, pre-cable, pre-Internet, where the legends were made. And magic resides where legend exists."

Magic or not, this much seems true: the process of Larry's rise to greatness moved rather quickly. Larry Bird himself said that he "just didn't care enough" to make any huge efforts to improve his basketball playing going into his sophomore year, trying to get out of doing any hard work at practices. The results were predictable. "I was on the B team as a freshman, but about the only time I'd get in a game would be at the end," Larry remembered. And yet, something finally clicked, maybe that little bit of magic that others talk about. I would argue, however, that it was a convergence of several elements that made Larry seem to explode onto the scene.

Although some of these important converging elements have been touched upon in the many Larry Bird biographies and in Larry's own autobiography, these accounts do not go into great depth in relating his game-by-game experiences before and during his high school breakthrough year—again, helping to create a false sense that Bird's success must have been pure magic, a belief that has persisted to this day. To address the void of information and discernment about Larry's early years, this book, using the new sources previously mentioned, explores more closely the forces that came to converge in the 1973–1974 Indiana high school basketball season, elements that include the state's and the region's powerful high school basketball culture at that time, the previously unexplored impact of county and regional high school rivalries and individual competition, the influence of Larry's two older brothers, Mike and Mark, and the essential impact of Springs Valley High School coaches Jim Jones and Gary Holland on Larry's basketball development.

That some of the above items have been given short shrift can be seen in biographer Lee Levine's argument that Larry received less high school basketball exposure in the state because "he was playing weaker teams." This could not have been further from the truth. After all, we are talking about Indiana high school basketball, and the region in which Larry and the Springs Valley Blackhawks played featured a hotbed of highly competitive teams and players, the drama of these rivalries building around county contenders Orleans and Paoli, conference foe Loogootee, and nearby big school Jasper. Many of the players Larry went up against went on to play in college at Division I schools, and the teams he went up against had long traditions of success and sparkling records.

Amazingly, for all the many articles and books out there about Larry, there has yet to be a detailed book or article written that examines in depth the story of that remarkable 1973–1974 breakout year and the years leading up to it. Lee Levine lamented this crucial void, noting, "It is ironic that the greatest player from the greatest basketball state is assigned so small a role in the state's basketball history." This book sets out to address this missing but important piece of the Larry Bird story and to place it within the context of the communal nature of Indiana high school basketball. For sure, it is a new, and in places, somewhat different angle from which to view Larry Bird's high school days. This approach, however, allows Larry's story to exist in its fullness, a story that honors and celebrates an important part of a quickly passing generation.

Bidden or Unbidden

It has been said that Hoosiers love high school basketball because it touches upon the importance of community, the Indiana citizen's devotion to egalitarianism, and a Hoosier's love of the underdog. The practice of the latter notion was apparent by the 1930s when United Press International began taking an unofficial survey every year during state tournament time to discover the "People's Choice" in state basketball tournament play. The *Muncie Evening Press* explained how this annual pick was always of a lesser known team of the smaller Indiana high schools, a team that caught high school basketball fans' fancy, one that played "the part of tournament dark horses by knocking off the bigger boys." Hoosier sports historian Herb Schwomeyer pointed out that narratives about Indiana high school basketball have long celebrated all the above values to the point of creating a cultural mythology, so that over the decades Hoosier communities of every size flocked "to their local gymnasium to cheer on their team." This communal element was so pronounced, even in Larry Bird's day, that every time teams performed in an Indiana high school gymnasium, they played before not only screaming fans but also before a gym chock-full of ghosts

These were not quiet spirits. They were terribly restless, the players, teams, and loyal fans who filled the gymnasiums down through the decades, constantly being conjured by coaches at high school basketball practices. These former players and their names were also recited by the fathers of players before a big game, at local gathering places, and at the games themselves. When Larry Bird played high school ball, a Valley fan might note a "Marv Pruett" move to the basket, call out the name of Coach Rex Wells, or mention Frankie Self's last-second layup in overtime against Vincennes. Then there were the painful moments. Ghosts that lingered most—the unexpected loss in a sectional tourney, a sprained ankle of a key starter, a missed free throw, a memory of defeat. These older elements, like the layers in an archaeological dig, must be exhumed—conjured, even—to bring clear eyes to see and understand the forces that shaped young Larry Bird. Bidden or unbidden, ghosts were always there.

One could easily argue too that from the onset, Indiana high school basketball was the most competitive, skilled, and sophisticated in the nation. James Naismith, the inventor of the game of basketball in Massachusetts in 1891, noted, after attending the Indiana high school state basketball tournament in 1925, that although the game was invented in the East, Indiana was by far "the center of the sport." The *Indianapolis News* reported that year that basketball's founder had "presented the tournament winners with the shields and emblems given each year at the conclusion of the tournament" and that Naismith had been astounded at the sheer energy unleashed at the "fast paced games." Most amazing to Naismith were the huge crowds that attended over a four-day period, a number equaling more than fourteen thousand raving fans, an enormous gathering for those days.

Such crowds were not surprising to Hoosiers. By the mid-1920s, the state's high school basketball tradition had already solidified around stories of the great teams, coaches, and players who had come before. Franklin High School's "Wonder Five" was the prime example of this legend-making process at the time of Naismith's visit, having won three straight state titles beginning in 1920. The core of the squad stayed intact after high school, playing for local Franklin College, going undefeated even while playing against large university schools and winning back-to-back the Indiana college/university championships.

So passionate was the yearly state tournament drama in March that the event came to be known as Hoosier Hysteria. The phenomenon is difficult to explain to an outsider, but perhaps The *Evansville Press* sportswriter Tom Tuley described it best in 1970 when he called it "a trip to the moon, a ride across the heavens on a crazy thunderbolt, lightning bottled in a jug, a community gone mad." But there was a history in getting to this juncture. As better roads and highways appeared and newspaper sports reporting expanded, so did the intensity of the state's high school basketball and tournament traditions. By the late 1940s, one Indiana newspaper, the *Seymour Daily Tribune*, carried a long editorial, celebrating the state's deeply rooted high school basketball culture and arguing that the game was about much more than quickly forgotten entertainment. "The first round of Hoosier basketball hysteria is over. With 779 teams in the state starting in the sectional tournament during the week and 64 have survived." Basketball in Indiana, the writer went on to say, "is something more than a high school activity. It has become a community affair. Basketball develops a community spirit that should be helpful to citizens in reaching decisions on all civic matters."

In 1949, the region where Larry Bird grew up witnessed Jasper High School's improbable journey to the Indiana state final game, an event that rocked the state's sports world. The Jasper team had ended the regular season with a so-so 9-10 record but then managed to make it up the ladder all the way to the final game of the state tournament, winning one close nail-biting game after another. The final game was the most ex-

The Franklin, Indiana, high school basketball team, a group that won three state tournaments in a row in the 1920s and whose starting five players would forever be known as the "Wonder Five."

citing of all, with diminutive guard Bob White's long field goal giving the unrated Jasper Wildcats a 62-61 state championship win over Ray Eddy's Madison, Indiana, club. A day later, fifteen thousand fans inundated the small city of Jasper to welcome back their heroes. But it was tiny Milan in 1954, with only 162 students, to be the first small school in almost forty years to win the state tournament on Bobby Plump's last-second shot against powerful Muncie Central. The unlikely win cemented the dream for every small school in the state that anything was possible at state tourney time.

Even winning a sectional, the first rung of the state tournament, was a big deal, especially for the smaller schools. A sectional championship or the rare undefeated regular season would be forever enshrined in a community, both in ongoing narratives and lasting memorials, the former taking place in the local eating places and community meeting spots, the latter in the form of a huge team photo hanging on a wall just inside the school gymnasium's main entrance. On the lowest level, certain regular season successes were almost as satisfying. Smaller schools, like the one Larry Bird attended, were typically happy

The 1949 Jasper, Indiana, Wildcats basketball team's great showing in the state tournament, including gaining the championship after a poor regular season, made them a Hoosier legend.

to break anywhere above .500 and to beat at least one of their main rivals in regular season. Upsetting a much larger school only added to a team's season success and likely secured another year of service for the coach.

As time passed, local high school basketball traditions in Indiana grew only deeper, with even the older stories—some vague, some forgotten—still lingering like the shadowy presence beneath the tip of an iceberg.

Throughout the decades after basketball's introduction to the state of Indiana, several forces continued to drive the growing intensity of the sport. One involved the media. At the height of single class play in the 1960s through the early 1970s, every local and big-town newspaper had a large sports section, often with multiple sportswriters who wrote lengthy, colorful columns about sporting events and athletes in a way that the reader would think that everything depended on the outcome of a particular game. Most Bird biographers, for example, credit the *Jasper Herald*'s colorful sportswriter, Jerry Birge, for first noting Bird's amazing play in the '73–'74 season and writing long, detailed columns about Larry's achievements long before others joined the bandwagon. Such detailed local media reports hardly exist today, but in that golden age of Indiana high school basketball, it was these sportswriters, like the bards of old, who spun the stories of teams and individuals, setting the themes and chronicling the consequences of human actions during the Indiana high school basketball season. Their rich stories and often colorful headlines ultimately helped create the wonderful legends that still softly echo in small Indiana communities today.

Newspapers certainly flourished in Larry Bird's part of the world before and during his time of growing up, their thick sports pages offering up detailed analyses of basketball contests.

But newspaper sports articles and reports were not the only force out there stirring up the Indiana high school basketball world. Local fans were always loyal and hot-headed when it came to their teams, but, conversely, quick to criticize one of

ASSOCIATED PRESS ★ UNITED PRESS ★ INTERNATIONAL NEWS SERVICE ★ AP WIREPHOTO

WEATHER TODAY
Partly Cloudy

THE INDIANAPOLIS STAR Section 1

"Where the spirit of the Lord is, there is Liberty"—II Cor. 3-17

VOL. 51. NO. 289   ★ ★ ★ ★ ★   SUNDAY MORNING, MARCH 21, 1954   FIFTEEN CENTS

MILAN WINS STATE NET TITLE

Little Milan High School's state championship victory on a last-second shot by Bobby Plump made the headlines of the *Indianapolis Star* in 1954. The team's story, forever known as the "Milan Miracle," would be a potent basketball tale even in Larry Bird's younger days and the basis for the movie Hoosiers.

their own players or coaches if they believed a mistake had been made in play or strategy. In this regard, Indiana high school basketball was egalitarian, community fans feeling like they had an important say-so about their team. And God help the official whose call may have changed the course of the game, the losing team's fans often responding in a way that required law enforcement to intervene, the winning team's fans chuckling about the call.

Of course, unique local eccentricities and a community's larger geography and history further added to the emotional level of fan support. The long narrow valley where French Lick and West Baden nestled was a rather remote area of southern Indiana, part of the Lost River region, for many years one of the poorest areas in the state. The physical landscape is one of high hills and deep valleys riddled with natural springs, caves, and unusual rock monoliths, and includes the counties of Orange and Martin, along with the northeast portion of Dubois County. In this region, Larry Bird's high school played against schools in Orleans and Paoli in Orange County; Loogootee, on the western edge of Martin County; and Jasper, the county seat of Dubois County, twenty-five miles west from Bird's home.

Although the physical landscape of the Lost River region offers a rich year-round beauty, it also suggests a dark and haunted cultural past. In fact, one does not have to look far to understand Larry Bird's own hard-headedness, confidence, and distrust of outsiders. The southern area of Indiana was initially settled

KEEPING SCORE

With Jerry Birge

Jerry Birge of the Jasper Herald was one of the many splendid Indiana sports-writers of the 1960s and 1970s who helped create the legendary stories of Indiana high school basketball and was the first regional sportswriter to sing the praises of Larry Bird in his breakout senior year.

around the early 1800s, primarily by people from the upland south, a clannish, tribal-like population who had often established strong ties through intermarriage and religious affiliations before coming into Indiana from the south. Both Larry's father's side and his mother's side came from this cultural heritage. Mostly uneducated, emotional, and fiercely proud, these upland southerners would quickly gather to protect their own in times of trouble, to the great exclusion of outsiders. Violent family feuds, outlaw gangs, and vigilante justice were frequent in the early frontier days, an Indianapolis newspaper in 1885 describing the isolated area as being "wild and broken, abounding in hills, valleys and rocky fastnesses, with numerous caves in the neighborhood to aid evildoers to hide from the light of day."

By the early 1900s, much of this violence had disappeared, and the area was opening up to the rest of the world as better roads, budding industry, and more railroads appeared. However, French Lick, West Baden, Paoli, Orleans, and to a lesser degree, Loogootee, did keep a few remnants of their frontier heritage, especially regarding aggressive loyalty to community, a trait that easily morphed into rabid support for their basketball teams.

In the mid-1890s, basketball came to Indiana through the YMCA system and quickly spread to the college, high school, and local independent team levels. Fan bases seemed to form overnight around these teams, and with the fan base came intense rivalries. Tension between sports teams and their fans ran even higher when schools were close by each other, as in the case of West Baden and French Lick, the towns where Larry grew up. These twin communities had formed around two mineral water resorts in the mid-1850s, the waters bottled and sold nationwide. French Lick called their brand Pluto Water, named for the mythical god of the underground. The resort there had a devil-like statue of Pluto, complete with pitchfork and tail, in their foyer, and the French Lick sports teams took the name Red Devils in his honor. West Baden sports teams took the nickname Sprudels, after the labeled name for their brand of "healing water," a German word relating to carbonated bubbles. The West Baden and French Lick basketball rivalry went back to the introduction of the game to the state.

This great tension would extend into the next several decades, only growing more profound. A former French Lick player from the 1950s recalled a "very bitter rivalry between French Lick and West Baden, and you didn't go to West Baden yourself—you always went with two or three guys; same way whenever [West Baden] guys came to French Lick."

Rabid followers only added to the conflict between Indiana high school teams and sometimes stirred up internal issues that divided a community. It would be an understatement to say that local Hoosier high school fans, especially those with so-

EXECUTION OF SAM ARCHER.

The Last of Orange County's Desperadoes Pays the Penalty of His Crimes.

Outlaws such as Sam Archer were common in the last half of the nineteenth century in the Orange County region where Larry Bird was born in 1956. While an extreme example, their presence suggested the emphasis in the region on rugged independence and individual confidence.

cial/economic status in a community, expected to have a strong say-so regarding their teams, including how the coach should instruct and which team members should be played. During a fan-driven basketball disturbance in Larry Bird's community in the 1950s, a Springs Valley newspaper would come to call such fans "drug store coaches," but not every fan saw this type as a bad thing. A Springs Valley sportswriter pointed out, "When a fan expresses their opinion on parts of a game or on a team, they are usually tagged a drug store coach, but I think these fans are the ones who really love the game and their team, and keep the spirit high year after year." Unfortunately, such squabbles among fans driven by the strong feelings of a few could tear a community apart.

In the winter months, high school basketball was a constant topic in almost every little diner, mom-and-pop grocery store, and coffee shop in Indiana. In Larry Bird's original hometown of West Baden, those types of places would have included, among others, Agan's Market, The Villager Restaurant, Shorty's Pool Hall, and The Pizza Cellar, across the street from Shorty's. A stone's throw away, in French Lick, there was Flick's Restaurant, where Larry's mom worked as a cook for a time; Carl Roll's Barber Shop; Brownies Service Station; and the City Drug Store, among others. At these West Baden and French Lick establishments, talk about basketball could sometimes grow hot, as there was much riding on games—bragging rights, money, and sometimes a coach's job. A coach's strategies, even when his team won a particular game, were discussed in detail, and damned or praised anywhere people gathered. In fact, more than a few school board elections revolved around getting rid of or hiring a particular coach.

West Baden, the immediate world that Larry Bird was born to in 1956, along with nearby French Lick, had long-established basketball histories and devoted fan bases. The latter community, however, with a population of two thousand, was twice as big as neighboring West Baden. As noted, the lowest prize a high school team could hope to achieve at state tournament time was to win a sectional title. Before Larry Bird's birth, West Baden had gained

The French Lick High School basketball squad in 1948. Stories of former teams such as this group were passed down to future generations, such tales perpetuating the love of basketball in small-town Indiana communities.

only a single sectional title in 1935 and French Lick three—1942, 1943, and 1946—but neither of the small high schools could gain much winning traction after French Lick's accomplishment just after the end of World War II.

Despite this lack of success in the sectional rounds of play, both communities loved their high school basketball squads. A 1950s writer in the *Springs Valley Herald* summed up that adoration, along with the sport's importance to the two communities, noting high school basketball "isn't as important as getting born, or married, or dying. But in its own line, it is important enough. It is a game paced to the American way of life: fast, hard, a happy combination of individual and team effort, a means of developing our youth in body and in spirit of clean living." The writer went on to declare the game brought together the "common interest of all, young, middle-aged, and old." Ultimately, he believed the game left fans "with light hearts. We look forward to many a jump ball, free throw, and late rally with a quickening pulse."

There was also a dark side to the basketball culture. Like other groups of Indiana small-town basketball fans, West Baden and French Lick followers held high expectations for their teams. When disappointed, they often went after the coach or harshly voiced any other factor they believed to be the cause of a bad season. The local *Springs Valley Herald* newspaper did not always help matters, as in one situation after a game going after a poor performance by a West Baden team in a front-page article in the late 1950s. "Baden's shooting was very poor and their concentration of score was really unbalanced. They'll wonder where their record went if they continue to miss the net."

A more dramatic chastisement was directed at the French Lick team when the Red Devils failed to do well in the 1955 Huntingburg sectional. Shortly after the 1955 sectional ended, the *Springs Valley Herald* carried an eye-catching front-page article about French Lick High School's dismal basketball season—"The Public Wants to Know!"—pointing out that the school had gone through four coaches in four years. The opening of the piece set the stage. "The uproar among residents

The 1950–1951 West Baden High School basketball team. The Sprudels had a sometimes bitter rivalry with close neighbor French Lick.

of French Lick that followed the very poor showing of its high school basketball team in the sectional tournament at Hunting-burg last week seems to be louder than any previous outbursts of indignation by students, parents, and fans."

The *Valley* editorial did not so much blame the coaches as it did the school administration for emphasizing seniority and scholarship over letting better underclassmen play. "It seems that scholarship rates a boy at French Lick a much better chance of being on the varsity than does ability. The material at French Lick the past few years has been better than average for a school of this size—if the better boys had been permitted to represent the school." Comments from readers about the article varied, but one French Lick high school player strongly disagreed with what the critic had said. "Yes, French Lick has had four coaches in four years but it's from your own kind of stupidity and 'Drug Store Coaches' which forces them to leave town."

One of these coaching situations would linger over the French Lick basketball program like a dark shadow, a situation that came to intertwine with the ultimate Hoosier high school basketball story.

In 1950, French Lick High School hired a twenty-two-year-old recent graduate of Butler University, Marvin Wood, to be the school's new head basketball coach. At Butler, Wood had played for Hoosier coaching legend Tony Hinkle, who preached a controlled, structured style of play that included a stall game. Wood quickly engaged his young French Lick team in this more sophisticated type of strategy, one that demanded confidence, total floor attention, and good passing.

At first French Lick players and fans, used to the more pop-ular run-and-gun style of basketball, found the game Coach Wood taught to be an issue. Hoosier high school fans expect-ed lots of motion and plenty of basketball shooting that pro-duced excitement throughout the entire game. On top of this, the French Lick players, unfamiliar with the slow-down style, found it difficult to learn and to carry out.

By the end of the first half of the season, the frustrated Red Devils had a 3-7 record, but Wood persisted. Meanwhile, a local sportswriter pointed out that the players often seemed confused, although they did not seem to be giving up trying. Apparently, at least according to the newspaper, the fans had not given up either. "To the credit of the local fans, it must be said they still show a strong faith in the abilities of the Devils and hold hopes for a strong finish and a good tournament record next year." What this really said was that Coach Wood had another year to achieve enough success to keep his job.

The next season held much promise, although not every French Lick basketball fan had bought into the delay game. Several of the local "drugstore coaches" still complained. It helped Coach Wood's situation, however, that in mid-season, the Red Devils won six games in a row. During this run, Springs Valley sports reporter Bill Wright, in his sports column, "Basket-Bawlings," argued that the stall strategy was the team's "sharpest weapon." After a win over Loogootee, Wright noted how "the Demons got rolling and built enough of a lead to go into that well known stall." At the end of the regular season, Wright made yet another positive observation about the delay game. "This stall the team uses is the most powerful and amusing thing we've seen a team of Devils use in several years. It is commanding from the word go and is hard to disrupt once it's in action. Look for it to win more and more games for us."

French Lick ended up with a 10-8 record going into sectional play, this time at the Huntingburg sectional, a school that now boasted one of the largest gymnasiums in the area, where strong sectional teams like Jasper, Huntingburg, and Winslow played. French Lick fans were excited, however, in great part because of the team's "million-dollar stall" that Bill Wright argued was used "so effectively." Wright went on to brag, "The possession game literally wrecks the opponents in the screaming closing minutes of the game."

Enthusiasm was high when the fired-up Red Devil fans filed into the gym to watch their team play a smaller school, Ireland, in the very first game of the sectional. Many believed the French Lick squad would easily win their first game over Ireland and go on to win the championship. But then French Lick lost to

Ireland, 41-37, never having a lead in the latter half of the game from which they could launch their famous stall tactic. Red Devil fans left the gymnasium more angry than disappointed.

Marvin Wood did not come back the next year to coach at French Lick. Let go, he fortunately found a job at a smaller school in southeast Indiana. There, he continued to work with his players on a stall pattern he called "cat and mouse." He took his team to the state finals in his first year there, but lost in the morning session. The next year, with his team a point behind in the state final contest, Wood signaled his players to hold the ball for four minutes as the state-final game clock wound down. Then, with the clock almost at zero and the game tied, Bobby Plump pulled up and scored the most famous basket in Indiana high school basketball history, giving tiny Milan High School a state championship over big-city school Muncie Central. Milan was the smallest school ever to win an Indiana state basketball tournament, and Gene Hackman would later play the part of Coach Wood (under a different name) in the movie *Hoosiers* in 1986. French Lick's loss of Coach Wood had been Milan's gain.

By 1955, French Lick had gained the reputation of being a tough place to coach, and for all the *Springs Valley Herald*'s passionate front-page articles about the need to improve the performance of the French Lick high school basketball team, the biting narratives did not seem to fix the problem. Two seasons later, in the 1956–1957 regular season, French Lick went 9-9 and lost in the first round of sectional play, this time to a weak Dubois team, by twenty points. Meanwhile, that same year, archrival West Baden, under the direction of Coach Rex Wells, went 11-6 and played in the Huntingburg sectional final game after beating three other very strong teams.

After West Baden's stirring sectional finish, where the Sprudels finally lost to big-school Jasper in the final contest, the *Springs Valley Herald* carried an upbeat article about the West Baden team's successes, calling the squad "Wells' Wonders." Against mighty Jasper, who would go on to advance to the semi-state, the West Baden squad "had to play with knots in their legs from the previous grueling games. The Sprudels were like a sharp knife with the polished edge taken away. How in the world these boys stood the pace we'll never know, but it does go to show what determination and plain guts can accomplish. To these boys I would like to say, and I feel all the fans in the valley will agree, we think you are wonderful, and we are proud to live almost in hollerin' distance of such a fine bunch of young men."

The editor, while more prone to root for French Lick in the past, probably had good cause to be positive about the West Baden team. Just before the sectional tournament began, a newspaper headline in the *Springs Valley Herald* announced that a group of citizens had formed a committee to examine the possibility of consolidating the two high schools.

It is an interesting coincidence that during the 1956–1957 basketball season, Larry Bird entered the world on December 7, 1956, and that the basketball traditions of West Baden and French Lick were about to end and a new basketball tradition was about to emerge. It would be by this latter tradition that Larry, and other Springs Valley players and coaches, would have their successes and failures measured. But first came the painful process of school consolidation.

The move to consolidate schools involved the towns of West Baden and French Lick, along with three township school districts. There was strong initial support for uniting the five units, citizens understanding such a merger would only increase financial stability and add a wider variety of curriculum. Soon, however, key leaders in French Lick began campaigning against consolidation, an action that aggravated the Valley newspaper editor. The *Springs Valley Herald* began blasting the anti-consolidation movement on a regular basis, claiming the group's true issue with the merger had to do with not wishing to lose their power and influence. The anti-consolidators, however, said their only hang-up had to do with the proposed new name for the school unit—Springs Valley. The French Lick leaders wanted to keep the French Lick school name.

Rather quickly, opposition to the new school plan faded,

falling like a house of cards, and it was high school basketball that greatly helped the cause of the new school movement. Fans from both towns pointed out that neither French Lick nor West Baden had been able to beat nearby Jasper, a situation that had long stuck in the craw of the Orange County folks. Nor had either team won the Huntingburg sectional for over a decade. Suddenly, with a talented crew of players under coach Rex Wells coming from West Baden, many French Lick fans saw a chance to improve the overall possibility of both a better regular season record and better tournament successes. French Lick would also be the home of the new high school when it was finished. Quickly, the new unit decided on a school name and mascot—the Springs Valley Blackhawks. School colors would be black and gold.

Although consolidation did increase school enrollment to a little less than four hundred students, Springs Valley was still small compared with several nearby schools. Jasper was over twice as large, and county rival Paoli had more students as well. The new Valley school, however, would have the third-highest enrollment among teams in the Huntingburg sectional, quite a jump.

For all the excitement about the merger, old loyalties to the former West Baden and French Lick basketball teams did reemerge and linger for a brief time. Many basketball fans showed up at the Springs Valley basketball games still wearing their old school colors: West Baden fans in blue, French Lick fans in red. Still, school and community leaders continued to plunge on at the beginning of the 1957 school year to bring the two former high schools together.

Jasper sports fans certainly kept a close eye on the new school's sudden appearance, with a *Jasper Herald* sports reporter giving the Blackhawks a detailed write-up when the 1957–1958 season started. The writer noted that the newly consolidated squad was a likely "big basketball threat" to surrounding teams and that Coach Rex Wells was blending seven of his former West Baden boys with four French Lick players. The article also picked up on major logistical problems for the Valley athletic department. The two former schools had to revamp the schedule "in order to make only one 18-game card" and "new uniforms were needed, and they could not be ordered until funds were allocated to the athletic department." Most pressing, although home games would be played in the larger French Lick gymnasium, even that facility was so small that visiting fans would be able to find only a few seats.

The day before Springs Valley's very first basketball contest against the Shawswick Farmers from Lawrence County, the *Springs Valley Herald* made an optimistic prediction. "Tomorrow night's tilt will be the first opportunity for most of you fans to see your new school corporation in action. You will see how young citizens from two communities can be molded into one bigger operation. Not only to become better sports but to become better educated as well."

It was the sports aspect, however, that quickly captured everyone's interest.

Valley school administrators tried to handle the problem of a shortage of seats for outside fans by sending extra tickets beforehand to the visiting school, thus reserving several seats. There is a story, however, that Shorty Reeder, owner of Shorty's Pool Hall, printed counterfeit game tickets for that first game and told Valley buyers to get there early. When the fans from Shawswick showed up, the French Lick gym was already packed full of rowdy Springs Valley fans. That situation was just the beginning of Shawswick's problems.

The Jasper sports reporter had been correct about the Blackhawks being a big threat in the region. The Valley team blasted the Shawswick Farmers 55-40, with Marv Pruett, a West Baden boy, hitting 50 percent of his shots and garnering twenty-one points. The Bedford *Times-Mail*, however, referred to the winning squad as the French Lick team, likely adding fuel to any fire that might have lingered from the merging of the French Lick and West Baden schools. All that animosity was blown away forever in the team's next game against the Jasper Wildcats, which the previous season had advanced all the way to the semi-state round of the fabled Indiana state tournament. Valley led the Wildcats at every quarter stop, with Butch Schmutzler joining Marv Pruett as a co-leading scorer.

After these two sweet victories, Jim Ballard wrote a front-page article for the *Springs Valley Herald* with the big banner headline "New School, New Yell, Two Games, Two Fell." Ballard's narrative simply gushed. "The kids and nearly all the grownups in this community are just plain tickled pink. The consolidation in our schools has the folks in the valley hoppin' and poppin'." The writer noted that after Valley beat Shawswick, the victory over Jasper "broke a twenty-three-year record when they whipped the Jasper Wildcats Tuesday night 45-38. Until Tuesday night's defeat, Jasper boasted of not having lost an opener for twenty-three years."

Ballard also went on to praise the Springs Valley school band for their playing at intermission during the game with Jasper, although the band had yet to get new black-and-gold uniforms that reflected the two schools' merger. Nevertheless, "The members seemed to take a different air with consolidation and performed with snappy movements."

The excitement continued. Valley's third straight win brought yet another front-page banner headline—"Sprudel + Pluto = Dynamite!"—along with another enthusiastic sports editorial by Jim Ballard. "The Hawks, who have developed into a bundle of dynamite, are creating a panic in the Valley. The panic of which we are speaking is the mad scramble for tickets to see those touted young men play this highly regarded Indiana sport." The writer also tossed in a hit at the French Lick leaders who had opposed the school merger at the beginning of the process. "Who would have thought just one year ago when the Citizens Committee started the job of consolidating the two schools of our community that the outcome would be so great,-so soon. Not only in the sports world, but it has given the children new hope, new life, a new school."

Perhaps the most interesting portion of the narrative was a prime example of how a Hoosier newspaper writer could bring basketball immortality to a team, the coach, and its star players in one single, colorful article:

There can be but one answer to the success of the Black-hawks. The credit belongs to Coach Rex Wells. There are very few men around our community who could have taken a bunch of boys, who just one year ago were rivals, and mold them into one smooth working machine. When we say smooth, we mean smooth. If you haven't seen Bob McCracken run his arm an elbow's length above the hoop for a rebound, then you haven't seen anything. If you haven't seen Butch Schmutzler and Marvin Pruett stop, spin and throw in a two-pointer on a fade-away jump shot, then you haven't seen anything. If you haven't had a glimpse of little Frankie Self, then fans, you are just not a basketball fan. He is a bundle of dynamite all by himself.

Led by Marv Pruett and company, Springs Valley just kept winning basketball games—on through the entire regular season. After winning the Huntingburg regional in state tournament play, they were named "People's Choice" by the United Press. The Noblesville *Daily Ledger* declared, "Springs Valley is the most talked about team in the Indiana high school basketball tourney today. Springs Valley is not only undefeated this year but, having just been formed this fall from French Lick and West Baden schools, it can boast of never having lost a prep basketball game in Indiana." After winning at the semi-state level, the Blackhawks were finally defeated in the morning session of the four-team state finals by Fort Wayne.

For the Springs Valley Blackhawks and the two communities the team represented, the season was a Hoosier high school basketball fairy tale come true. Ironically, the amazing success of the team, its twenty-five-game win streak and state finals play, would cast a great shadow, a tough yardstick by which all Blackhawk teams would now be measured.

Coach Wells was the first coach impacted by the team's late-1950s accomplishments, and this in a positive way. After losing only two games the next year in regular season play and losing in the finals of the sectional to Huntingburg by a heartbreaking single basket, Wells moved on to coach at a bigger school. Hav-

Marv Pruett, leader of the Springs Valley team in 1957–1958, set all-time and single-game scoring records at Springs Valley that stood for fifteen years until Steve Land, "the forgotten Blackhawk," came along in 1973, Larry Bird's junior year.

ing a less sterling group of returning players for the next year may have prompted the move, but the new position was also a step up to a larger school.

Given Rex Wells' amazing record in that two-year stretch, Valley school board members faced a monumental task in finding an equal replacement. Adding to this was the difficulty a new coach would face after Wells' successes. Regarding the latter point, Jim Jones, who began his coaching career at Springs Valley in 1960 working with eighth-grade and freshman teams, believed Springs Valley, by the early 1960s, was a tough place to coach any way it was cut. "There was always criticism when Valley lost, and we always had a very strong schedule playing Washington and Jasper early and coming off football season. It was usually Christmas before we were really healthy. Of course, poor coaching always added to the mix."

Marvin Wood's success at Milan, after being let go at French Lick, also brought out an astute observation from a newspaper reporter in Bedford about coaching success when it came to Indiana high school basketball—"There's a lot of luck in coaching."

Finally, the school board members did find someone they believed to be a strong candidate to replace Wells, a handsome young man who had been an Indiana high school All-State performer in both basketball and football, Gene Flowers. He certainly possessed the right Hoosier basketball pedigree. In high school, Flowers had started on the powerful Muncie Central basketball squad, being on the playing floor at the 1954 state final game when small-school Milan's Bobby Plump coolly put up a last-second shot that shocked the Indiana high school basketball world. Flowers went on to play basketball at Indiana University. Valley school leaders were sure they had found a winner. One later Valley coach in the system remembered that Coach Flowers preached the run-and-gun style of basketball play, a kind he had known at Muncie Central and at IU, but "Springs Valley lacked the athletes to play this kind of ball." Flowers only broke even over the next two years, although he did help produce a fine shooter, Jack Belcher, who tied the single-game scoring record of thirty-nine points in 1960 that would last for over a decade. Belcher went on to Louisiana State University after graduation to play for the Tigers, who played tough Southeast Conference competition. As for Coach Flowers, perhaps Valley's record-breaking loss, 97-60 to Jasper in the 1961 sectional, led the novice Blackhawk coach to move on to a job at another school.

After Gene Flowers' exit, Rex Wells, a West Baden native to begin with, returned to Valley to coach, doing a bit better than Coach Flowers had, ending up at 12-8 at the end of the 1961–1962 season. Then, to everyone's shock, Wells stepped away from coaching to become the high school principal, announcing his retirement from coaching before the 1962 basketball season began. That move once more left Springs Valley administrators and school board members scratching their heads, wondering who they might find to lead the Blackhawks back to glory. What made that process even more difficult was captured in a *Jasper Herald* article, a report that suggested a solid, established coach from another school might look twice before taking the Valley job. "Springs Valley," the paper explained, "will lose more players via graduation than any other Huntingburg sectional coach. Eight of Valley's first ten are seniors." Most fans and coaches in the Valley school system, including Jim Jones, expected the choice of a solid outsider, one with strong past successes.

Winding Them Up and Letting Them Go

Jim Jones grew to become a gifted Indiana high school basketball coach, respected by those who played for him and those who played against him. In a Louisville *Courier-Journal* sports piece when Jones was at Springs Valley, one regional coach spoke of Jim's simple but effective tactics. "His teams play it slow, move the ball around and wait for you to make a mistake on defense, then they go in and score. They're the type of team that won't beat themselves; they make few mistakes." Another area coach, when asked what kind of season the Springs Valley basketball team might have that particular year, offered a more picturesque description of Jones' coaching. "They are always so fundamentally sound. Coach Jones just winds them up and lets them go."

Larry Bird, in his autobiography, *Drive*, recognized Jones as being his primary teacher when it came to his learning the fundamental skills of basketball. "Jones is the man I have to thank for drumming basketball fundamentals in my head. He taught me every basic maneuver there is and once he would show me something, it would just seem to click in my mind." Among many other things, Jones taught the young Larry Bird to use reverse pivot moves, to box out to get rebounds, and to use his left hand as well as his right to double movement possibilities. At times when Larry was in high school, the coach seemed all but omnipresent, always coaching, forever giving helpful tips. "Jim Jones was always around, showing us something." Larry came to discover that when Coach Jones said to try something to improve a basketball skill, "it worked." In short, one could argue that had there not been a Coach Jones, there might not have been a Larry Bird.

Interestingly, the details of Coach Jones' early career, the stories suggesting how he came to his own coaching insights in training players and in game strategies, skills that powerfully guided Larry Bird, are not well understood. Part of this void of knowledge may stem from one of Bird's own perceptions about Springs Valley teams of the past that he shared in his autobiography. "The first year they merged the high school in West Baden and French Lick into Springs Valley in 1958, the basketball team went all the way to the Indiana state finals. After that we didn't have much of a basketball reputation." Larry Bird's downbeat view about what followed the 1958 championship year may have discouraged later sports historians from researching deeply into Coach Jones' accomplishments. Thus, this period deserves some scrutiny.

The time between the 1958 state tournament season noted by Larry, and Coach Jones' last year he coached at Valley, Larry Bird's junior season, spanned fifteen years. During eleven of these years Coach Jones served as varsity coach. Jones' Blackhawk teams won five sectionals, including three in a row, and a regional title from which the team advanced to the semistate. Jim's always tough squads also frustrated bigger teams like Jasper at every turn. So well, in fact, did Valley perform in the Huntingburg sectional during Jim's tenure that one Jasper

Springs Valley starting five at the 1958 state finals.

sportswriter suggested it had been a powerful group of Jasper folks pulling strings in Indianapolis, where the Indiana High School Athletic Association (IHSAA) was headquartered, that got Springs Valley moved to the Paoli sectional in 1970.

Great coaches also produce players who are college-level material. In Jones' case, he had Blackhawk players recruited at all the college levels of play, including, among others, Vincennes University, Oakland City College, Hanover College, Indiana State University, and SEC's Louisiana State University.

In Larry's defense regarding his negative assessment, he was the first to admit he paid little attention to basketball traditions on any level. He told in his autobiography that he had watched only one college basketball game on television when he was younger and hardly went to high school varsity games until he played as a sophomore on the junior varsity. Meanwhile, Jones would, in fact, carve out a solid career at Valley, to the point where he was able to move on to bigger schools when he was ready, but the road to his achievements was far from easy and not without one major heartbreak.

OOLITIC BEARCATS

Larry Bird's most influential coach, Jim Jones, is pictured in a 1954 photo of the Oolitic, Indiana, high school Bearcats basketball team. Jim is number 54 on the front row.

Springs Valley Set to Pull a Milan in IHSAA's Big Show

Jim Jones grew up in the little town of Owensburg, Indiana, in the eastern hills of Greene County. Despite growing up in a very rural area of the state, Jim was indoctrinated more than most young kids into Indiana basketball. His father coached basketball at Owensburg High School for a short while in the 1940s, leading a team nicknamed the Indians, although sportswriters often humorously referred to the team as the Burgers. The school was one of the smallest schools in the state.

Jones retained many deep memories of the Owensburg gym, the one in which he first played basketball, remembering it as antiquated and small "with potbellied stoves and wooden backboards." Jim loved the game, and having access to an indoor gym enabled him to play year-round. When Owensburg High School closed around 1948 and the Owensburg kids were sent to Oolitic, Jim still went into the old gym alone, whenever he could, to shoot around — the empty space, the soft, seeping sunlight through dusty windows, offering peaceful seclusion.

There was another factor that turned Jones on to basketball. Jim started high school at Oolitic in 1954 during the heyday of Indiana University's "Hurryin' Hoosiers" era of play, IU having won the national basketball title the year before. Living close to Bloomington, Jones was able to go to IU games, where he got to experience not only the red-clad, screaming fans, filling him with excitement, but also the college-level coaching tactics. Jim's own high school basketball career was exciting as well. By his sophomore year, he was starting on the Bearcats junior varsity squad, and in his junior year he played sixth man and sometimes started for an Oolitic team that won a sectional, a very rare occasion in the sectional dominated by big school Bedford.

After high school, Jim went to IU, where he hoped to participate in the sport he loved most, baseball. "I might have eventually made the team," he recalled, "but I did not have any encouragement, so I gave it up." Baseball's loss was Indiana high school basketball's gain. Graduating in 1959, Jones, who held a degree in business education and PE, began beating the bushes for a job. That next fall, a former IU classmate contacted Jones and told him he was leaving his position at Springs Valley and there would be an opening. In the fall of 1960, Jim was hired at Springs Valley to teach business classes and coach the eighth-grade basketball team. He was also made the school's basketball scorekeeper. An early picture of Jim Jones in the faculty section of the Springs Valley school yearbook shows a boyish-looking man wearing a big smile, a smile that suggested he was there for the students. But that same big smile belied the intensity Jones brought to coaching.

Jones did not ride a player or holler at them. He truly enjoyed helping youth of all ages become good at the game, having started and worked in a Biddy Basketball program in the Valley area for young grade school kids. He was someone who easily became a positive father figure for any boys who were missing out on having a strong and helpful older male in their lives. But these features were often not enough to guarantee successful high school coaching seasons. Coaches at smaller schools had to become great students of the game to be successful, lacking the many solid players year after year the big schools had. Fortunately for Springs Valley, Jones was a natural coach.

Coach Jones broke down all aspects of the game. There was, for example, his "ten ways to shoot a layup, and thus a shot for every occasion." He also preached to his players the essential need to work hard on being able to go to the left or right when dribbling to the basket, this skill giving the offensive player an advantage over the defender, "making the defender uncomfortable rather than the other way around and putting the offensive player in control." Jones also worked to know his teams' strengths and weaknesses and those of his opponents. If the other team had a greater number of strong players, his team "had to hide," that is, slow down the game and work on lots of good passing, taking only good shots and making few mistakes. In the end, however, Jones knew that success came not so much from how hard one played in a game as from the intensity a player was putting into practice sessions and at working at shooting skills while not in school.

During Jones' first two years at Valley, he moved quickly through the coaching ranks, from eighth-grade and freshman basketball coach to the assistant varsity position in the 1961–1962 season under Rex Wells. The fact that Jones had more responsibilities than most assistants can be seen in a *Springs Valley Herald* article just before the 1961–1962 season began, the report noting that Jim was "using calisthenics and drills, emphasizing various fundamentals to round the charges into playing condition."

Only high school players, coaches, and student managers of that day would understand the sensory pleasures of those first season practices, the sound of gym shoes squeaking on the wooden floor when a player made a sharp cut, the feel of summerlike sweat in the early fall, the smell of resin put on hands and feet to keep them dry, and the astringent slap to the nose of the balm the student manager rubbed on sprained ankles.

At the end of the '61–'62 playing year, Wells made his unexpected move out of coaching, becoming the principal at the high school. But that wasn't the only surprise. Before the Springs Valley school board members could argue among themselves about what successful high school coach they might snatch away from another school, Wells shocked the board members, the community, and Jim Jones by insisting the young novice assistant coach be hired for the vacant varsity basketball coaching position. Wells had good reasons for his decision.

As eighth-grade coach of the "Little Hawks," Jim Jones was always able to come up with great season records, including an incredible 18-2 season. That year his young charges beat an exceptional Jasper eighth-grade team in the regular season. Valley then went on to sweep through the prestigious sixteen-team Jasper Grade School tournament, the sixteen-team Loogootee Grade School tournament, and the Orange County Grade School tourney. So successful were Jones' eighth graders that even the *Springs Valley Herald* began posting front-page articles about the team, along with photos. In one report, the article noted, "The little Hawks, under the tutelage of Coach Jim Jones, did an outstanding job in all departments that led to victory. They displayed a lot of finesse and ability in rebounding and floor play, along with a deep desire to win for their coach and school." Larry Bird could have easily explained what finesse in rebounding was all about. Coach Jones, Larry reported in *Drive*, "hated it when we failed to box out on the boards."

There was another plus for making Jim Jones the head man at Springs Valley. If Jones was made varsity coach, he would be working with the same youths who had played so well for him as eighth graders and as freshmen, giving him an advantage over any outsider coming in to coach. To Wells, it was a no-brainer. Jones wasn't so sure. While aspiring to become a head coach, he also knew he was young and untested at the varsity level in an immediate region that was thick with excellent veteran coaches—future Indiana Basketball Hall of Famers like Jack Butcher

Coach Jones began his very successful coaching career as eighth-grade coach at Springs Valley.

at Loogootee, Sam Alford at South Knox, and Guy Glover at Bloomfield, to name a few. Then there would be big-school Jasper to think about, always waiting early on the schedule and looming again in the Huntingburg sectional. "Jasper always made me fearful because of their pride. I never saw a community that had so much pride," Jones remembered. Nor did the Springs Valley community's expectations lighten the load, Jones recalled. "Valley fans expected us to be up every year, just like 1958." Finally, if Jones took the job, he knew he would have few upperclassmen to work with, the previous year having seen the loss of eight seniors. Perhaps Jones realized he was going to take the job when his main thoughts quickly turned to how a coach might build the upcoming Valley team around Lonnie Ziegler, a promising six-seven senior who seemed only to get better with every practice. Jones decided to take the job.

In early November, the *Springs Valley Herald*'s Sports Corner column reported on the upcoming 1962–1963 basketball season, how the fans were "anxiously awaiting" the Blackhawks' opening game with the Huntingburg Hunters. "Valley coach Jim Jones," the article explained, "will be fielding his first varsity game." The fact that the Blackhawks would be playing in their new facility, a sunken-floor-style gym holding almost three thousand fans, only added to the excitement.

Jones was surely nervous, knowing a first game, even if lost, could still set a positive tone for the rest of the season if the team played well and played its opponent close. What Jim could not change was Valley's previous season record, a reasonable 12-8 campaign. This accomplishment, while modest, would be the initial benchmark by which Jones would be measured. On the other hand, there was also the likely chance that Valley fans would cut a first-year coach a little slack, but wins against perceived weaker teams and victories over archrivals such as fellow county schools Orleans and Paoli were almost essential. A win over nearby Loogootee or Jasper would be cream. After the regular season, sectional play would be yet another arena where Jim Jones' accomplishments would be severely scrutinized.

There was one last element. Whatever pressures were to

come from the local drugstore coaches, Jones had a coaching philosophy that set him apart from most, one that took time for fans to understand and accept. "To me," Coach Jones recalled in an interview, "the regular season games were exhibition contests that helped us prepare for the state tournament. I did not mind losing a few games in a season if we learned something that we could work on to get better."

Jim Jones' inaugural high school coaching game against Huntingburg was a mixed bag. Playing at the Valley gym, the Blackhawks took an early lead and were ahead at the end of the first quarter. Huntingburg eked ahead and led by one point at halftime. In the second half, Springs Valley hung tough, but the Huntingburg squad was able to build a small lead in the third quarter and then went into a slow-down game. The Hunters won the contest by seven points despite Lonnie Ziegler's solid performance.

Things grew worse. Jones' team lost their next four games—to Washington, and to two rivals, Loogootee and Orleans, and to Winslow by a single point. Finally, the Blackhawks beat Pe-

Jim Jones' first high school varsity team, the 1962–1963 Springs Valley Blackhawks. Jones would have great success there and at two larger schools, eventually being inducted into the Indiana Basketball Hall of Fame.

tersburg, and four games later, managed to defeat Orleans in a holiday tournament in three overtimes. More losses than wins followed.

Jim's squad did beat county rival Paoli by a basket but was clipped by Jasper in a close game in the next to last contest of the regular season. After the Paoli tilt, the drugstore coaches seemed to come out of the woodwork. The *Springs Valley Herald* sports column noted how the majority of fans second-guessed Jones' last-second shot strategy, the fans thinking the always dependable Ziegler "would be set up for the final shot under the basket." Instead, Jones went with Jeff Reynolds. When Reynolds set to shoot, he was a great distance from the goal, causing more than one Valley fan to let out a groan. When asked about this after the game, Jones patiently explained to the sports reporter that Reynolds "was the shooter in our out-of-bounds play. The only thing being the shot was supposed to be closer to the hoop." Fortunately, Reynolds hit the last-second basket and Valley won.

The Jasper loss finally pricked the bubble of Valley fans' growing frustration about a lack of wins. In the last two minutes of play, and with the Wildcats ahead by a single point, Valley's six-seven Lonnie Ziegler was called for his fifth personal foul. An explosion of boos erupted from the Valley side of the gym, a few fans becoming vocal, calling the referees names and making threats. After Ziegler's exit, Jasper pulled away to win by five points in what had been a nail-biting game, but the agitation among Blackhawk followers continued even as people left the gymnasium.

The next day the *Springs Valley Herald*, in a front-page editorial, blamed the embarrassing action of some of the Valley fans on "John Barleycorn" (drinking) and warned that such behavior might jeopardize the team in the future, causing the IHSAA to bring a sanction against the school. Such was the situation as Jim Jones watched his first regular season of coaching draw to a close.

Jones had little time to digest his team's 5-15 regular season exploits, the Huntingburg sectional looming on the horizon. He knew he needed a strong run in the tournament to stay ahead of the Springs Valley naysayers, which meant at least making it to the final game. Such a run seemed highly unlikely. An Evansville sportswriter wagered that only Jasper and Huntingburg had a real chance of winning the Huntingburg sectional, with Dubois and Ireland cited as dark horses.

Jones and his players, however, were about to catch a little bit of lightning in a jar.

The draw for all the Indiana high school sectionals took place in February and witnessed Springs Valley drawing St. Ferdinand in the first round of the Huntingburg location. The Crusaders had more wins in the regular season than the Blackhawks, but the Valley squad had posted a seven-point victory over Ferdinand in the regular season. Whichever team won the return game at the sectional would likely face favored Jasper.

Coach Jones breathed a sigh of relief as the Blackhawks walked off the Huntingburg gym floor after gaining a 78-67 win over St. Ferdinand. Meanwhile, in the same bracket, Jasper trounced tiny Birdseye. Valley fans could hardly wait for the Springs Valley/Jasper rematch. The game, however, turned out to be anticlimactic, Springs Valley leading the entire game and winding up smashing the Wildcats in a 72-59 victory that was oh so sweet. Lonnie Ziegler tallied thirty-three points in the win, and the Blackhawks took the easy victory on some amazing sniping. Valley shooters, in the words of the Jasper sportswriter, were "hotter than a $5 pistol."

The Blackhawks had no time to celebrate. They would play small-school Ireland the next night in the finals of the Huntingburg sectional. The Spuds were on cloud nine, having had a great regular season with fifteen wins and only five losses, and were hungry to win their first sectional. But there were many doubters. Ireland's schedule had been made up of small schools like their own, and the Spuds started five players, all of whom stood at only five feet nine inches tall. They were, nevertheless, amazingly quick and possessed great court sense, and their guard duo of Dave Small and Joe Lents may have been the best pair of guards in southern Indiana that season.

Springs Valley began the championship game as cold shooting as they had been hot shooting the day before, missing all eleven of their attempts from the field in the first quarter while making three free throws. But not much damage was done to the Valley team, as the Ireland coach decided in the first quarter to play a slow-down game to counter Valley's height advantage, a tactic they continued throughout the game until halfway through the fourth quarter. An *Evansville Courier* reporter noted that during the prolonged stall, "Dave Small displayed his dribbling ability to the dismay of the [Springs Valley] crowd." The score was 8 to 3 at the end of the first period and 9 to 8 in favor of Springs Valley at the half. In the second half, Springs Valley had the lead a few times, but surprisingly, played a slowdown game as well. When the final horn sounded, Ireland led by one, 20-19.

After the game, the Springs Valley dressing room was as quiet as a tomb, the air so thick with what might have been that it was hard to breathe. Many years later, Dave Small recalled how the Springs Valley game did not unfold the way the Ireland team thought it would. "Our plan was to slow it down because Valley was so much bigger than we were. I remember wondering why Springs Valley was taking their time on offense too, and not trying to open it up and run. So, with both teams slowing the game down, there wasn't going to be much scoring. They ran off as much clock as we did." Jim Jones later told Small the reason he slowed the game down on his end was that he did not think the Blackhawks could run with the Ireland squad because Lents and Small were too quick and fast. Small realized that the game "stuck in Jim's mind for a long time." Jones, for his part, would always berate himself for not having had his team unleash a full court press. Luckily, getting to the final sectional game was enough for the Valley coach to keep his job.

The next day, the low score of the contest caught the eye of state sports reporters, the *Indianapolis Star* observing, "Just about everything stood still but the clock at Huntingburg where Ireland outlasted Springs Valley." But then the Spuds' amazing run after winning the Huntingburg sectional, all the way to the semi-state level, would become another Indiana high school basketball legend. The people at the *Springs Valley Herald*, however, were so downcast at the outcome of the 1963 sectional that the paper failed to carry any details of the Ireland/Valley game, other than to give the score.

After 1963 sectional play was over, Coach Jones had a few things of his own to mentally unpack, perhaps including painful thoughts of what might have been had he only changed a decision or two. As the *Jasper Herald* pointed out, "The title game was so close all the way that the team that made the fewest mistakes would be the one that would carry off the hardwood prize." Jones, meanwhile, would be in a no-man's-land of uncertainty until the next season progressed and the win/loss ratio started to reveal itself. He could not have known the mountaintops and the low valleys that awaited him.

It is hard to imagine what kind of life Larry Bird would have had if Jim Jones' coaching had been absent from the equation. As one early *Sports Illustrated* article suggested, without all the converging elements that came together in Larry's early life, he might have been "pumping gas or working in the Kimball piano factory" like many other young men in French Lick. Yet, Coach Jones' part in Larry's story could certainly have been absent had Jim not put together a solid year in his second season of coaching, a task that looked bleak as that season started. Gone was six-seven Lonnie Ziegler and several other senior players. The *Jasper Herald*, perhaps happy with the circumstance, reported Coach Jones would have only "two seniors on the 10-man varsity squad." Fortunately, Valley's first game was an overwhelming victory for the Blackhawks as they took out Huntingburg by almost twenty points. The next contest, however, was a loss to rival Loogootee by almost twenty points. These two game outcomes set the tone for Coach Jones' second year, a back-and-forth win/lose rhythm, with more than twice as many losses as victories.

Toward the end of that tough season, fans grew disgruntled

after an embarrassing loss to lowly Shawswick, a team that had not defeated Valley in several years. After the win, the Shawswick fans "responded to the victory as if it were a sectional championship win," running out on the floor and carrying the winning coach off on their shoulders. Some Valley fans that night thought their team did not seem ready to play, but Coach Jones put on his best face in a Valley newspaper piece the next day, noting, "Every team has one night during the season that nothing goes right, and everything is off, and Friday night was it."

Lee Levine—in his study of *Larry Bird, The Making of an American Sports Legend*—captured perfectly the very tough kind of situation Jones now faced: "In Indiana, everyone thinks he's a coach because he either played basketball or studied the game." In that atmosphere it was not "unusual for a high school to have four or five and sometimes as many as seven coaches in a ten-year period." One of the winningest high school coaches in the state, Howard Sharpe, noted in a more personal way, "You got to win, the wife can't even go to the store if you don't win."

Just in the nick of time, the Blackhawks won their last two regular season games by wide margins, one of them a satisfying romp over Jasper. But these last two important successes left the Blackhawks with a record only one game better than the year before.

Although no one publicly or privately told Jim Jones that he would be fired if he did not do well in tournament play, Jones felt this was the case. Looking at the February draw for the Huntingburg sectional, the Springs Valley coach could see he would have to win four games to gain the championship. The good news was that Valley would not meet tourney favorite St. Ferdinand until the title match, if at all. Like the Ireland Spuds from the year before, the St. Ferdinand Crusaders had a once-in-a-lifetime team and were picked by many to take home all the marbles at Huntingburg. At 18-2, the Crusaders had already beaten every team in the tourney during the regular season, except for Jasper, whom they had not played. If this weren't enough push, the Crusaders were highly motivated by another reality: they had yet to win a sectional.

Midway through the season, the Crusaders had clipped the Blackhawks by three points in a nip-and-tuck battle. The five starters for the Crusaders had all played together the year before, and by the time the 1964 sectional rolled around, they operated like a well-oiled machine. Lee Joe Werne was their outstanding shooter, but any of the other starting players—Jim Werne, Bill Hagedorn, Dennis Oeding, or tall, broad-shouldered Fred Drach—could score. Jim Werne, for example, had iced the regular season game against Valley by coolly stroking in six straight free throws in the closing seconds of the contest. As the 1964 sectional tourney approached, fans in the small town of Ferdinand were about to explode with excitement, understanding their team was one of those small-town basketball squads that seemed to come along once in a generation, a team that might be able to go deep into the state basketball tournament. Meanwhile, Coach Jones knew that only a deep run by Springs Valley into the state tournament, an unlikely scenario, would save his job. In the Blackhawks' favor, the team had eight players—Charles Harris, Warren Owens, Logan Ballard, Jeff Reynolds, C. B. Charnes, Dick Royer, Keith Worthinger, and Ronnie Collins—who continued to listen to their coach and worked extra hard on learning to play good defense, to take good shots, and to not throw the ball away. The team won their last two regular season games, indicating to Jones that they were really starting to jell. Jones told no one about his sudden sense that this team was destined to do something great.

One factor that was beyond the control of any coach when sectional tournament time came around involved the bracket setup of sectional games. In mid-February 1964, six teams received a bye in the Huntingburg sectional—Ferdinand would match up against big-school powerhouse Jasper in the second round of play, while Dubois faced Ireland and Birdseye would go up against Winslow on the second night as well. Teams without a bye included Springs Valley, who played Otwell in the tournament's very first game. The winner would go on to play one of two other non-bye teams, Holland, or Huntingburg, in the second round. This meant Valley would have to win four tough games to win the championship. Slowly, through sectional week, playing out the brackets, Springs Valley and Ferdinand battled their way toward each other.

In their opening game, Springs Valley was nervous. They allowed a much less talented Otwell squad to keep a substantial lead in the contest until the game's final stages, the Millers, according to the *Jasper Herald*, throwing "a giant scare into the favored Blackhawks for three quarters." But Jones' prior intense training of his Blackhawks crew in regular season practices had prepared the Valley team not to panic. They just kept pecking away, playing their game, and won the contest. Ferdinand, meanwhile, suited up the next evening against tradition-rich Jasper in the Crusaders' first contest. The Crusaders won easily, Ferdinand's very first-ever victory against big-school Jasper. Ferdinand fans were ecstatic and grew more rowdy and excited as the tourney progressed. The Crusaders beat Dubois in a much tougher game to advance to the sectional finals. The Crusaders basketball team now stood at 20-2.

After beating Otwell, Springs Valley had to overcome Huntingburg and then the Winslow Eskimos to get to the final game. Beating Huntingburg was a walk, but Winslow, like Otwell, hung tough through much of the game. A Jasper sports reporter asserted Valley "was not nearly as polished" as the Winslow five and that the Eskimos' Jim Marshall simply "dazzled" the fans. Out-dazzled or not, the well-coached Blackhawks managed to get a solid lead in the fourth quarter and then slowed the ball down, forcing Winslow to foul and winning the contest by ten points on free throws.

The stage was now set for what would be termed by the *Ferdinand News* "the most exciting final game in Huntingburg sectional history." St. Ferdinand High School fans could all but taste a sectional championship, and the school teachers got little done during sectional week, allowing the students to prepare for a huge pep rally the day before the final game with Springs Valley. A giant banner hanging on an end wall of the St. Ferdinand gymnasium summed up the attitude of the school and community, their hope for a first sectional championship: "THIS IS OUR YEAR." But the Springs Valley team and community had its own urgent motive for winning the sectional tourney, and had an honest banner been hung in the Valley gym, it might have said "SAVE OUR COACH."

The next day the *Evansville Courier* would call the St. Ferdinand/Springs Valley double overtime game "heart-stopping." For one team, it was heartbreaking. The *Ferdinand News* reported the contest in detail, an almost complete play-by-play narrative, beginning with how "a capacity crowd of 6,246 screamed and cheered for their favorite team as the lead changed hands 22 times and the score stood even 15 times." A Jasper sportswriter was more picturesque about the amazing closeness of the contest, asserting, "The championship game was as close as pages in a book." Excluding Valley fans, most of the attendees likely rooted for small-school Ferdinand.

Big Fred Drach, standing six-six, got the opening tip for Ferdinand, but Valley stole the ball back and scored the first basket of the game on a Jeff Reynolds field goal. Then Jim Werne and Tom Ruhe scored for the Crusaders, bringing every Ferdinand fan to their feet in one breathtaking motion, rising and letting out gym-shaking cheers. But Springs Valley quickly responded, taking a small lead, giving the Valley fans a reason to go wild. After a quick Ferdinand time-out, the Crusaders surged back into the lead. Fred Drach's basket ended the first quarter, his field goal pushing the Crusaders ahead 20-17.

The lead changed hands eight times and the score was tied five times in the second period, leaving the score knotted at halftime 34-34. Ferdinand scored first in the third quarter and never trailed in the period. At one time the Ferdinand squad took the longest lead of the game, 47-40. Fred Drach, playing his best game as a Crusader, including making ten out of eleven foul shots, did much of the damage.

At the end of the third round, Ferdinand hung on to a slim 56-52 lead. The final quarter of regulation play was a carbon copy of the other three quarters, the lead going back and forth so quickly, it strained one's neck watching the scoreboard. Then, with just over three minutes left in the game and Valley leading by a single point, ace Ferdinand player Bill Hagedorn fouled out. The *Ferdinand News* reporter called Hagedorn's loss "a stinging blow." Drach came back, however, with two free throws and a goal for Ferdinand, and just like that, the Crusaders had the lead. Valley regained a one-point edge until Crusader Dennis Oeding hit a free throw to tie the game 70-70 in the last seconds of regulation play.

Valley got the ball as the first overtime began and ran a delay game. Ferdinand got back the ball but was unable to score, and Warren Owens put the Blackhawks ahead with two free throws with sixteen seconds left. The *Ferdinand News* reported, "Seven seconds later Fred Drach saved the game for Ferdinand with two free throws," ending the first overtime with the teams tied 72-72.

Springs Valley's cool, steady play, their lack of mistakes, all forged in Coach Jones' tough practices, finally prevailed. Throughout the game, the Blackhawks shot well from the field and super well from the free-throw line, hitting twenty free shots in a row in the second half. The boys from the valley led the entire second overtime period, winning 77-74.

The day after the loss, the *Ferdinand News* lamented how close the Crusaders had come to winning the sectional, a win "just a heartbeat away." But the article also reported the team's amazing accomplishments—a first-time conference championship, a holiday tournament championship, twenty-two wins against three losses, a team season scoring record, and a new individual scoring record gained by Lee Joe Werne. The piece ended by noting how the Crusader squad was escorted home by "Town Police, State Police, and the Ferdinand Fire Department" and that "Strangers in Ferdinand would have thought the Crusaders had captured the sectional crown when the team and their coaches returned home Saturday night and were greeted by the entire community of basketball fans who showed their pride in their Crusaders and coaches for a tremendous effort which ended just a heart-beat away from victory." Only in Indiana.

Even after the amazing sectional windup, Jones had yet to feel safe about his coaching employment. Sitting down after the sectional win, he figured his team would have to win the regional and then the semi-state and advance to the state finals to break even for the year. Jones, his fingers crossed, began getting his Blackhawks ready for the regional tournament.

The Huntingburg regional featured four schools, two of which — the Loogootee Lions, at 19-4, and Bloomfield, the favored team at 20-3 — had already soundly beaten Springs Valley in the regular season. Valley played the North Knox team in the first game, however, so Jones knew his team would have to contend with only one of the other two teams. Jones also realized the Blackhawks had now put together six strong games in a row, including the last two games of the regular season, giving him confidence that his team was peaking at the perfect time. The North Knox game proved this to be true, as the Springs Valley players kept their cool even as the lead changed fourteen times. With less than a minute left in the contest, the patient Blackhawks had a scoring explosion, including eight straight free throws, cruising to a 72-60 victory. Loogootee took out the favored Bloomfield team in the second game with an even easier conquest, 84-69.

In the final game of the Huntingburg regional, the gym was packed beyond capacity. Coach Jones spent the pre-game locker room time calming his troops, but in his own mind he knew he needed another almost flawless game from his team against Loogootee, the Lions being directed by a basketball strategist as sharp as Jones, Jack Butcher. Jones' troops delivered. The Blackhawks shot at a .600 clip for three quarters against the Lions and then went into a controlled game that made the Lions have to foul. The final score was 89-64 Valley.

The Springs Valley team, coming into tournament play with only six wins, had done the unimaginable, winning the Huntingburg regional, leaving the Blackhawks standing with only fifteen other Hoosier high school teams going to the semifinal level of play, the old Sweet Sixteen. Valley was also the smallest school left in the tourney.

The Valley community went wild, loving every minute of it, the local newspaper carrying the headline "WE'RE THE GREATEST—WE'RE THE KINGS" after the improbable sectional win and "THEY SAID IT COULDN'T BE DONE—THEY DID IT—HAWKS STILL SOAR" after Coach Jones and his team took the regional.

Southern Indiana sports reporters, on the other hand, were dumbfounded after Valley's regional victory. An *Evansville Courier* writer observed, "An underdog from the start of the sectional action a week ago, the team from the French Lick-West Baden area has, in the words of young Blackhawk coach Jim Jones, 'Made each tournament game its best one.'" An *Evansville Press* writer, Tom Tuley, was even more perplexed. "A month ago, most experts figured Springs Valley couldn't have beaten a team consisting of four midgets and a cheerleader. It's no joke now." Almost all the tournament victories, the reporter went on to say, "were considered upsets, for Loogootee and Ferdinand, and nearly everyone with a basketball beat Jim Jones' Blackhawks during the season. There's no logical way to figure out how or why. It wouldn't be any fun if you could."

Seymour ended the Blackhawks' dream run in the first round of semi-state play, 86-71, but even after the game was over, Jones knew he'd have his job at least a little longer. The sportswriters knew this to be true as well. The *Evansville Press*, in an article headlined "Jones Isn't Gone Yet," reported, "An impeccable source said officials notified Coach Jim Jones late in the season that his contract would not be renewed next year. Then Jones' Blackhawks won their last three regular season games and pulled upsets throughout the sectional and regional tournaments to gain the Sweet Sixteen for the second time since 1958."

In truth, Jones had spent a great deal of his coaching capital working to perfect the method of using the regular season to prepare his teams for tournament play. It was a strategy not likely to have been initially popular with the fans. But his style took hold as the sectional wins accumulated. Over the rest of the decade, Springs Valley basketball teams under Jim Jones' direction would dominate the Huntingburg sectional, winning the prize three more times after the 1964 victory, in 1965, 1966, and 1969, much to the chagrin of Jasper. Jones' overall record in those Huntingburg years would be four titles with sixteen wins and three losses in overall tourney play. It was probably Valley's domination of the Huntingburg sectional that, more than anything else, kept Jones his job and made him a fixture as the Springs Valley coach.

One Bedford sports reporter captured well Jones' unique coaching style, noting his teams were often without individual stars, but always seemed to have several players who contributed to the team's winning. "The Hawks play a pressure defense with Coach Jones using as many as seven or eight players to keep everything going." The 1969 sectional championship at the spacious gym in Huntingburg would be one of the sweetest for the Blackhawks. Valley came into the tourney that year with fifteen regular season victories and proceeded to easily mow down Jasper, Dubois, and a 17-3 Holland squad. After Valley's sectional triumph, Jones told *Jasper Herald* sportswriter Jerry Birge, "This was one of the most satisfying wins of the season. It is always very satisfying to knock off two teams like Jasper and Holland to win the sectional."

Unknown to Coach Jones, trouble was brewing.

Up in Indianapolis at the Indiana High School Athletic Association headquarters, the group that directed high school tournament play, wheels were turning, and not in Springs Valley's favor. Although the exact reasoning behind moving Springs Valley from the Huntingburg sectional to the 1970 Paoli sectional will forever be shrouded in darkness, there were those who believed some of the Jasper elite used their influence to make it happen. Jerry Birge, a big fan of Coach Jones and his accomplishments, however, pointed out another powerful reality in his sports column. "We've suggested the switch the last two years due to the fact Paoli is just a few miles down the road and Huntingburg is a good twenty-five miles along a curving, dangerous road."

Jones was disappointed, to say the least, although everyone,

including Jones, would have bet money Valley would more easily dominate the Paoli sectional than they had at Huntingburg.
But the move messed with Coach Jones' comfort zone, the competition at the Huntingburg sectional having always factored
into his overall basketball season strategies for almost a decade.
In an interview with sportswriter Jerry Birge, Jones shared his
feelings about the move. "We hate to be leaving Huntingburg
because we have always enjoyed participating there. There is no
tourney around compared to Huntingburg. The atmosphere is
great, and we have gotten to know the coaches, fans, sportswriters, and broadcasters. We feel we are leaving behind the best
all-around competition you can find at the sectional level."

But Birge, like other coaches and sportswriters in the region,
believed the Valley coach would be placed in an advantageous
situation at Paoli, "moving into a tourney with considerably
less competition. The Blackhawks will have a shorter trip for
the tournament, but they are not jumping with glee over leaving the Huntingburg tournament having had uncanny success
there." With great confidence, Birge went on to predict, "Teams
assigned to the Paoli sectional this year will quickly learn about
Valley's tournament success story." Coach Jones, apparently not
a student of the old Greek myths centering on hubris, agreed,
telling Birge at the end of the interview that the Blackhawks
would bring to the Paoli sectional "the best schedule, the second biggest school, and without a doubt, the most basketball
tradition." Jones added, "We should be the favorite or co-favor-
ite every year at Paoli."

As far as Jasper's fate after the change, the Wildcats went
on to win five consecutive sectional titles in the 1970s, with
good-riddance to the Blackhawks.

The 1969–1970 season found Jim Jones attempting once
more to wind a team up and let it go. He had a veteran crew
back from the Huntingburg championship team, two of them,
seniors Rex Willoughby and Greg Charnes, having started for
the Blackhawks since they were freshmen. The regular season

again ended at 15-5, but the Blackhawks just as easily could have been 17-3. The Hawks beat Loogootee, a team destined to go to the state finals that year, and a highly ranked Bloomfield squad, and got past the Paoli Rams in that school's holiday tournament. The Rams, however, were able to turn the tables on Valley toward the end of the season, winning in an overtime at Springs Valley, 53-50. This Paoli victory set the stage for a new level of rivalry between the Orange County neighbors.

The Rams finished an up-and-down regular season at 13-7 but had a nice streak going as state tournament time approached, having won their sectional two years running. An Evansville sportswriter caught the buildup of tension between Paoli and Springs Valley as sectional play drew near. "A new face but an old rivalry confronts the sectional here, as Paoli and Springs Valley prepare for a showdown." Rams coach Mike Cooper was excited by the upcoming collision, telling the reporter, "After we beat them the last time, our kids are ready to beat anyone." Cooper went on to explain how the win against Valley at the end of the regular season was "a morale builder for us."

Jim Jones' last hurrah at the Huntingburg sectional in 1969. The next year Valley was moved to the Paoli sectional. Sophomore, Mark Bird, sits on the bench to the far left.

Meanwhile, as the '69–'70 regular season ended, the *Evansville Courier* rated Springs Valley "one of the best teams in southern Indiana," predicting they "should not have any trouble" winning the Paoli sectional and "reaching the regionals." Jerry Birge at the *Jasper Herald*, agreed, writing, "Watch Orleans and Paoli if you wish, but watch the Hawks cut down the nets."

These sportswriters probably were not closely following the end of the regular season. Jim Jones' team suddenly found itself struggling, losing three of its last four games.

Normally, Jones had his players at top form at the end of the season and ready for state tournament play, but the overtime loss to Paoli on Valley's home floor and then the surprise two-point loss at the Blackhawks' last game against Brownstown, a team Valley had blasted earlier in the year, likely eroded some of the team's confidence. Regarding the latter contest, a *Jackson County Banner* sports piece even suggested Jones had been outcoached for a change. "Springs Valley had downed Central by 24 points in the regular season, but Brownstown came back with a new style of play and turned the tables on the Blackhawks."

Ever the tactician, Jones also fretted about Springs Valley's draw in the upcoming sectional at Paoli, where both his team and the Paoli Rams were placed in the same bracket. Jones also believed that playing times could make an important difference, telling a Louisville *Courier-Journal* reporter, "The arrangement of teams doesn't make that much difference, but you do have to consider the position—whether you play Wednesday or Thursday or the first or second game Saturday. Those are significant factors." He then told the reporter he was afraid his team "was in a slump" after the Blackhawks barely beat Orleans in their opening sectional game. The coach's words turned out to be prophetic.

The Blackhawks were almost without fail deadly at the free-throw line, thanks to Coach Jones' emphasis on his players shooting lots of free throws in practice, but not in the game against the Rams. The closely contested battle was tied at the end of three quarters, 38-38, Valley hanging in only by virtue of their field goal shooting. Paoli, however, pulled away in the final quarter, beating Springs Valley in a semifinal game, 61-48. Valley players, coaches, and fans left the gym in silence, completely stunned.

The next day the *Springs Valley Herald* sports page called the game "a sorry loss" and took argument with the Rams' head coach, who claimed that Springs Valley lost the game because of Paoli's great defense. "It didn't look that way from where we sat. The Hawks outscored the Rams by 8 points from the field and any other day, as they have proved through the year, they could have hit those free throws." Tiny Milltown, with ninety-seven students, then beat the Rams in the championship contest. The Millers, led by Jerry Conrad, would advance to the semi-state that year.

The Springs Valley team and their coach took little solace in the Rams' loss to small-school Milltown in the sectional final. The thrashing Paoli had given the Blackhawks was more than a defeat; it was an embarrassment, a catastrophe. Coach Jones had been quoted in the Jasper paper the year before saying that Springs Valley would likely dominate the Paoli sectional for years to come and the Blackhawks entered the sectional play with a great record. But Coach Jones soon had a larger issue with which to contend—only two sometime starters would be returning the next season. One was a six-two skinny blond kid whose last name was Bird and whose first name wasn't Larry.

Number 33

Every major biography of Larry Bird touches upon his difficult early life of poverty, his parent's eventual divorce, and his father's alcohol issues. Lee Levine in particular frames his book about Larry by constantly referring to studies showing how an alcoholic parent often causes their children to desperately seek ways outside the family dysfunction to give them a sense of control in their unpredictable environment. The family dynamic that has been missed, however, by Levine's work and others is a detailed account of how influential Larry's two brothers, Mike Bird and Mark Bird, were on Larry's rise to basketball greatness. Mark's own high school and college career offered Larry a clear example, a road map to follow in times of youthful difficulties.

Joe Bird was home on leave from the army when he married Georgia Kerns in September 1951. The couple could not have imagined how quickly their lives would be filled with children. In five years, Joe and Georgia would produce four heathy babies. Mike Bird was the first born, followed less than two years later by Mark. Linda came next, and then Larry, born on Pearl Harbor Day in 1956. Two other sons, Jeff and Eddie would follow over the next ten years.

The Bird family lived in West Baden at this time, the most predominate force in their lives being a lack of money. Their difficult financial situation, however, was not much different from what many families experienced in hilly Orange County, Indiana, one of the poorest counties in the state. As Larry noted in *Drive*, "I know we didn't have money, but it didn't seem as if anybody else did." Nevertheless, Larry said, "Money was always an issue in our lives." Later, when Mark Bird received an athletic scholarship to play basketball at Oakland City College, the family got their first glimpse of a possible way the cycle of poverty might be broken.

Joe and Georgia Bird's first four children - Mike, Mark, Linda, and Larry - are shown in this photo taken around 1960.

Sports quickly grew to be the center of the three young Bird brothers' lives. Long before they were involved in organized high school sports, sandlot baseball, basketball, and football kept the three brothers out of trouble and filled their lives with activity. "There was never a day," remembered Larry, the brothers didn't do something involving sports.

Initially, baseball was the sport the three most loved to play, but the birth order situation might have seemed unfair to Larry at first. When he was around five and six, he began pushing to play baseball and softball with his older brothers, but because of his young age, he was not allowed to be a regular player with all the older boys around. And when Larry did finally get to play some, his older brothers showed him little mercy, "constantly trying to beat me at any sport we were playing" and making light of his mistakes. It was tough, unbending competition. Mike and Mark were solid athletes in a culture where many young boys worked hard to be the best they could be at any sport, and they never let up on little brother Larry. "If I was up at home plate, they would pitch harder to me than anyone else," Larry remembered.

But the difficult and extreme competition among the brothers likely caused Larry to work that much harder, desperately hoping to catch up with Mike and Mark someday.

As the two older Bird brothers moved into early adolescence, they played on a host of Little League– and Biddy Basketball–type sports teams in the Valley area—baseball, basketball, and football. Georgia and Joe Bird were surely glad these kinds of sports activities were available, because they burned off excess energy and kept their sons out of trouble. It was also an inexpensive endeavor. At this point in time, what they did not plan on was the adoration their two oldest sons' participation in high school sports would bring to the boys and to the family.

The family's circumstances also suggested the difficulty the Birds faced not only in their struggle to get by but in how they were sometimes viewed by others. Georgia once shared in a *Sports Illustrated* interview, "My kids were made fun of for the way they dressed. Neighbor boys had basketballs or bikes. My kids had to share a basketball."

Her boys being good at sports would come to help soothe some of that sting.

Levine noted in *Bird: The Making of an American Sports Legend* how the high school basketball culture of Indiana permeated every aspect of the state's small-town communities. "Only religion and the economy rival the influence that basketball has over most communities across the state." The situation caused communities to start grooming players early. Coach Jones, for example, had established a Biddy Ball League for fourth, fifth, and sixth graders "to give the kids a basketball when they're in the low grades." Like any endeavor that ranked highly in a community, status soon became involved, and for a poor family like the Birds, a son's achievements on the basketball court, bragged on even more in the local newspaper, gained community recognition. This surely brought the Bird family to hold their heads a little higher when they were out and about in French Lick.

Oldest brother Mike was the trailblazer for the Bird boys in high school sports, his name popping up on the *Springs Valley Herald* sports page whenever he scored a touchdown in football, got a base hit or a home run in baseball, or let go "a pretty shot" in basketball. Mike was quiet, wore glasses, and sometimes revealed a sweet, shy smile. The first mention of his sporting talents in the local newspaper involved his being the leading scorer for the Springs Valley eighth-grade basketball team in 1966. Later, Mike got noticed in the local paper for his football skills, catching a sixty-yard throw for a touchdown in one instance. His best achievements, however, were in baseball, where he was the team's leading hitter his senior year, making the elite Jasper All Regional baseball squad at the third base position. The *Jasper Herald* reported that against the powerful Jasper team, Mike "had two of Valley's three hits, including a double, drove in one of their two runs and scored the other one himself." But Mark Bird could knock the leather off the ball too.

Larry's oldest brother, Mike, suited up for a Valley basketball game. Mike was an accomplished high school baseball player, too, being chosen for the All-Sectional and All-Regional baseball teams in 1969.

In the Bedford *Times-Mail*, the two brothers were mentioned in the same breath, Mike Bird singling "to score his brother, Mark."

During the 1968–1969 and 1969–1970 basketball seasons, both Mike's and Mark's names began popping up in the basketball sports reports in the local newspaper. After a victory over a Bloomfield squad, for example, a reporter described Mike Bird's "two incredible shots from either side of the basket." In another article, one that must have thrilled the family because it involved a game against rival Jasper, the *Springs Valley Herald* reported how Coach Jones, upset that his starting five had let the Wild-cats grab an early ten-point lead, "went to his bench and insert-ed Mark and Mike Bird who sparked a Valley comeback that saw them cut Jasper's lead to one, 23-22, with 3:58 remaining in the first half." When Mark Bird scored a basket close to the end of the first quarter that put Valley ahead of the Jasper Wild-cats, Blackhawk fans rose to their feet and cheered. Although Valley ended up losing to Jasper, Georgia Bird would be getting plenty of positive comments about her boys at her job for the next few days.

The Bird family, along with the rest of the Valley community, would see both Mike's and Mark's photo with the Springs Valley varsity basketball team just before the Paoli sectional in 1970, Mark standing in the middle of the top row and Mike sitting in the bottom row. This photo was flashed across not only news-papers in French Lick but on the sports pages of Evansville, Jas-per, and Bedford newspapers.

There were other positive sports reports about the brothers. After Springs Valley's embarrassing loss to Paoli in the 1970 sectional, the *Springs Valley Herald* noted, "Mike Bird, who came into the game late, was one bright spot for Valley as he made some mighty fine rebounds and chalked up some pretty field goals as he played his last game of his senior year." Some-times a sports announcer would get the two brothers mixed up, as seen in one newspaper report of a Valley game. "When the P. A. system announced that Mike Bird was starting the game, the announcer, like many of us, mixed up the Bird boys' names. Mike did get into the game later. It was Mark who was the start-er. Both boys turned in good games." Mark scored seven points that contest, and Mike "hauled down 8 rebounds," the second most by a Valley player.

It was obvious that hardworking Mike Bird was a sentimen-tal favorite of both fans and sportswriters. At the end of his senior year, Mike received the Attitude Award at the Springs Valley basketball banquet and had his picture featured in the newspaper. Mark Bird, a junior that year and a sometime start-er who had averaged almost ten points a game, played even better than Mike, performing at a level a couple of notches higher than his brother. And Mark would be back the next year, eventually gaining his own special place in the Springs Valley High School basketball tradition. Because of Mark Bird's impact on his younger brother, Mark's rise to Blackhawk glory deserves special attention.

"If anybody in our family appeared to be heading for a career in basketball," said Larry Bird in his autobiography, *Drive*, "it was my brother Mark." Like any classic second born, Mark probably worked extremely hard to find a place in the crowded family and in the bigger world of the West Baden/French Lick community. And being good at high school basketball in Indiana certainly offered a ticket for Mark to receive such positive recognition.

As Mark grew older, he participated in the various sports leagues available, doing well at football, baseball, and basketball. A football injury eventually took him out of that sport, and he concentrated on baseball and basketball. As noted, basketball offered the fastest path to local high school sports fame, and even regional recognition. A player who performed a memorable deed in an important game, like scoring the winning basket in the last seconds, would likely be remembered in ongoing basketball narratives that were told and embellished over the years at local community gathering places, especially around tournament time. In fact, becoming part of the rich tradition of high school basketball in the valley would be an epic event for a young man in that part of the country, especially one from a poor family. The competition was fierce. After all, only five players could be out on the floor at a time.

Mark's natural skills and his hard work paid off. He was suiting up for varsity play by his sophomore year, although he mostly played on the junior varsity squad and rarely got into a varsity game. He was typically the leading Blackhawk scorer in the junior varsity games, one *Jasper Herald* reporter noting he scored sixteen points in a loss to the Jasper Kittens. This would have been an in-between time for Mark, his chances for greater success still unknown. He did, however, receive an important distinction, one that quietly spoke about his joining the small exclusive varsity group. Now he would be wearing a permanently assigned numbered jersey the rest of his varsity Springs Valley playing days—number 33.

It must have been very exciting for Mark Bird and his family that next year, as Springs Valley players, fans, and Coach Jones carried high hopes for the 1969–1970 season. It had to be assuring too to know that Valley had an even better chance of winning the Paoli sectional than they had expected in Huntingburg, or so the thinking went. Before the Blackhawks' first game, Mark was listed in the Bedford paper "as a returning letterman," the next-to-the-last name of a long list of possible players. The list was in fact a verbal ladder that Mark Bird soon began to climb.

The Blackhawks came blasting out of the blocks in late November 1969, swamping big-school Washington 80-47 in their first match. Orange County rival Orleans fell next, but in a much closer game, 64-60, with Mark Bird picking up four points, a clue that he had finally gotten into a varsity contest. In the next tussle, with North Daviess, Mark had eight points and older brother Mike Bird three. Then seventeenth-ranked and undefeated Jasper came to Valley, and the gym was packed beyond capacity.

It was a nail-biting, seesaw type of battle, a contest in which the Bird brothers were mentioned together in a sports page narrative for the first time. They were sent into the game where they "sparked a Valley comeback," shaking things up and turning the game around for at least two quarters until the stronger Wildcat team brought the Blackhawks back down to earth, winning 66-58. The next day thirteen-year-old Larry could not have missed the exciting talk around the Bird household about his two brothers being mentioned in a regional newspaper. But even better news was yet to come.

Mark Bird's big breakout games occurred in a situation where he would get even more hot publicity, at the four-team Paoli Holiday Tournament midway through the season. He came off the bench in the first game and scored twelve important points in a win against Brownstown. In the championship victory match against archrival Paoli, Mark Bird started and copped fourteen points, all on field goals.

Mark just kept getting better. Starting again, this time against Shoals, Bird shot a sizzling 73 percent and ended up the team's second-leading scorer with seventeen points. Valley was now 7-1 for the season, and excitement about the team grew throughout the valley. Then Mark's hot season turned cold. Valley continued playing well and Mark Bird continued to start, but his scoring pace, except for the Blackhawks' last two games in their regular season, fell off considerably. Bird ended up averaging ten points a game. In the bitter loss to Paoli at the 1970 Paoli sectional, Mark went scoreless.

At the beginning of the 1970–1971 season, one local newspaper sports reporter from Bedford assessed the chances of the Springs Valley team, noting the Blackhawks had lost several strong players from the 16-6 season the year before and that the one returning three-year starter, Jeff Willoughby, would likely lead the team. Mark Bird, who was now a senior, was mentioned in passing as one of three returners with a year's varsity experience.

Coach Jones knew he had a weaker crew than the year before and honed in on beating Valley's main rivals in the regular season, Orleans and Paoli in Orange County, Jasper over in Dubois County, and, to a lesser degree, Blue Chip Conference foe Loogootee. Jones also explained to one reporter that although he loved to beat Paoli and Orleans, "a win over Jasper just about makes a season in basketball." Defeating the Wildcats, however, would be a daunting task, as they were highly rated in the state.

The 1970–1971 season turned into a roller-coaster ride. The Blackhawks won their first game against a tough Pekin Eastern squad, 54-49, then ran into a buzz saw against the Washington Hatchets, 74-59. The only good news after the loss to the Hatchets was that Valley had discovered a new shooting star. Mark Bird blistered the nets with his "steady pumping" of long, accurate jump shots for twenty-three points. In another contest a week later, a newspaper reported how Mark broke the game wide open "by hitting five straight field goals, giving Valley a 10-0 edge at the beginning."

It is interesting to note at this point how sports articles so often mentioned Mark Bird's shooting form—crowd-pleasing, high-arching tosses, often taken from far out and from either side of the goal, shots that almost always went in. Fans would hold their breath between the snapped release of the ball from Mark's slender fingers and its perfect drop through the basket. It would be just such a shot that younger brother Larry Bird would later perfect by his senior year in high school and go on to thrill college and NBA crowds with. Mark continued to be the top scorer for Valley in the regular season for most of the games, with sophomore Steve Land and senior Kevin Carnes helping as well. As Coach Jones hoped, the Blackhawks beat rivals Orleans and Paoli, but they got pounded by Loogootee. Against Jasper, rated number six in the state at the time of the contest with Valley, the valiant Blackhawks lost a heartbreaker, leading by five with just three minutes left, only to lose by a single point in the very last seconds in Jasper's packed gymnasium. It was a game most thought Jasper would easily win. The extreme level of Hoosier high school basketball hysteria at the Jasper/Valley struggle was noted by one sportswriter who explained, "The fans were

Mark Bird's hard work on improving his shooting made him one of Valley's best players. He would have a profound impact on younger brother Larry's basketball development.

so noisy with the aid of some drums that it was almost impossible to hear the referee's whistle. At one time four boys (2 Hawks and 2 Cats) were still battling away at one end of the floor and the referee had to go tell them he had whistled the ball out of play at the other end of the floor." Jerry Birge at the *Jasper Herald* reflected on how the contest "was a disappointing loss for Valley who played near-perfect basketball."

Mark Bird had an outstanding game against Jasper, scoring sixteen points, grabbing eight rebounds, and passing out four assists. He scored a basket with nine seconds remaining that put his team ahead by two. Then after Jasper scored two, Valley was inbounding the ball under their own basket. Everyone in the gym thought the ball would come to Mark. Instead, it was passed in to sophomore Steve Land, who had already scored twenty points. Land was fouled during his shooting attempt and made one of the foul shots to put his team ahead by one. Then Jasper's Manley scored the winning basket on the other end as time ran out.

Harry Moore, reporting for Orange County's *Paoli Republican*, was more intrigued with the upset that Springs Valley almost pulled off against the number-six-rated team in the state. "This is the best played Hawk game seen since the regional of a couple of years ago when Valley defeated New Albany. The Jones-men did it all this game. They out-hustled, out shot, and out rebounded the Wildcats." Moore was most mesmerized by Coach Jones' leadership. "Words cannot describe the superb coaching tactics of Jim Jones," Moore asserted. But it was a bewildered Jasper fan's comment to Moore after the game that really caught the reporter's attention. "We just can't understand it, how Jones can lose most of his players and keep coming back with a team like this."

Mark Bird's great shooting only got better, as captured in articles about the Blackhawks' victories over Huntingburg and Bloomfield that year. Bird opened Valley's scoring against Huntingburg with a long, beautiful side shot. The Hunters picked up a single point on a foul shot; then Mark got the ball on the other side from which he had just scored and hit another bomb. The arching shot, noted a reporter, "threaded the needle." Mark then went on to score six of Valley's next eight points, including a layup and two more stunning long bombs. In a win against Bloomfield, "Mark let go at the top of the circle as the horn sounded" at the end of the first period. "It was a swisher," bringing the fans to their feet. Bloomfield came back to tie the score. "Then Bird went to work, hitting four straight baskets."

Mark could play great defense also, as captured in a sports report of Valley's game against North Knox. "Bird played one of his best games, at least defensibly. He had the task of guarding 6-8 Bob Harkness. Mark rose to the occasion and held the big boy, who is averaging 25 points, to 13." In the meantime, Bird scored eighteen points to lead the Valley team, along with six rebounds and several assists.

Mark Bird, number 33, watches as fellow teammate Steve Land snags a rebound.

When shot from a distance, and with perfect accuracy, a basketball makes a special sound that players and fans alike appreciate. Mark apparently did this frequently, one sports article noting that in one series of no-misses, he hit several "swishers." Mark had another great game against West Washington, "giving the crowd a thrill with his 15- and 20-foot shooting, making his first four shots and for the quarter hitting five out of eight."

As the season ended, even the Paoli sportswriters were admitting that Mark Bird was playing "superb ball." Mark gave one packed gym, the paper noted, "a shooting exhibition, as he hit six of eight shots. Mark's shots came from all angles; from each side, top of the circle, and under the basket." In another contest, Mark was five for six from the field in the first quarter. This awesome shooting, a sportswriter declared, "demoralized" the opposing team. To the opposing teams, the loud swish of those arching shots snapping through the basket were the sounds of nails being driven into a coffin. In the next-to-the-last game of the regular season, Valley took another great team to the wire, losing to Salem by four with Mark Bird leading "a late rally" and knocking down twenty-nine points, hitting those long arching jump shots whose swishes made the fans go ahh, and, as usual, canning almost all his foul shots.

One would have easily expected Larry Bird, four years younger than Mike and three years younger than Mark, to be at every game he could when his older brothers played basketball, especially at Mark's games.

That was not the case.

Larry told in his autobiography how his mother, Georgia, would take all the siblings to Springs Valley basketball games—everyone but Larry—come rain or snow. Bird went on to explain his reasons for never attending a Valley varsity game until the very last two games of Mark's senior year. "I had little interest in basketball before I was thirteen or so. My mother would drive my brothers to the games. I wouldn't go, just didn't care to. I'd stay at home and watch TV. And I wasn't watching basketball either." Larry also shared that behind this lack of interest was another element: his great shyness around crowds.

Larry would finally break his record of no-shows and go see Mark play at the 1971 sectional tournament at Paoli, and, in the process, have his life changed.

The Springs Valley Blackhawks came into sectional play with a so-so 12-8 record, having struggled to win just three of their first eight games, but sticking to the course and winning nine games after the Christmas break. Coach Jones explained the up-and-down year to a Louisville *Courier-Journal* reporter: "We didn't do anything different to start winning. We just stuck to the fundamentals and kept improving."

When sectional play came around, Springs Valley was not

seen by most sportswriters as sectional contenders. But Harry Moore at the *Republican* had his own take on the Blackhawks' chances of taking the sectional title. "It seems like only yesterday this green bunch of Hawks took the floor. And here it is tourney time. Not many Valley fans dreamed their team would have a 12-8 record going into the tourney. The Hawks lost seven of 12 players via graduation last year." Moore believed that because of Jim Jones' coaching skills, "Valley must be considered a threat to cop all the marbles," adding that there would be great tension as "county rivalry always runs high, especially between the Hawks and the Rams." Coach Jones was especially hungry to capture the title too, given Valley's unexpected loss to Paoli the year before and Jones' boast in the Jasper newspaper that Valley would likely dominate the sectional at Paoli.

Mark Bird was responsible for many of Springs Valley's regular season successes, being the squad's leading scorer by averaging almost eighteen points and grabbing ten rebounds a game and by hitting almost 80 percent of his free throws. Fans were certainly hopeful, given that the Valley team's efforts had grown stronger as the season wound down, that they would see the old "be ready when sectional time rolls around" cycle that everyone, friend and foe, had grown used to. Then, at the very week that sectional play was to start, disaster seemed to strike. Mark came down with a major health problem, facing the possibility he would not be able to play. What happened next would bring Mark Bird a level of Springs Valley sports immortality, while little brother Larry Bird would have what he described later as an almost religious experience, one that changed the trajectory of his life.

Part II:
Getting There

The biggest and most pleasant surprise for Hawk fans was the play of sophomore Larry Bird.

— Harry Moore, *Paoli Republican*, 1972

Success and Crisis

Like one of the many twisting backroads in hilly Orange County, Indiana, Larry Bird's journey to basketball greatness did not run in a straight line; there were many tough situations he would have to navigate, skills and emotions he would have to master. Having two older brothers must have felt like both a blessing and a curse. On the one hand, his brothers' solid sports achievements cleared the way for Larry to be noticed, both on the playgrounds in the Valley when Larry was younger, and later, in school sports. Mike and Mark, however, would have carried a much different perspective regarding Larry's presence, and acted on it in ways that were not always pleasant to their little brother.

Larry noted in *Drive* that his brothers were basically his babysitters, since both parents were working. Mark and Mike played hard, as did the other Valley boys their ages who competed with them. But this environment created an initial hardship for the two older Bird boys since little brother Larry was relentless when it came to going to the playgrounds. It was surely distracting, trying to work a five- or six-year-old Larry into a sandlot football or baseball game, and impossible in the higher-skill-demanding basketball games, not to let his lack of age screw things up for the rest of the guys playing. Larry always persisted anyway. As time passed, the older two sometimes let their frustrations out on Larry. "Even though I was their little brother, they were constantly trying to beat me at any sport we were playing."

The older siblings also gave Larry a hard time or even ridiculed him with laughter "if I ever played poorly," Larry reported. Later in life, he understood this latter situation as one that made him try even harder to compete with and pass his brothers. The harassing did not sting much. Coming home for supper after a hard day of playing sports, the three exhausted but content boys

A shy, sensitive-looking Larry Bird, lower grade school age.

would likely arrive covered in sweat, dirt, and glory. Playing sports with older boys also probably gave Larry an edge in confidence when he began playing sports with kids more his age.

Larry always had one thing going for him: he was a big kid. His first-grade teacher recalled how Larry was quite a bit bigger and taller than the other kids. Going out at recess, Larry, in his excitement, would often accidentally knock down a fellow student.

In time, Larry would be big enough to shag basketballs for Mark, as his older brother endlessly practiced perfecting his jump shot. "All day long," Larry remembered, "he would shoot, shoot, shoot. He could really shoot the eyes out of it." What Larry watched unfolding, as he gathered the ball and passed it back to his brother, was Mark developing the uncanny accuracy sportswriters would later swoon over. Larry gazed as Mark, from long range let go shot after shot, the ball arching and rotating in the air toward the basket, Mark knocking down "six or seven in a row."

Larry could only watch in awe, taking in the graceful shooting form, watching the net dance, dreaming of making such a smooth shot. It was the model Larry would emulate. But that would come later. Larry remained an average shooter until he was fourteen, according to one biographer, but "Mark was the one that got me interested in developing my shooting," according to Larry.

It was not surprising that in their younger days all the Bird boys loved baseball. In the summertime, baseball and softball were the games the brothers played the most. There was a rich tradition motivating this interest. The high school produced solid teams, and years ago both the Chicago Cubs and the Chicago White Sox held spring training at the West Baden resort before major-league teams started going south and west. At his youngest, while being babysat by his brothers, Larry longed to keep up, and Mike and Mark finally let him do some of the pitching in sandlot baseball games. Larry carried an oversized baseball glove and cried when his brothers wouldn't let him bat. He would often play a lonely fantasy-type game of baseball by himself where he took a rubber ball or tennis ball and threw it up against a wall. He would imagine striking people out, doing this "for hours and hours until someone came to get me." Like his future high school coach, Jim Jones, Larry would later say, "Baseball was my first love." Speaking about basketball at

When Larry was younger, he watched his brother Mark develop good shooting form, inspiring Larry to do the same.

this time, Bird noted the game "was always around and I played it once in a while, but I was by no means obsessed by it."

In Little League baseball, Larry pitched and played short-stop, where he excelled. As he grew older, he played in the Babe Ruth League, again gaining attention for his skills. By his fresh-man year in high school, it looked as if he would be starting on the varsity squad playing third base. "I really wanted to play," Larry explained in his autobiography, "because Mark was on the team, and I was the only freshman." Then an event occurred that spoiled Larry's high school baseball career, a situation per-haps escalated by his resentment and anger whenever he felt he had been slighted.

One day after Larry had patiently waited for his turn to work in the outside batting cage, and had chased balls for all the oth-er players, the coach, when it was Larry's turn, told him to just take three swings and then pick up the balls and come in. Larry quit the team that day. He continued, however, to have a love for both baseball and softball, especially when playing softball on teams with Mike and Mark. In fact, this interest almost came to tragedy when Larry, shortly after signing with the Celtics, reached out to grab a hard softball line-drive Mike had hit, the catch breaking one of Larry's little fingers in a way that could never be completely fixed. Larry also served as an assistant high school baseball coach his last semester at Indiana State at West Vigo High School, while doing his student teaching to finish his college degree, and he played one game for the varsity Indiana State team.

As a youngster, Larry was happiest when he was busy with sports. When the summers were over, and his beloved baseball and softball games were no longer in season, he turned to pee wee football in the fall and the Biddy Ball basketball league in the short days of winter. Levine, in *The Making of an American Sports Legend*, believed the Valley area of Larry Bird's youth was an almost perfect place to grow up and learn to play the game of basketball. Levine especially emphasized the Biddy Ball program as being an essential part of the process. The Bid-dy Ball program at Springs Valley included fourth-, fifth-, and

While Larry was playing high school ball, he was also helping in the Biddy Ball program that had done so much to help him develop basic basketball skills. Larry, a junior in the photo, is in the second row from the bottom, on the right.

sixth-grade players, coached by their high school heroes under the watchful eye of basketball perfectionist Coach Jim Jones

The high school players involved during the three-year span of Biddy Ball for Larry would have included players from one of the Huntingburg sectional championship teams, thus offering added excitement for the young would-be stars. Several teams were formed, so that after the Saturday Biddy Ball practices, competitive games were played. Larry performed for Agan's Market. To top it off, Biddy Ball teams played at the halftime of Valley varsity games.

Both Jones and his assistant, Gary Holland, were committed to teaching the fundamentals to their devoted little charges. Larry Bird later gave total credit to the program for instilling "the fundamentals into us." These fundamentals included learning to shoot with proper form, dribble the ball with either hand, develop passing techniques, and box out when rebounding. Then came more advanced work—learning to carry out back door plays, pick and roll, and use the backboard on lay-ins.

Playing in the Biddy Ball league should also have prepared Larry to take directions from coaches, but it initially failed to do so. Larry could act out if he felt slighted or his frustration with his own play got the best of him. Nevertheless, in the Biddy Ball process, Jim Jones entered Bird's life, becoming a strict but essential father figure, perhaps along with older brother Mark Bird, the most important key to Larry's later successes. On the other hand, Larry had his own natural drive for the sport.

Close neighbors in West Baden remember a young Larry Bird dribbling a ball on the way to and from the old West Baden school, the bouncing ball an extension of the slight blond boy's body, the taut rhythmic thumps reverberating up and down the street. At some point, an older woman neighbor named Kerby complained to her family, "That boy is never going to amount to anything. All he knows is how to bounce a basketball."

It was while Larry was playing at one of the local outdoor courts in the West Baden/French Lick area in his early youth that he picked up and eventually developed a shot that would later thrill high school, college, and NBA fans, and frustrate defensive players for years to come. In the move, mostly taken when he was in one of the two far corners, Larry, holding the ball with both hands, would pretend to pass the ball behind the head of the defensive man, only to pull the ball back and shoot when the player turned around to see where it had supposedly been thrown.

As a young boy, Larry picked up the move from an older man who worked at the local French Lick resort and played with the younger kids on his off hours before the older teenage kids got there and took over the outside court. Because he was so much taller than the younger boys, the man could reach the ball behind their heads and then bring it back and shoot.

Larry took the move and made it his own.

By seventh grade, Larry had joined organized grade school play. A yearbook photo of Bird with the seventh-grade team shows a thin, shy-looking boy wearing the number 14. He may have looked shy, but a *Jasper Herald* sports report of a game between Springs Valley seventh graders and archrival Jasper indicated a 37-35 win for the little Blackhawks. Larry was the leading scorer for both teams with twenty points. The second-leading scorer was Mike Luegers, future Jasper star and Larry Bird rival.

Number 14, Larry Bird, with his seventh-grade team. He would be dismissed from his eighth-grade team late in the season for disciplinary reasons.

This was the same year older brother Mark Bird earned a varsity letter at Springs Valley High School and received the number 33 as his jersey number.

Sports reports featuring Larry's eighth-grade year indicated he continued to do well. At the prestigious sixteen-team Jasper Grade School tournament, Larry led his team with fifteen points in a win over Winslow. In the next game, against Huntingburg, Larry was again the leading scorer in a Blackhawk victory. Jasper finally knocked out Valley in a semifinal match, Mike Luegers being the top scorer for Jasper and Larry for his team.

These glowing reports about Larry's play, however, fail to reveal another issue, a crisis that brought his playing days in grade school to an abrupt end.

There were several issues in Larry Bird's life that could have caused his aggressive acting out at organized basketball games. One was the uncertainty created by his father's working situation, a circumstance probably driven by Joe Bird's drinking. Larry noted in *Drive*, "It seemed as if Dad was always switching jobs." Also, the family always seemed to be moving. As Larry himself observed, "We moved quite a bit for different reasons. Sometimes it was because of the rent, sometimes because we could get a better furnace, and once simply because it was the house my mom really wanted to live in."

During Larry's eighth-grade year, the family had moved from West Baden to French Lick, leaving the sites and rhythms Larry had been used to all of his childhood, especially the nearby playgrounds where he had spent so much time in sports. That Larry believed the house they were moving into was haunted probably did not help matters. He had hit puberty, too, and new levels of energy and restlessness probably were upon him. Then again, Larry's aggressive behavior could have been caused by one of the family's many hard financial episodes, or just the fact that Larry had an explosive temper, as did both his brothers and his father. Whatever the cause, it was trouble.

Levine noted that even as a kid, Larry "often lost his temper when playing Biddy Ball." By Bird's seventh- and eighth-grade years, "He was notorious for getting into altercations with other players, getting technicals because of overly physical play, screaming at the officials, using profanity, and slamming the ball down on the court or at other players." Larry would also cry tears of frustration and anger if his team lost. There were even times he would dramatically storm off the court. Finally, Larry was benched for two eighth-grade games by his coach after some unacceptable behavior, this shortly after his family had moved to French Lick.

Puberty is a time when a young male begins to form an identity, an essential task if the young man is to succeed in life. Since basketball was beginning to become important to Larry, a sudden growing part of his early identity, his acting out on basketball courts may have been driven by his frustration with his own basketball performance, his trying to play at the level his mind was now demanding. In some basketball programs, good players might get by with misbehaving, and Larry was good enough in some instances to be noted early on. Both head coach Jim Jones and his assistant, Gary Holland, later explained how they were aware of Larry's advanced court sense in Biddy Ball and in grade school basketball contests. Holland thought Larry's exceptional reading of the court came from playing with his two older brothers, who were themselves accomplished players. Jim Jones meanwhile discerned how the grade school youngster would let the player he was guarding go and "steal the ball from someone else." This, Jones knew, was an unusually high level of basketball perception. Jones realized too that Larry had a tuned-in anticipation concerning what an opposing player was going to do, and had picked up this essential skill "so much faster than anyone else." And all the coaches knew about Larry's older brother Mark, who was a solid player, and the fact that good basketball players often run in families.

Still, Larry was not on anybody's radar as a possible superstar. Springs Valley always seemed to have a few savvy young players in the mix, players whose natural skills caught the eyes of the coaches. Brad Bledsoe, a year behind Larry in seventh grade, remembered Bird as someone who seemed to play basketball "all the time, but that was true of several of us at that age. Nothing seemed to stand out about him. He was just another kid who played hard-nosed basketball, like many of the rest of us."

Whatever special skills coaches may have caught, Larry wasn't going to be enabled by the Valley coaches when he threw a fit. This became apparent when the Blackhawks' eighth-grade coach promptly kicked Larry off the team after Bird missed a practice. An eighth grade scorebook suggests how Larry's sometimes extreme reactions might have been quickened in one particular game, as it was the last time Larry's name is listed in the Valley scorebook that season. Valley was playing the always tough Loogootee Lions. The scorebook shows that Larry, who was his team's leading scorer, kept the Blackhawks in the game in the first quarter. In the second quarter, however, Loogootee's center, Wayne Flick, went on a scoring spree, pushing his team to an all but insurmountable lead. To add to Larry's frustration, he fouled out early in the third quarter, and Loogootee breezed to an easy win. The dual between eighth grade players Wayne Flick and Larry Bird is made more interesting by the fact that Larry would be frustrated by Flick's defense in a key basketball contest in Larry's senior year.

Interestingly too, Larry's dismissal may have been one of the reasons seventh graders Brad Bledsoe, Doug Conrad, and Mike Cox were moved up to play with the eighth-grade team. Bledsoe was the biggest benefactor of this move, using the skills he gained in more rigorous competition during his last two years of grade school to gain a starting position on the varsity team half-way through his freshman year. Larry, a year ahead of Bledsoe, was still playing on the junior varsity team when his sophomore year started.

These must have been dark days for Larry, struggling with questions involving the very core of his being, shamed by being thrown off the team. But history shows that among high achievers, the adolescent crisis of constructing an identity is often marked by a dramatic turning point. Larry Bird would experience two such events in one year, gaining his first fledgling senses of his true self, an identity that he would claim and on which he would build for the rest of his life.

Epiphanies

It is the opening scene in Larry Bird's book *Drive* and how I imagine it. Thirteen-year-old Larry is restless and uncomfortable. Not well traveled—in fact rarely leaving his French Lick, Indiana, hometown—he is stuck several hours away in Hobart, Indiana, taken there by his mother, who is visiting her sister. This city is a busy, noisy industrial community full of hazy air just south of Lake Michigan. Steel mill country. It's a hot summer's day, the sun straight up in the sky, its light as strong as a death ray.

An unfamiliar odor lingers in the air, and Larry perhaps wrinkles his nose as he explores along the narrow streets. Sudden familiar sounds—the rhythmic thunk of a basketball on concrete, someone being razzed for missing an easy shot.

Larry follows the sounds, finding the game a mere block away, the area a simple concrete court with ragged nets hanging on the goals and a few blades of sickly grass pushing through a seam of cracked concrete. Eight kids, no uniforms, just shirts and skins. All are bigger and older looking than Larry.

A heavyset kid has to leave. The biggest kid looks at Larry.

"Hey, we need someone to make the teams even."

Larry pulls his T-shirt over his head, rolls it into a ball, and tosses it on the scraggly grass. He's even thinner than he looks in his shirt. Straight up and narrow from his feet to a head of shaggy blond hair.

The other kids know one another's strengths and weakness, who will probably shoot, who will pass, and who will just hope they don't screw up. On the second trip down the court, Larry hits a long shot. Nothing but net. Someone winks—a lucky shot.

Larry steals the ball and sinks another basket. The other team switches a bigger man to guard Larry, but Bird is on a streak, making shot after shot and playing better than he ever has before. When the game is over, several kids come up and ask Larry, "What's your name?"

The results were life changing; this was the day, Larry later explained, he fell in love with basketball. So powerful was the moment that Bird remembered it in detail. It was the beginning of his realizing he hardly ever missed a shot. "Even though I was playing against bigger kids, it seemed as if everything I lofted went in. The kids on my team started slapping me on the back and telling me what a great player I was, and I just loved it. That was it. I was hooked on basketball."

Hooked or not, the Springs Valley coaches had not forgotten Larry when school came back into session, neither his bad behavior on the court and in practice nor his advanced understanding of the game. Before the basketball season started, Coach Jones had his assistant, Gary Holland, approach Larry's mother. Gary was soft-spoken and kind, more easy-going perhaps than Jim Jones and great at taking care of all the little details. Gary told Georgia Bird that if Larry could control his temper, he would become one of the best players in the state. Holland later noted he had exaggerated Larry's potential, or so he thought, to get Larry's mother on board. It must have worked.

While Larry's Hobart experience had given him a new sense of himself, one that seemed to tie into playing basketball, he had not arrived at fully committing to being the best basketball player he could be. But he did have some sense of what it might be like to play varsity basketball at Valley. He had watched his first Springs Valley varsity basketball game when oldest brother Mike played his final game, a title championship contest in the Huntingburg sectional that Valley won. "That would have been in 1969," Larry recalled, and Larry would have been in seventh grade. After this, Larry became aware of Mark's blossoming into a solid basketball player and eventually into a Springs Valley star.

Despite his previous acting out in organized basketball games in eighth grade, Larry came back to play on the Springs Valley freshman squad, dealing much better with his temper. A freshman football injury, however, may have limited his playing time. Larry noted in *Drive* that he did not get to play that much as a freshman, winding up "on what we called the B team." Freshman Tim Eubank, who played on the Paoli freshman basketball squad, remembered Larry as "kind of a runt" in size in his freshman year. "You would never have thought he would be a good player." Yet, one *Springs Valley Herald* article showed Larry scoring nine points in a freshman game against Shoals. Another sign of success on the basketball floor occurred at the end of the season when Larry received the freshman free-throw award, hitting, according to the *Valley Herald,* "65 percent of his free tosses." But even then, as Larry later said, he could still take or leave basketball "during my freshman year." It would take Mark Bird's most important basketball performance to create a life-changing revelation for Larry.

As noted earlier, Valley had an up-and-down season Mark's senior year, coming into the sectional at 12-8. Plus, the Blackhawks still carried the embarrassment of losing the Paoli sectional the year before. To Jim Jones, however, the vibes at the end of the season seemed good, the team coming together at the last moment like so many other successful Blackhawk squads of the past. The Valley team had also received a lucky draw, having to win only two games to take the sectional championship. If they did play archrival Paoli, it would be in the title game.

Then, Mark Bird suddenly and unexpectedly became ill.

Valley was certainly not a one-man team. Seniors Kevin Carnes and Jeff Willoughby, along with budding sophomore Steve Land, were essential parts of the hardworking squad. But Mark was the team's leading scorer. Without his average of almost eighteen points a game, plus his rebounding and assists, Springs Valley would be hard pressed to win.

Valley faced Leavenworth, 13-8, in their first sectional game, and if Mark did not play, the Blackhawks would be in great danger of doing something that was very rare: losing a first-round game in sectional play. Sportswriter Russ Brown of the Louisville *Courier Journal,* in search of a compelling human-interest story, certainly found one in Mark Bird's situation while following the Paoli sectional. "Jim Jones," he wrote, "likes to think that

Mark Bird is exemplary of the types of boys he has on his Springs Valley Basketball team. At 6 feet 2 and about 150 pounds, Bird is a slender wisp of a boy." Bird, the sports reporter went on to explain, also suffered from pleurisy, and the illness had popped up just as the tournament was starting. It was "a disease that sometimes makes breathing difficult and painful—and he was trying to fight off an attack when Springs Valley made its debut against Leavenworth."

Larry is somewhere among these nervous Blackhawk fans, watching his brother Mark with great apprehension in the 1971 Paoli sectional final.

Coach Jones was unsure if Mark would even be able to play a single minute, telling the reporter, "Mark was really sick." Mark, however, played despite the pain. It was the tournament, and he did not want to let the team or school down. But even then, at the start of the Leavenworth contest, Mark Bird "could hardly run," Coach Jones remembered. Steve Land, a sophomore, recalled how the trainers "wrapped Mark tightly around his chest so he could breathe better. I was almost sick with worry and didn't think he would be able to play."

As the game started, Larry Bird sat helplessly in the stands, worried too about his brother, hoping his illness would not affect his game too badly. In Larry's mind, however, the worst that might happen, the nightmare of all possibilities, was that Mark might make a mistake in a close game that would cause Springs Valley to lose the contest.

Larry felt some relief when Springs Valley built up a nice lead. The Blackhawks led by nine going into the fourth quarter. Then Leavenworth came back, "having Springs Valley on the ropes with 12 seconds remaining," reported one newspaper. Valley's opponent had two shots to break the tie with just nine seconds left in the regulation time, leaving the Valley fans and Larry frantic. Both attempts failed. Then Mark, who had seventeen points in the game, led his team to a 71-69 victory in the overtime squeaker.

A photo of Larry when he began to grow aware of his brother Mark's basketball skills.

The next day the Louisville *Courier Journal* reported that Valley "narrowly escaped an upset at the hands of Leavenworth, thanks mainly to Mark Bird, who scored seven of the winner's 12 points in the overtime." The newspaper also carried the headline "Bird Hero in Overtime."

Valley's final game of the sectional against the previous year's champion, Milltown, was even more dramatic, with Mark Bird once more the savior.

From the opening tip-off, Milltown played a slow-down game, but Springs Valley still took an eight-point lead at the end of the first quarter. The Millers came back to tie the Blackhawks by halftime and led, but just by one point, when the

Hero Mark Bird, with his 1971 teammates, celebrating winning the sectional championship.

fourth quarter started. In the final quarter, Milltown continued to hold the ball, making the game even more nerve-racking. Almost all the fans were standing. Valley finally got their hands on the ball and scored, going up by one point. The Valley fans' cheers were so loud, smaller kids put their hands over their ears. Then Milltown ran down the clock before going ahead 51-50 late in the game. At this point, Mark Bird, worn out from playing in his second nail-biting game in two days and still not at full strength because of his illness, was fouled. Bird stepped up to the line, the noise of the crowd seeming to shake the gym's very walls.

No one was more nervous that night in the Paoli gym than Larry Bird, who remembered sitting in the stands being "so scared we were going to get beat" that he was almost sick.

Mark calmly made both free throws, and Valley won the game, 52-51.

When the final horn sounded, the gym exploded with the shouts and screams, and hoots and hollers of Valley fans. With Mark's baskets, Jim Jones and the Springs Valley basketball program had thrown off the yearlong shadow of its loss to Paoli in the previous sectional. There simply could not be anything sweeter.

Suddenly, the fans flowed like water from a busted dam, pouring from the bleachers onto the floor and surrounding their team in a wild celebration. While all this was occurring, an unexpected and powerful emotion swept over fourteen-year-old Larry Bird. Tears streamed down his face. Something had clicked—several things, in fact—that brought Larry a new and important insight concerning the role basketball might play in his own life.

As he cried, he also worried, wondering, "What's wrong with me?" Then he answered his own question — "This is what I've been missing my whole life by not going to these games." Larry later told biographer Mark Shaw, "Everyone was cheering for him [Mark]. I wanted to be that guy; I wanted the people cheering for me."

After the awesome victory, a communal one as much as a team success, came another wonderful surprise for Larry. "Mark was a hero and when we were riding back on the bus,

Mark sat right next to me. Everyone wanted Mark to sit next to him, but he came right over next to me. He made me feel so good when he did that."

When the championship trophy was given the night of the final game, Mark, as one of the co-captains, proudly stood on one side, holding the tall trophy. The photo made the front page in the next issue of both the *Springs Valley Herald* and the *Paoli Republican*. Then Mark had one last high school game hurrah. In the first game of the regional at Huntingburg, a contest between Valley and Salem, his play enabled the Blackhawks to tie the game with less than two minutes to go. It felt like the sectional final game all over again. But Valley ended up having to foul, and Salem squeaked by for the win.

A week or so later more photos and articles about Mark appeared on the front page of the local papers—Mark making the All Sectional, All Regional, and Blue Chip Conference All Star first teams, a list of Mark's many records and accomplishments in an article about the Springs Valley High School sports banquet, and the announcement of Mark's scholarship to play basketball at Oakland City College.

Mark's athletic scholarship to Oakland City likely had an especially important impact on Larry and on the Bird family. Being the first in a family to go to college can seem like an almost impossible dream to people who have lived in poverty. This achievement was a crowning glory, and perhaps one not completely understood by Mark or the family. Larry noted in *Drive* that when Mark went to college, he told the family not to worry about added expenses. "When I get out, I'll be a big businessman and take good care of you." To the Birds, Oakland City College might as well have been Harvard.

As all of Mark's accomplishments sank in, Larry's fledgling identity began to merge with his older brother's. Larry realized that he too wanted to be the kind of hero Mark had been. Before the next season started, the season after Mark scored the winning free-throw shots in the sectional championship, Larry was "hooked on basketball." In *Drive*, Larry emphasized, "I hardly wanted to do anything else. I wasn't sure how good I was, but

I just knew I couldn't get enough of it." This desire would take over the rest of his life.

Just as the larger story of Coach Jim Jones' essential influence on Larry Bird has not received the attention it deserves, so it is with the story of how big brother Mark Bird impacted Larry's journey to basketball greatness. It is ironic too that Mark would be somewhat forgotten, having been the first one in the family to gain community recognition for his high school basketball performances, accomplishments that surely brought positive recognition to the Bird family. But in the end, Larry's shadow was too great. Nevertheless, just as one could easily ask if Larry Bird would have been the iconic basketball player he became without Coach Jim Jones, one could also ask if there would have been a Larry Bird without Mark Bird's role in his brother's life.

Keep an Eye on Mark
Bird's Little Brother

The beginning of the 1971–1972 Springs Valley basketball season found sophomore Larry Bird standing just over six feet tall and weighing 135 pounds. Larry had spent the summer constantly playing basketball, and he was surely breathless with excitement as high school practices began. Bird may have been even more excited when he found out that he would not only be playing on the junior varsity squad but also dressing out for varsity games. Just like Mark had done his sophomore year, Larry could now hope to be occasionally put into a varsity game where maybe he would make a few baskets and pull down some rebounds, accomplishing enough success to get more varsity time. Larry also asked for and received his brother's former varsity jersey number, 33, an indication of how much his growing sense of his own developing identity now matched Mark's heroic path.

Few today would recognize Larry in the varsity team photo taken that year. The picture shows him barely fitting into his loose jersey, looking back at the camera, vulnerable, and standing just behind a seated Jim Jones as if seeking protection. But despite his almost sweet, and certainly fragile, look, he now possessed the beginnings of a personal playbook about who he was and what he wanted to accomplish.

Larry may have had trouble getting into one unusual preseason workout routine, the activity taking place early in the mornings. The nature of Jim Jones' preseason morning workouts was captured in an article in a regional high school basketball magazine called *Hoopla*, written by staff writer Charles McPherson. "If a person would pass outside the Springs Valley High School gymnasium around 7:30 some weekday morning, he might assume that the sound emitting from the Blackhawks' haven resembled that of bouncing basketballs. His assumption

The 1971-1972 Springs Valley Blackhawks. Sophomore Larry Bird, wearing his brother Mark's jersey number 33, is standing behind Coach Jones in the official varsity team photo.

would be absolutely correct. When most high school students are just in the process of getting out of their beds, there is a dedicated group of young men 'in the valley' who are working to improve their basketball skills." Coach Jim Jones admitted to the reporter that his early morning practices each day usually brought some moans and groans from the players. Jones explained, however, that "The one-hour practices in the mornings gives the boys a chance to do a lot of individual exercises as well as work on fundamentals. This leaves our afternoon practice to devote to basic offensive and defensive patterns that we are using." The school also provided the team players with breakfast, and Jones asserted that "If it wasn't for the morning practice, some of the boys would be coming to school without any nourishment at all."

On the cusp of the 1971–1972 season, the Bedford *Times-Mail* carried a detailed article about the Springs Valley basketball team. Coach Jones explained it would be "a rebuilding year," but the sports reporter noted Jones' reputation "of developing a [winning] combination each season." The piece also listed the players scheduled to be in the varsity group, with

Larry listed last at number thirteen. The *Hoopla* article about the morning practices mentioned juniors Steve Land and Jay Charnes as sure starters, followed by juniors Tony Clark, Marlin Campbell, Danny King, and Louis Nigg. Two brothers, Dave and Jim Bush, who had recently moved in from Michigan, were also mentioned. But no Larry Bird. As noted, Larry would be playing only junior varsity games starting out. In his reserve uniform, he wore number 12.

In his sophomore year Larry continued to be inspired by his brother Mark, seen here as a college freshman basketball player, number 32, at Oakland City College.

Early in that season, destiny decided to play a frustrating game with Larry. These events, however, would help fine-tune his identity even more, Larry casting the episode, in the words of Lee Levine, "as the kind of heroic beginning that often anticipates a special career." Valley played their first game at Pekin Eastern. Both the varsity and junior varsity lost their games, but the greatest damage occurred in the junior varsity tilt. It was a seemingly shattering moment for Larry Bird, whose ankle was broken early in the contest, a player having stepped on Larry's foot when Larry was going up for a rebound.

At first the damage was not apparent. Larry came out of the game and tried to walk the pain off on the sidelines. At half-time, Coach Jones looked at the injury and announced it was probably just a sprained ankle. The swelling ankle was taped up and Larry went back into the game. He made it up and down the court only a few times, however, before he came out. An X-ray the next day revealed two cracked places and some torn ligaments. It took a week for the swelling to go down enough so that a cast could be placed on the injury.

However downcast Larry was about the broken ankle, he got busy modifying his practice of basketball, participating in shooting drills where there was an absence of movement. He also talked neighborhood kids into retrieving the basketball for him on the playground, Larry shooting while propped up on his crutches. These almost-every-day practices improved his accuracy and range. And, as with most dark events, there were other silver linings.

Larry began expanding his game beyond scoring, working on his dribbling and passing skills while stationary or "hobbling" around in his cast. He would throw the ball against set objects, grabbing the returning ball for his next throw. When he did return to the regular practices without his crutches, players asked him in wonderment, "Where did you learn to pass like that?" Larry later reported that more than anything else, he discovered from his adversity "that I loved to pass." It became an unexpected joy on the court, Larry getting a charge out of seeing "the gleam in my teammate's eyes" as that player ran down the court after scoring off a Larry Bird pass.

Larry may have also had a secret drive for wanting to get back on the playing floor; his older brother Mark was doing well at Oakland City College, occasionally making it into sports articles in the local papers and the larger Evansville papers. But the most striking article appeared in an *Indianapolis Star* report about an Oakland City College game, citing Mark for bringing "a big lift" to the team in an important win by hitting four straight shots in a row.

Mark was once more bringing glory to the Bird family, and Larry surely longed to do the same.

After Larry's cast came off, literally falling apart from all of his activities, he begged his coaches to play him as soon as possible. Seeing how much pain Larry's movement still caused, and knowing how out of shape he was, junior varsity coach Gary Holland was reluctant to let him do so. Instead, he required Bird to be able to run a set of difficult practice sprints called "suicide drills" under a certain time before letting him into a game.

By the time Larry was able to run the drill in the allotted time, only a few junior varsity games remained in the season. But Bird was ready. One newspaper box score in the Bedford *Times-Mail* in early February showed Larry scoring eight points in a junior varsity contest against Huntingburg's "Little Hunters," the Blackhawks winning 45-31.

Harry Moore, the sportswriter at the *Paoli Republican*, had watched most of Valley's games that year, including the last few in which Larry Bird played on the junior varsity squad. Just before the beginning of play at the Paoli sectional, Moore penned a prophetic observation in the sports page. "Don't be surprised if you see sophomore Larry Bird enter the game. Larry, little brother of last year's Valley hero, Mark, has come on strong in the late going. He can shoot the ball with anyone, and pressure just doesn't seem to bother him."

The stage was set.

It was not one of Jim Jones' better regular seasons. Valley had beaten a strong Washington squad in the second game of the season, after a first game defeat, then lost four straight games. They broke even in their four-team holiday tourney. The Blackhawks then defeated Shoals, only to then lose five games in a row. Next, they beat Huntingburg, Steve Land knocking down thirty points for Valley. But in their last six games, the Blackhawks went 2-4.

There were some positives in the mix. Assessing Valley's

chances as sectional play approached, one newspaper report noted Springs Valley junior Steve Land was averaging eighteen points a game and grabbing an amazing fifteen rebounds a contest. Many people thought Land would likely break some team scoring and rebounding records in the next season. The same article pointed out that Valley had two other strong juniors in Tony Clark and Danny King. John Carnes and Beezer Carnes were solid sophomores, and Valley even had an up-and-coming starting freshman, Brad Bledsoe, who had great shooting accuracy. Interestingly, Larry Bird was not even mentioned in this conversation.

Basketball sectional time in Indiana brought a festive mood to schools and communities. Players, coaches, and fans saw their hopes rising, the season rebooting, regular season records meaning nothing. Harry Moore at the *Paoli Republican* gave Valley fans even more hope on the verge of sectional play when he explained that "Coach Jones thrives on tournament tradition. This year's squad is extremely young and that is why their record isn't good. However, these young players are fast becoming veterans."

Before the dust settled, no one would come to fit the latter notion better than Larry Bird.

Valley's first sectional battle was against West Washington, a team the Blackhawks had lost to in the regular season by only three points. When the contest started, Larry was riding the bench, finally out of his leg cast and proudly wearing his brother's old jersey, number 33.

Although this game has been immortalized by Larry Bird biographers and in Larry's own book, the reports about its dramatic ending vary in the exact details. Research for this book showed Valley had built up a solid lead by the end of the first quarter, 22-11, and by twenty points in the second half before West Washington made a run and pulled to 36-23 at halftime. One of the elements that made Indiana high school basketball so exciting, an event that could all but snap a fan's neck, was how quickly a game could turn around. When the second half started, West Washington exploded, hitting shots and grabbing rebounds, taking a two-point third-quarter lead and shaking the Blackhawks and their fans to the core.

The fourth quarter continued to be a nail-biter, the lead swinging back and forth several times, the fans out of their seats, screaming support for their teams.

At some point during the nip-and-tuck game, Larry, unexpectedly, heard his name being called and did not realize for a moment that it was Coach Jones telling him to check into the game. "My heart," Larry later said, "started pounding and I threw my warm-up jacket off and was at the scorer's table before I knew it."

It was not surprising Larry was so nervous. It was his first time in a varsity game, a contest of the highest stakes in the intense world of Indiana high school basketball.

Up to the last few seconds of the contest, Steve Land had clearly been the hero of the game, finishing with a game-high twenty-three points and piling up an astounding twenty-one rebounds. "Steve was just tremendous throughout the game," observed one sports reporter. But then came the defining moment of the contest.

With a few seconds showing on the clock, Bird was fouled, his team leading by a single point. Larry calmly knocked down both free-throw attempts, and Valley went up by three. A last-second shot by West Washington ended the game with Valley on top, 58-57.

Larry's free throws had made the difference.

Bird explained in *Drive* that "The first time I get the ball, I launch it from about twenty feet out and it goes in. The crowd goes absolutely crazy while I'm passing everywhere, rebounding and sinking all my shots." Near the end of the game, Larry was fouled with his team down by one. It was the ultimate pressure packed moment. Larry recalled, "I go to the free throw line and I try to pretend it's 6 A.M. in the gym back home and these are just two of the five hundred free throws that I shoot every morning. Swish! Both shots are good and we win the game by one point. Pandemonium! The next day's headlines read: Bird Steals the Show."

Newspaper reports reveal slightly different versions of the unfolding of the game. The Bedford Daily *Times-Mail* reported the next day, "With 37 seconds showing on the clock, Larry Bird, a sub for the Hawks, hit two free throws on a 1-and-1 situation to give Valley a 58-55 lead." The Bedford box score showed Larry making one of nine field goal attempts and the two free throws. The Louisville *Courier-Journal* had its own version, noting, "Bird's two free-throws were the clincher," and headlined the article, "Land and Bird Propel Springs Valley, 58-57." The same report, however, had Larry making two field goals out of nine, instead of the one out of nine reported in the Bedford paper.

Since he consistently reported on the Valley team in detail, Harry Moore, at the *Paoli Republican*, likely had the most accurate account. In his version, Coach Jones had put Larry into the game early. "The biggest and most pleasant surprise for Hawk fans," Moore explained, "was the play of sophomore Larry Bird. Coach Jones used Bird early, and Larry, who had never played varsity ball, responded like a veteran." Moore reported Larry made two crucial baskets from rebounds. Then, "With 13 seconds remaining, Bird was fouled. At that time Valley was nursing a one-point lead. Larry stepped up to the line and canned a pair. That insured the Hawk victory."

Freshman Brad Bledsoe, who had earned a starting role on the Blackhawk team just after Christmas, remembered Bird's unexpected contribution as well. "Larry's play in the game was a surprise, a big boost." Interestingly, at this point, Brad Bledsoe was the younger player Coach Jim Jones had his eye on, calling the freshman "our most consistent player since we moved him to varsity."

In the next sectional contest, Milltown beat Valley 70-59, knocking the Blackhawks out of the tournament. In that contest, Larry came back down to earth, scoring a single field goal while big Steve Land notched twenty-six points for Springs Valley. Looking at Valley's entire season, Land, a junior, was clearly the Blackhawk player who stood out. He was the leading scorer and rebounder and set a conference single-game rebounding record. Behind Land were solid players like senior Kevin Carnes, junior Danny King, and freshman Brad Bledsoe. Because of his early injury, Larry had played in just a few junior varsity games toward the end of the season. In the two varsity games in sectional action, he scored a total of eight points, although his contributions in the first sectional game were dramatic. Nevertheless, the Bedford and Louisville newspaper articles about Larry's play at the Paoli sectional, along with reports from the two Orange County newspapers, would be the first of hundreds of sports reports telling of Larry Bird's amazing heroics on high school basketball courts. These accounts were the first narratives where Larry would read about himself in media and those in his immediate area would read. It was a clear acknowledgment of a perhaps small but still gallant accomplishment in the basketball-crazed state of Indiana. Larry was getting his name in the papers like big brother Mark at Oakland City College.

Biographer Lee Levine pointed to outside pressures that caused Larry to dedicate himself to basketball, arguing that growing up in Indiana socialized Larry to totally channel his drive into the game, and that the family's financial situation "dictated a kind of survival mentality that made winning in basketball much more important to Larry than most kids." The newspaper narratives that Bird read after his heroic actions, however, likely created another psychological element as well. These narratives, along with Larry's earlier Hobart experience at an outdoor basketball court, and his witnessing Mark's scoring the winning foul shots at a championship sectional game, may have come together to help solidify his own construction of an early but solid personal identity. Altogether, these factors would now propel a dedication to basketball that can only be described as furious. As Larry noted in *Drive*, after scoring the winning points in the sectional game and reading about it the next day, "From that point on, basketball was all I thought about, all I wanted to do. I couldn't wait for school to let out for the summer so I could play ball."

For Larry, identity had finally become destiny.

On the other hand, Larry was hardly, if at all, on anyone

else's radar after Valley was knocked out of the 1972 sectional tourney. Springs Valley had experienced a poor season and the region had several seemingly more gifted sophomore players than Larry at that point, players such as six-eight Dave Smith at Milltown, who tallied twenty-eight points in Milltown's thumping of Springs Valley in the sectional that year, and six-six and still growing sophomore Curt Gilstrap, of Orleans, who led his Bulldogs to the Paoli sectional championship that year.

Harry Moore called Gilstrap "a demon on the boards and a regular scoring machine." Another very productive six-eight sophomore, Mike Luegers, over in Jasper, was making his coach and Wildcat fans happy with anticipation about the next two seasons. Finally, there was a freshman, Bill Butcher at Loogootee, who caught Moore's attention, the Paoli sportswriter calling the youthful Butcher "another star in the making at Loogootee." At best, sophomore Larry Bird had been, in the words of sportswriter Moore, "a pleasant surprise" to his coaches and the Valley fans.

Meanwhile, after being booted out of the sectional by small-school Milltown, Coach Jones, a figure one of Larry's biographers called the "high priest of Valley basketball," was assessing his next year's season. Jones was fast approaching his tenth year at the helm, and the 1971–1972 campaign had brought him one of his poorer records. On top of that, the Valley coach had to live out another season without a sectional championship, Coach Jones' most important yardstick of success. Fortunately, when it came to upcoming players for next year's campaign, he had much to be excited about. Returning starters included the solidly built six-five Steve Land, coming back as a senior, along with two other seniors to be—a six-four player named Tony Clark and a tough little guard, Danny King, who seemed to get better with every game. Another starter from last year, James Carnes, a junior, and the sharp-shooting sophomore-to-be Brad Bledsoe would also be returning. On the downside was some up-coming tough competition. As noted, county rival Orleans, champions of the 1972 Paoli sectional, looked to be the primary contender for the sectional crown again, having a strong cast of players to

Land and Bird propel Springs Valley

Larry Bird shares a sports headline with Steve Land in the Louisville *Courier-Journal* in 1972, the very first time he was feted in a headline.

enhance big-man Curt Gilstrap. Paoli had a giant of their own in rugged junior Tim Eubank. Jasper, which had gone to the semi-state, would be returning big junior center Mike Luegers, a guarantee the Wildcats would have high state ranking at the beginning of the 1972 season. Jones also knew Loogootee, another always consistent winner and Blue Chip Conference foe, would be loading up and would have its own "high priest," brilliant coach Jack Butcher, directing the Lions. What Jones had yet to factor in, however, was the amazing and unexpected increase in one Valley player's basketball skills, Larry Bird's.

When Larry said in his autobiography that he was shooting or playing every day for long periods of time that summer of 1972, he was not kidding. He would later ponder this obsession, how he continued to play even when he was "aching and so tired." Gary Holland, Larry's senior year coach, recalled that summer and how other boys playing with Larry would get tired and go home, and Larry would just wait for someone else to show up at the outdoor courts and continue playing.

When there was no one there to play a game with, Larry shot basket after lonely basket in solitude, even into the twilight and beyond. Occasionally, someone saw him playing by himself after dark, propelling a basketball repeatedly toward a rusty iron goal with ragged netting while summer cicadas serenaded the thin young teenager. Springs Valley player Tony Clark recalled even seeing Larry shooting around by himself in the rain, Larry's hair pasted to his head.

One steady playing partner that summer before Larry's junior year was fellow Blackhawk basketball member Michael Cox, Bird remembering how he and Cox "would just play and play and play. When we'd sit down, we'd still be dribbling the basketball." Bird also sneaked into the high school gym whenever he got the chance, taking shots there too for hours at a time.

While Larry's personal zeal for improvement with almost round-the-clock practicing on outdoor playgrounds continued, Coach Jim Jones' coaching passion also entered the picture. Although high school coaches in Indiana were not supposed to direct any summer practices, every player knew the coach was always around, watching to see if they were shooting and working on key skills. Jim Jones, for example, according to Bird, "was always around" that summer. Larry recalled that when he and Mike Cox worked out, Jones might stop by the playground, "showing us something," telling the two sweaty players he was leaving but that he would be back. Then, "He might come or go two or three times."

Perhaps sensing their great potential, Jones seemed to work extra hard with this team that summer. And of all the things that Coach Jones told his players to motivate them to give their all, the one that spoke the loudest to Bird was the idea that there was always someone out there taking one more practice shot, running one last sprint. Those images, Bird remembered, became a dark specter that drove him to the limits of practicing to improve his performance.

The tough practice regimen did not stop once school began. If anything, the intensity increased. Player Brad Bledsoe recalled the consistent running "Coach made us do in practice. It was brutal, but we were never out of shape once the season started." Indeed, once the season began, basketball became a Valley player's life. Larry got to school at six o'clock in the morning to shoot free throws. After school, there were grueling practices with Larry often staying afterward to shoot around some more. Finally the season started.

Part III:

From Despair To Glory

Springs Valley can't be touched.

— *Evansville Press* sportswriter, 1973

This is as good of a shooting club as I ever had.

— Coach Jim Jones describing his 1972-1973 team

Going by Land

Fifteen-year-old junior Larry Bird came to Springs Valley High School's official basketball practice in the early fall of 1972 a bit taller, heavier, and stronger. He stood at six three and weighed 155 pounds. Although his physical stature had increased to some degree, his basketball skills had grown astronomically. Coaches, team members, and fans, however, had yet to understand the depth of Larry's new level of play. They would soon learn.

At first, even Larry was unsure of his abilities or his possible role on the team. He decided at the start of the season to use his passing skills and rebounding efforts to help the team win, and to concentrate less on his scoring. Larry was also wise enough to recognize the hierarchy of older players.

Sportswriters apparently agreed with Larry's not particularly strong assessment of himself. None of the writers mentioned his name as a likely leader of the Blackhawks in early articles that talked about the team's chances for success. Interestingly,

Larry Bird began to show his great potential in his junior year. In the varsity team photo that year he stands in the middle of the top row.

however, one newspaper account at the beginning of the season listed Larry as potentially playing all three positions—forward, center, and guard—an indication of his versatility. But in another article, Bird was not even recognized as a possible starter. This probably made sense given his lack of playing time in his sophomore year the season before, save for going into the first two games in the sectional and scoring a few points, including the winning foul shots.

One Blackhawk player's name was on every sports reporter's mind: big senior Steve Land. Land, who also excelled academically and played tight end on the football squad up until his senior year, had caught the eyes of sports reporters early on in his career at Valley. One noted how Steve as a sophomore had led all scorers with twenty-five points in a particular game but added, "It's hard to say if this was Land's best game. It was score-wise, but in the Jasper game he looked great." Even as a sophomore, Steve was also good enough to make both the All-Sectional and All-Regional tournament teams. A scoring and rebounding machine, Land earned a place on the conference and sectional all-star teams his junior year, leading the county and the Blue Chip Conference in scoring, averaging nineteen points a game. Land's rebounding his junior year was just as impressive, the total for one game setting a Blue Chip Conference record of twenty-five grabs. Land also won the team's MVP trophy that year. One interesting sign that Steve had caught the eye of sportswriters by his junior season occurred when a sports reporter used his last name in a witty fashion in a sports headline—"It was a Landmark Victory"—to described Steve's thirty-point output. More witty uses of Land's name in headlines were soon forthcoming.

Jasper's six-eight Mike Luegers remembered Land as "being almost impossible to stop if he got the ball anywhere around the post. He had good hands, great footwork, and had one heck of a head fake. He was simply deadly around the ten-to-fifteen-foot range." Paoli's junior big man, Tim Eubank, was impressed as well. "Steve was huge and a great player even in eighth grade. By his senior year, he could take over a game. He simply owned the lane."

Steve Land had already made a name for himself during his sophomore year when he played alongside senior Mark Bird. Here he scores over a Salem player in Huntingburg regional play in 1971.

At the beginning of the 1972–1973 season, when Bird was a junior and Land a senior, Coach Jones, although typically a cautious man, all but gushed in an early interview about his up-coming team, telling a Bedford paper news reporter, "We've got the biggest team we've ever had. We've got a lot of depth, and of the nine returning lettermen on the team, all started at one time or another." The Blackhawks also had at least four good shooters, a rarity on any team.

The Bedford reporter certainly understood Jones' situation, saying that "Optimism is oozing from the Blackhawk gymnasium," and that the team was "loaded for bear." Interestingly, Al Brewster, the main sports columnist for the Bedford Daily *Times-Mail*, failed to mention Bird among the possible varsity squad. Thus, it may have been a bit of a surprise to many when, as the time drew closer for Valley's first game, Jones had selected his starting five, and six-three Larry Bird was one of them.

Larry's rise in status was fairly spectacular, considering he had played in only two varsity games the year before and scored a total of eight points. His quick rise, however, spoke to his hard work preparing for the season during the summer months. The other starters were six-five Steve Land, six-four Tony Clark, Danny King, and James Carnes.

Jones told Dave Koerner at the Louisville *Courier Journal* that having nine boys back who had started at one time or another would be a challenge in terms of keeping everyone happy. As it turned out, the squad would evolve into Jones' smoothest group of players. Jones explained to the sports reporter one change that ended up bringing great success to the team. When Steve Land played post at the center position, "He was always doubled teamed, so to make better use of his ability, we moved him to the outside where our patterns fit him better." The reporter noted this arrangement helped Land to become the team's leading scorer.

At this juncture, Jim Jones was beginning to move into his prime as a great Indiana high school basketball coach. Steve Land recalled that the coach "was always in a coat and tie at the games, and he was never out of control. He kept his program folded like John Wooden did, communicating to the players on the floor by giving out a quick whistle and a simple hand gesture. He might have gotten loud, but he never yelled or screamed. He never threw anything, never threw off his jacket, and never embarrassed himself or a player."

Up until this time, Jim Jones had accomplished many things at Springs Valley—winning sectionals, going deep into state tournament play, developing several players who received college scholarships— but one accomplishment, a rare gem in Indiana high school basketball, had escaped his grasp, although it was not something he publicly made a big deal about. The rare gem was going undefeated in a regular season. Jones' mentor, Rex Wells, had pulled off the trick his first year at Springs Valley. Jones had always indicated, however, that regular season wins were not important to him, that these games were simply a rehearsal for state tournament play. A glance at the 1972-1973 season schedule, however, suggested that several oppo-

Steve Land grabs a rebound while classmate Tony Clark looks on. Tony drove Larry Bird to his first visit to the Indiana State campus a few years later.

nents would be down to one degree or another. Winning every regular season game was surely on the coach's mind.

There was one subtle sign early in the season that Coach Jones had thoughts of a perfect regular season. Before the first game was played, Steve Land remembered how the team begged Jones to get the school to buy new basketball warmups, including pinstripe pants, a request Coach Jones playfully said he would gladly do, "if you guys go undefeated through Christmas."

The results of the first and second games of the season brought some reality to the hope of winning every contest. Pekin Eastern came to the Springs Valley gym with a 5-0 record and one of its best teams ever. The Blackhawks, however, got revenge from a loss the year before to Pekin, outscoring them in every quarter but one, and winning 77-60. The Bedford paper headlined senior Steve Land's great performance, adding that he "led all scorers with 26 points." Larry Bird followed with twelve points and Tony Clark garnered eleven.

Valley's second game against the Washington Hatchets at the spacious Washington gym was notable for how Larry's play was spotlighted, the first time Bird would receive his own splashy headline.

And what a headline.

It was a hell of a nip-and-tuck battle. Valley blew out to a big lead before the Hatchets tightened things by halftime, 40-36. In the third period, sportswriter Harry Moore wrote, "Bird soared." Larry bombed in four high-arching shots in a row from the corners, reminiscent of his brother Mark, putting the Blackhawks up by four when the final quarter began. In the last stanza, Washington tied the score, then went ahead by four with 1:10 left in the contest.

Then, like lightning, Steve Land scored. Danny King stole an inbound pass and made another basket. The game went into overtime.

As the overtime got underway, Steve Land won the opening tip. Steve went on to score four of the Blackhawks' last eight points, leading his team to a thrilling 74-72 victory. Land and Bird, however, would share the scoring honors, each getting sixteen. The next day the *Evansville Press* headlined "Springs Valley nips Washington." Harry Moore, at the *Paoli Republican*, however, could not hold back on his wordplay, writing the long, capped headline, "On Thanksgiving Eve Blackhawks Bury Hatchets By Giving Them The Bird."

Valley had little time to celebrate. They faced a tough undefeated Orleans crew next, a team that had come within a whisker of getting to the regional title game the season before and had rugged Curt Gilstrap and feisty Mike McClintic back

ON THANKSGIVING EVE
Blackhawks Bury Hatchets By Giving Them The Bird

Larry finally gets a sports headline of his very own in his junior year season.

for another campaign. It was a tense rivalry. For the Bulldogs, Orleans beating Valley was like Valley beating Jasper. An Orleans win against the bigger school was a major accomplishment, a season maker. Indeed, county basketball rivalries in rural southern Indiana drove the enthusiasm of players, coaches, and especially fans. Such rivalries were enhanced by proximity, kinship, and tradition. A victory gave a team, their families, and their community bragging rights at unexpected run-ins in towns, at church functions, and at family get-togethers. The bottom line was this: Orleans and Valley always gave their all when facing each other.

After the game, the Louisville *Courier-Journal* sports page picked up on the Blackhawks' dismantling of their county rival, a team that just the year before had thumped Springs Valley 66-35. The playful *Courier-Journal* headline read "Land's Sakes. Springs Valley Bumps Orleans." Indeed, Steve Land was the big gun again, racking up twenty-eight points while Larry Bird was in second place with eleven markers. Harry Moore, in the Paoli paper, reported that the Orleans/Valley game was close until the third quarter, when Valley's defense shut the Orleans Bulldogs down. Larry picked off twice as many rebounds as Land, but Gilstrap grabbed two more rebounds than Larry, a glimpse of the competition between those latter two to come.

The Blackhawks had jumped a big hurdle in beating Orleans, stirring the hopes even more for an undefeated season.

The Blackhawks' fourth contest was played at French Lick, with Valley taking apart North Daviess 67-48. The opposing team attempted to slow down the game and took an 11-9 first-quarter lead before the roof caved in. James Carnes took scoring honors with twenty-one points, followed closely by Steve Land with twenty. Bird had six for the contest, but if Larry was upset with his lack of scoring production, he couldn't dwell on it for very long. The Blackhawks would be traveling to do battle with yet another undefeated team, their primary rival, the Jasper Wildcats.

Something about Jasper rubbed Valley coaches, players, and fans the wrong way—the always noisy Jasper gym, complete with the constant beating of drums to distract opponents, and the availability of only two hundred tickets for the visiting team were maddening realities. One former Jasper player believed "our home court was worth ten points every game. Like many high school gyms at that time, we had what sounded like a hundred-piece band, a gym packed with three thousand fans, with some spectators sitting right on top of the out-of-bounds lines. It was a very intimidating place for opposing teams, and the noise level was deafening. My ears would ring for a few days after a home game."

Some of the dislike might also have been cultural. While the population of French Lick and Orange County were predominately descendants of laid-back upland south pioneers, Jasper folks, and those in most of Dubois County, were primarily hardworking people of German American descent. The Jasper community was also one of the most prosperous in the region, while Orange County was one of the poorest in the state. Conversely, Jasper's only dislike of Valley was probably the fact that Springs Valley teams often won in head-to-head basketball competitions.

Jasper fans may have hoped that Coach Ed Schultheis and the Wildcats would defeat the Blackhawks as they had the year before. Instead of more glory for the Wildcats, however, a new basketball idol for the already rich Springs Valley basketball tradition emerged from the shadows that eve-

Larry and his Springs Valley team ran up against one of southern Indiana's best players, Mike Luegers, when the Blackhawks came to town to play Jasper in 1972.

ning in the packed and deafening Jasper gymnasium.

The day after the contest, *Jasper Herald* sports editor Jerry Birge called the "talented Steve Land" the hero of the game, the stocky Blackhawk dealing "the damaging blow at the start of the final eight minutes as he hit two from ten feet out and added two free throws for a 60-52 Hawk lead." The game, however, was a nail-biter almost the entire way.

At the start, dependable Wildcat junior Mike Luegers made three quick baskets, and Mike Keusch and Dave Weidenbenner made two baskets each to help their team take a 21-18 first-quarter lead. The lead changed hands eleven times that quarter.

Jasper seemed to be putting the game away in the second half, stretching the lead to 35-26 shortly before halftime. At this

A hot game in the early 1970s in the always crowded Jasper gymnasium. Visiting fans were limited by Jasper's ticket-distribution method, and Valley teams often found it a tough place to play.

juncture, the noise from the Jasper supporters was earsplitting. One sportswriter noted, "The Wildcat fans loved it. They were really whooping it up. And the drums were drumming."

The drums did grow a bit quieter as the Blackhawks cut the

deficit to four at the half.

The rest of the game was not for the faint of heart. Jasper held on to its lead until the end of the third period, when Steve Land hit a thrilling eight-footer as the horn sounded, giving his team a two-point advantage and bringing Blackhawk fans to their feet, the basket stopping the drums for a short while. At the start of the fourth period, Land won the tip from Luegers, then scored when he got his hands on the ball. Steve then swiped a bad Jasper pass and scored again. Larry Bird grabbed another errant Wildcat pass and propelled a sharp, perfect pass to Land, who was then fouled in the act of shooting. Land cashed in both free throws.

Birge reported that in the final analysis, Jones' troops played "a near-perfect floor game," committing only eight turnovers, shocking a strong Jasper team and winning 69-62. The Blackhawks certainly had a good shooting eye that evening, at one pointing making fourteen foul shots in a row. Steve Land along with Valley's Danny King did the scoring damage against Jasper, Land gaining twenty-three and King fifteen. Clark added twelve. Larry Bird tallied eleven. Most importantly, Land had limited Luegers' scoring in the pivotal fourth quarter. But Jasper was not without some outstanding achievements. Stan Giesler scored twenty-two points, and Mike Luegers led Jasper in rebounding while knocking down twenty-one points.

Louisville, Kentucky's *Courier Journal* also touted Valley's exciting victory over Jasper, headlining "Land Spurs Springs Valley" and calling Steve Land "Valley's top gun." The Louisville piece also highlighted Land's third-quarter last-second shot, calling it the turning point of the contest.

For all his detailed information on the exciting game at Jasper, Jerry Birge, along with the Louisville sportswriter, did miss one Springs Valley asset that *Paoli Republican* reporter Harry Moore caught. It was an advantage that only increased as the season continued. Moore wrote, "This is one of the best Hawk passing teams we have seen. Larry Bird never missed an open man. Land had two good passes from Bird, then Larry hit Danny King." Bird later explained that the game was, in fact, another turning point for him in his quest to be the best basketball player possible. "We played a game over at Jasper, one of our big rivals. I was only averaging about ten points a game, but I was doing everything else." Coach Jones, however, was not happy. He took Larry aside at halftime and told Bird that if he didn't start shooting the ball, he was "not going to play anymore. You are hurting the team by not shooting when you're open." Larry took the direction to heart. "From that point on my game changed. I had to start scoring more, so I did."

In truth, while Larry did score seven points in the second half of the Jasper game, he was still slow to take Coach Jones' ultimatum to heart in the next few games.

Another interesting sports comment appeared in the Bedford paper after the Jasper win, an observation that indicated the Blackhawks would soon be catching the eye of surrounding communities and sportswriters in the rest of the state. The Bedford reporter noted, "Jim Jones, Springs Valley coach, has things going his way since the Blackhawks Saturday night upended the Jasper Wildcats 69-62. The win, too, was at Jasper where the Wildcats seldom lose."

Undefeated Valley's next contest was against a red-hot Barr Reeve club that stood 7-0 and had won an astounding twenty-six straight regular season games at home up to that point. Many thought, too, that the Blackhawks would be ripe for a loss, coming after the hard-fought victory over Jasper. Coach Jones, who typically never overstated his team's potential, felt otherwise, telling an *Evansville Courier* reporter before the game, "This is as good or maybe a little better shooting club than I ever had."

The coach was right. Barr Reeve was the fourth team Valley knocked from the unbeaten ranks, and although the final score was 72-69 in favor of Springs Valley, the game was not close. What made Coach Jones especially happy was that the scoring for the Blackhawks was evenly divided among three players who each got sixteen points, and another gaining fourteen. Larry tallied only six points, but Harry Moore pointed out that Bird still "played a whale of a game on the boards and on defense, making several steals." Moore also went on to praise the entire team. "Hard work has molded this year's edition of Hawks into a fine team. All last summer the boys were hard at it and it has paid off handsomely." One can be sure the Blackhawk players remembered all that hard work in the sweltering heat of the summer.

One of the often unnoticed and underrated difficulties a high-performing team faces involves playing much weaker teams. It is difficult to get up for such games, and embarrassing upsets occasionally occur. Further, nothing much is learned when a high level of competition is missing. In general, these contests tend to be dull events, despite an often-high scoring win. This was the case in Springs Valley's next two games in the Blackhawks' holiday tournament. Nearby Shoals was the first hapless victim, losing 105-46, Coach Jones playing all twelve varsity members and all but one ending up scoring points. This was also Larry's best game so far, scoring-wise, as he knocked down twenty-five. Steve Land was not far behind with twenty-two.

Fans thought the final tourney matchup with Brownstown would be a much closer game. It was not. Valley was now playing almost flawless basketball, running over Brownstown 85-48, with Bird playing well in every facet of the game—scoring, rebounding, defense, and passing. Then Valley played Shoals again in a regular season game, mowing them down 92-43. Again, every Blackhawk played.

The undefeated Blackhawks played Shoals in their first game after Christmas, bursting out of the dressing room decked out in their new pin stripe warmups, as promised by Coach Jones and pounding their opponent. North Knox was Valley's next victim. The contest was another runaway for the Blackhawks, a game they would easily win 97-59.

At some point in the contest, after Steve Land had made almost all his attempts in the first half, someone realized he was very close to breaking the old single-game scoring record for Springs Valley. It was a record shared by Land's cousin Jack Belcher and by Marv Pruett. Both Belcher and Pruett had scored thirty-nine points in a game.

The Springs Valley squad quickly got behind the effort to assist Steve in setting a new record. Land, however, certainly did his part. The *Springs Valley Herald* reported, "Steve kept pouring them in from everywhere on the court." Harry Moore noted too that Larry Bird was not idle, being, well, being Larry Bird. Besides getting twenty points, Bird "dazzled the crowd with his nifty passing. On one occasion he faked a shot and passed off. It had the official fooled. He was looking for the ball when Land put it through the hoop."

Land did set the single-game scoring record, one reporter describing how "Steve was outstanding in this game. His buckets weren't gimmies. He worked for them. He got several tip-ins and several from 10 to 15 out. He hit 18-29 attempts and was five-for-five at the line. During the first half Land hit nine of 11 shots." The Bedford *Daily Times-Mail* captured the importance of Steve to the team at this time when they carried the playful sports page headline "Hawks Are Going By Land." Although Steve Land's place as one of Springs Valley's very best players would soon be overshadowed by Larry Bird, in 1972–1973 Land was king, especially in the first six difficult games of the season. By this time Steve was drawing interest from Ball State, Indiana State, Hanover, College of William and Mary, and Tulane, among other schools.

After the North Knox victory, the Springs Valley team and community received a nice surprise. The Blackhawks had broken into the state top-twenty basketball rankings in the single class arrangement of that day, holding the seventeenth position, the only school in that part of the state on the list. The local paper congratulated the team, noting, "This is quite an accomplishment as Valley is considered a small-town team. This

Hawks Are Going By Land

Overlooked in the Valley:

A playful Louisville *Courier-Journal* sports headline features Valley's Steve Land in Coach Jones' best season at Springs Valley.

group of young men deserve the ratings and hope to see it climb higher as the season progresses." The team celebrated the ranking by going out the next game and steamrolling West Washington, 95-70. Of the eleven players on the varsity, all but two scored. Six were in double figures. Bird and John Carnes had eighteen, to lead the scoring parade, and Steve Land sixteen.

Valley's new ranking quickly caught the eye of the newspaper with the largest number of sports pages in southwest Indiana, the *Evansville Sunday Courier and Press*. Their report about Springs Valley's impressive play included a full-page story, one packed with photos of the team and of different players, including one of just Steve Land, whom the reporter called the team's leader. A column-long narrative observed that the exceptional team and the possibility of an undefeated season was just what Jim Jones had been waiting for. "Most coaches do hope to go undefeated at one time or another," the writer noted. Then the article related some historical context. "Springs Valley, which made a landmark appearance in the state tournament by going unbeaten until the afternoon game in Indianapolis in 1958, may be on its way to still a better year. It's hard to believe that even Jones would consider his present team as good as the '58 squad, but the Blackhawks rolled past all comers in the first half of the current year and have set themselves up as the odds-on favorites to capture the Paoli sectional."

Springs Valley was now 11-0, and had climbed to an enviable position in the state basketball ranking. The *Evansville Press* had them at the sixth spot in the southern half of the state. Coach Jones, however, may not have been happy with the lack of strong competition in the team's last five games, a situation he knew could backfire when his squad finally ran into a strong opponent. As noted, playing weaker teams can dull a good team's sharpness and throw off the winning rhythms that are earned in close, tough games. The report of Valley's victory over West Washington is a case in point. The Bedford paper noted how "outclassed" the losing team was. Every Blackhawk varsity member played and six scored in the high double figures. "The Hawks also had a wide 54-26 edge in rebounding. And they were helped by 26 West Washington turnovers."

A review of the Valley scorebook stats strongly suggests the dramatic situation. When playing in their first six games against solid teams, contests that helped the Blackhawks develop into a strong, dynamic squad, Valley won by an average of only ten points. In the next five games the Blackhawks won by an incredible 48.6-point average, with the starting players being replaced early on by bench players. In these instances, the sharpness of the starting five could only dull.

Coach Jones probably thought he was lucky playing a down 5-7 Corydon club the next game, a squad still tough enough to challenge the Blackhawks, making them bear down, and, in the process, getting them ready for upcoming Loogootee. The *Springs Valley Herald* reported just before the contest, "Corydon has been an in-and-out team this year," setting the stage for a bitter disappointment. Blackhawk sophomore Brad Bledsoe recalled signs of possible disaster before the contest. "We were probably overconfident, but in truth, it was a tough gym to play in. It looked like the inside of a barrel and the fans were intense. It didn't help that a window was broken in our dressing room, and it was ice-cold in there." Steve Land felt the dressing room situation was "psychological warfare by Corydon, meant to throw us off." Land may have been right.

Corydon blew ahead 21-8 at the end of the first quarter, and the Blackhawks were never in the game, losing 80-64 and getting out-rebounded 36-27. Worse, the Valley team made eighteen turnovers. The Louisville *Courier-Journal* pointed out that Corydon coach Jim Stewart used four different defenses to shut down Valley's usual hot shooting, but Coach Jim Jones argued that his team was simply "flat and they were really not ready. We made several turnovers the first quarter, they got us down and we never got back in." A Bedford reporter, however, got a real earful from Jones about his frustration with his team's play. "We just couldn't play defense tonight. They cut right through us, and our tempers flared. We just didn't play well at all."

The "temper" comment may have been directed at Larry Bird. Bird carried the scoring load for his team that night, getting twenty-one points, thirteen points coming in the second quarter. But he fouled out of the contest early in the fourth quarter, his frustration leading him to give the Corydon crowd the finger as he left the game. Valley also received two technical fouls in what turned out to be an ugly contest.

The *Paoli Republican* discussed the bitter loss beneath the front-page heading "Hawks Crest On Victory 11. Swept Off Roost By Corydon." Springs Valley's dream of going undefeated came to a crashing end, the article lamented, adding, "Saturday night Corydon caught Valley flat footed. It was just one of those games where a winner can do no wrong and the loser no right." A lack of rebounding, the paper added, was the "downfall." But then the piece also hit upon the many easy games Valley had played earlier. "Valley just hasn't had any competition since the Barr Reeve game." Mentioning the pressure that came with the short-lived top-twenty state ranking, the article finally pointed out, "Now the pressure is off."

Arnold Bledsoe, sportswriter at the *Springs Valley Herald* and Brad Bledsoe's father, argued that the loss "could very well be a blessing for the Hawks. It was better to get a game out of the system during the season than to wait until the tournament to fall flat." Bledsoe also noted the high caliber of the Blackhawk team, believing, "they will come back as strong as ever and maybe a bit wiser." With Orange County rival Paoli and Blue Chip Conference foe Loogootee coming up, the local sportswriter confidently declared, "I'm picking Valley over the Rams by 14 points and over Loogootee by 7."

Sports pages across the state were also quick to report on Valley's fall and the loss of the team's state ranking, the *Evansville Press*, for example, observing, "Springs Valley, unbeaten and No. 6 a week ago [in the Press' top teams in southern Indiana]. And this week? No. 11 after unranked Corydon ended the Blackhawks' 11-game winning streak."

But there were also some positive recognitions. After Valley's unexpected loss, a Terre Haute paper, the *Star*, carried a detailed article about Valley's and Steve Land's super accomplishments in the Blue Chip Conference, pointing out how Land was "way in front in the hoop scoring race with a 25.7 per game average" and added that the Valley team had set a record for field goals in a game and for the most points made in a single game. On a list of twenty leading scorers in the conference, Land was way ahead of his nearest competition. Several other Blackhawks were also on the list: James Carnes at number nine, Tony Clark at thirteen, and Larry Bird at the eighteenth position. The *Vincennes Sun-Commercial* summed up Valley's conference successes by headlining "Springs Valley Erasing Blue Chip Conference Records."

After the disappointing Corydon game, Jim Jones quickly began the task of resetting the season. An essential game with bitter county rival Paoli loomed ahead, then a big game at Loogootee, probably for the Blue Chip Conference title. And if the possibility of an undefeated season had indeed caused Coach Jones to stray from his philosophy of using the regular season to prepare for tournament time, he was surely ready to get his team back on track, focusing now on the conference and sectional titles. Those goals had always been the surer bet anyway.

Of Valley's two county rivalries, the one with the Paoli Rams was the oldest and usually most intense, sometimes verging on creating physical altercations among the fans. From some of the Valley fans' point of view, Paoli folks thought too much of themselves—living in a bigger and more prosperous town that had the county seat and possessing an especially ornate courthouse and square. Paoli High School also hosted the sectional tournament. This was an important advantage since Paoli would always have the benefit of home court in the tourney. On that cold Saturday night in late January 1973, however, as the Paoli team's bus slowly pulled into the Springs Valley gym's parking lot, the Rams' basketball team was struggling, mired down in a 3-10 season. The Paoli coach may have hoped that the recent Corydon debacle would help his team's cause, but if so, he was in for a disappointment.

Larry Bird was on a mission when Paoli rolled into town, bombing in nine field goals and making ten free throws for twenty-eight points, his largest single-game total yet, and leading his team to an 80-57 victory. Steve Land threw in fifteen points in the winning effort. The Paoli paper claimed that "few fans could remain involved to the finish of the game," with Bird and company "totally diminishing" the Rams. The *Couri-*

Steve Land breaks Springs Valley's all-time scoring record, one held since 1958 and set by the great Marv Pruett. Land's many records would not last long.

er-Journal declared in a gruesome image that the Blackhawks had completely ripped the Rams to pieces in the game.

Coach Jones had to be pleased with the victory, a sign, perhaps, that his players were getting back into a winning groove. They certainly needed to be in the groove. The next game was at Loogootee.

The Loogootee/Valley rivalry was interesting, one lacking the heat of Valley's more bitter competitions with Jasper and Paoli. In the latter case, for example, when Paoli native Gary Holland came to coach junior varsity at Springs Valley in 1969, some locals in Paoli vandalized his parents' store for their son's "betrayal" of the Paoli community.

In many ways, Loogootee was a mirror of Springs Valley. Both communities had a rich high school basketball tradition, but Loogootee had a louder, more aggressive coach, the legendary Jack Butcher. Jack got his share of technicals, perhaps sometimes doing so for tactical reasons. One reporter told of watching Coach Butcher over the years "kick chairs, toss warm-up jackets in the air, and do war dances," a complete contrast to Jim Jones' coaching style. And while Jack drew the most attention for his successes in leading small-school Loogootee deep into state tournament play in 1970 and for his many sectional championships, Coach Jones was probably as good a tactician, both coaches getting the maximum effort from their limited pool of players. Both Butcher and Jones preached the fundamentals of the game, and both knew how to use a delay tactic to level the playing field when playing bigger schools and better teams. In short, Valley/Loogootee meetings on the basketball floor were always exciting, nerve-racking events, the primary competition between the two schools usually focusing on the Blue Chip Conference championship. In the 1973 version, on a Tuesday night game in late January, played in front of a completely packed Loogootee High School gym, the battle would leave every coach, player, and fan in a heap of exhaustion.

According to the experts, Loogootee was in a "rebuilding year," coming into the game at 11-3 and on a five-game winning streak. Although lacking in height, the Lions had a dynamic set of guards, Bill Butcher and Alan Crane. Like Valley, they were disciplined, taking only good shots and blocking out on rebounding. The team also had one of those coaching father/son dynamics going, in the same vein as Indiana high school coaches Sam Alford and his son Steve, and Bob Macey and his son Kyle. And perhaps no other team in the state was as good as Loogootee when it came to playing a delay game.

Meanwhile, the same experts noted that Springs Valley had the dynamic Steve Land, a height advantage, and several good shooters such as Larry Bird, Tony Clark, and Beezer and John Carnes. Danny King had also begun stepping up as a fine playmaker at the guard position.

All bets would be off in this game.

Larry Bird was on fire the first two quarters, scoring sixteen points, keeping Valley within a single point of Loogootee at halftime. Steve Land was having a good night too in the first half, plowing his way under the basket to tally eight hard-earned points.

Interestingly, Loogootee junior forward Wayne Flick remembered little about Larry Bird's play that night and a lot
about Steve Land's, especially a key event occurring just a few
seconds before halftime. "Steve Land was a handful. Maybe six
four and 220. He'd just grind away, scoring and rebounding.
We were having trouble shutting him down in the first half."

At the time of the important just-before-halftime incident,
the Lions were up by one, bringing the ball down the court with
just a few seconds on the clock. But then Land stole the ball at
half-court and went down for what looked to be an easy layup.
It would have been the kind of basket that suddenly changes
the momentum of a game.

Loogootee's Wayne Flick got there just as Land was going up
to shoot. "I knew I had a foul to give so I made sure he didn't
score. It was a rough block, one where today I would have probably been thrown out of the game. Steve had to be restrained
but finally settled down. He missed both foul shots with no time
showing on the clock to end the first half."

The second half saw the first major coaching chess move of
the contest, Loogootee switching from a man-to-man to a zone
defense and sagging in on Steve Land to cut off his drive down
the baseline. The strategy worked. Steve did not score the rest
of the game. Coach Butcher also ordered a slowdown, his players working the ball around with great precision to take time
off the clock.

Coach Jones may have made his own chess move earlier in
the game, a gamble of sorts. Many basketball followers believed
Butcher worked the referees by loudly complaining about what
he believed to be bad calls. Such behavior, many argued, made
the officials more wary when making calls against Jack's team.
It was said Butcher would even risk a technical if he thought
it would make referees ease up on his teams. Perhaps this motivated Jones to boldly walk out to the ten-second timeline to
chew out a referee after Valley got a questionable call, easily
picking up a technical foul. The act did seem to liven the Blackhawk players in the first half. It is hard to say, however, how it
might have affected the officiating.

A rugged rebounder, Loogootee's Wayne Flick was a nemesis to both Springs Valley's Steve Land and Larry Bird.

In the second half the Black-hawks' shooting turned ice cold. After hitting 14-34 shots in the first half, they connected on only seven of twenty-eight in the second part of the contest. Amazingly, the game still came down to a last-second shot. Valley grabbed a brief lead with 5:48 to go in the fourth period before Lion center Mike Walls' basket put Loogootee back on top 49-47. There were only 46 seconds left in the game when Larry Bird hit a rebound shot to tie the contest, leaving fans on both sides hysterical. Loogootee had yet to score a field goal in the last quarter until Alan Crane hit a fifteen-footer with twenty-five seconds left, his twentieth point. Loogootee now had a 51-49 lead.

Ten seconds later, Larry Bird, while going for a basket that would have tied the game, was called for charging, sending Wayne Flick to the foul line on the other end. Flick missed the first free-throw attempt of a one-and-one situation, perhaps a bit of karma for his hard block on Land earlier. Valley's Tony Clark snagged the rebound.

The Blackhawks came storming down the floor, a few precious seconds still on the clock, Loogootee fans thinking the clock was running too slow and Valley fans thinking it was running too fast. The ball got into the hands of Beezer Carnes, who lofted a shot from fifteen feet, just to one side of the top of the key. Russ Brown, sportswriter for the Louisville *Courier Journal*, wrote the next day, "The ball spun in and out of the basket, then hung tantalizing on the back of the rim for a couple of seconds—while the crowd oohed and aahed—before finally rolling off into the hands of Loogootee's Bill Butcher as time expired." Kevin Smith, a young junior high student at Valley at the time, also remembered the ball spinning deep into the net, then spinning out, only to sit for a few agonizing seconds at the back of the rim before falling away. "You literally heard a collective moan erupting from our fans' section."

The Louisville sportswriter came into the Valley locker room after the game. "Coach Jones talked to him some," Steve Land remembered, "but I was so disappointed, I had nothing to say."

Loogootee Coach Jack Butcher, one of Indiana's high schools' best.

The other Blackhawk players felt likewise.

Like the immediate space after an untimely death, Valley players and fans pondered what might have been for some time—What if Steve Land had made the halftime layup? Would that have changed the momentum of the game? What if Larry Bird had not been called on a charging foul in those last few seconds and been given foul shots instead? What if Coach Jones had not gotten a technical? What if the ball had not spun out of the basket?

One would have thought it would be a game long remembered, but Valley's next year's battle with Loogootee was destined to become even more iconic.

There were six games left in the regular season after the Loogootee loss, and Jim Jones turned his attention to getting his team ready for sectional play. Valley needed some solid games to build up momentum, and they got them, along with Steve Land gaining another all-time school record. Just before Valley played Huntingburg in the Hunters' huge gym, however, Coach Jones expressed his concerns to Jerry Birge of the *Jasper Herald* about the state of his team. "We played five games in a row that we won easily, and we started to feel that we could do about anything we wanted to on the basketball floor, but suddenly we're no longer that sharp." Jones also explained the team's plight to a Vincennes reporter. "We haven't played good ball the second half of the season, and we deserved to lose both games we lost. We ran some big scores against some teams that weren't very good at the start of the season, and I think those big scores went to our heads."

Coach needn't have worried. In the very next game, Huntingburg fell to Valley's spread-out scoring barrage, Tony Clark getting fifteen points, Beezer Carnes snaring thirteen, and Land and Bird each collecting twelve. The Raiders did draw close at the very end of the contest, making a bit of a comeback, but the game ended 62-57 Valley.

Bloomfield, under Coach Guy Glover, was Valley's next victim. Glover was known for his savvy coaching, and the Cardinals had a solid record and a fine team, one that would measure how the Blackhawks were doing late in the season.

The answer came quickly: excellently.

Against Bloomfield, all five Blackhawks scored in the first quarter, and Valley won the game easily, with Land shooting for eighteen, as did Tony Clark. Danny King chipped in fourteen. Most of all in the contest, there were amazing flashes of what Larry Bird would be by the next year. "The Hawks," reported the *Springs Valley Herald*, "led throughout the game as Larry Bird took charge on both offense and defense to pace the

Larry Bird shakes his raised fist in disbelief after Loogootee has just gone
ahead in the last seconds of a game on a shot by Loogootee's Alan Crane.

Hawks with 24 points and 18 rebounds. Larry picked off six offensive rebounds and put four back in. Bird was also a demon
on the defense board with four full court passes that led to easy
buckets for the Hawks."

South Knox, another solid team, ran into an awesome offensive attack when they came to the Springs Valley gym for the
next game. In the first period, Steve Land had eight straight
points before South Knox knew what had hit them. After
Steve's fourth field goal, the game horn suddenly sounded, halt-
ing the contest, and it was announced that Land had broken
the Springs Valley all-time scoring record set by Marv Pruett.
Coach Jones came out on the floor and presented Steve with the
game ball, and the crowd gave the Blackhawk hero a rousing
standing ovation. Then the game proceeded as the Valley squad
smashed South Knox 88-66. Land celebrated his major new record by leading all scorers with twenty-two points.

After the game, the Blackhawk players all autographed Steve
Land's basketball. Perhaps it was Larry Bird's intense competitive spirit, shaped by all those times that his older brothers
worked him over in playground games that moved him to write,
"To number one, after me."

Sports reporter Harry Moore, sensing the swelling tide of

Springs Valley success as sectional time approached, reported after the South Knox victory that the Blackhawks had "put it all together in the two weekend games, not just for a couple of quarters but in all 32 minutes. This is the best Valley has looked since they defeated Barr Reeve Dec. 15." Further good news involved the team's amazing free-throw accuracy, a product of Coach Jones' free-throw shooting regimen in practice and before school. For the two games, the Valley players nailed an incredible 90 percent of their attempts, making 49-55. The French Lick newspaper also rejoiced. "Over the weekend, the Blackhawks looked like the Hawks of old. It seems the Hawks are getting back into the groove and will be ready for the sectional."

The next game against a physical Mitchell team was far from a perfect performance. In front of a packed Springs Valley gym, the Mitchell team jumped out to a steady first-quarter lead, knocking around the Valley players until Steve Land hit a thrilling shot that swished the net just as the first period ended, leaving the score 12-10 in favor of the Bluejackets. Meanwhile, Larry Bird picked up three quick fouls. Valley led by only six at halftime, and Valley fans were growing nervous. Then Bird came back in the second half to score fourteen points, and Valley pulled away to win by ten.

The point-scoring spread achieved against Mitchell surely made Coach Jones happy. Bird contributed sixteen, and three other players had ten points each. Just as exciting for the fans and Coach Jones was senior guard Danny King's growing floor leadership. His great play, according to Harry Moore, was keeping everyone "on the edge of their seats with his shooting and jumping abilities." King, another sports article reported, "will make some college a fine leader as guard," a prediction that later came true when Danny played at Indiana State University.

The Blackhawks traveled to Salem for their next-to-the-last regular season contest, and it was Tony Clark's turn to shine. He had a spectacular night, leading all scorers with twenty-two points, while Danny King nailed sixteen. Larry came out of the game after scoring fifteen but also having been called for a technical foul. Land was in the unusual spot of being the fourth-place scorer with fourteen points. Salem trailed the entire game and lost 83-64.

More important than the score of the contest was the sense building up about Springs Valley's post-season chances, a growing feeling that Coach Jones and his boys might go deep into the state tournament. The balanced scoring of the team and its smooth dynamic play was certainly catching everyone's eye. The Bedford *Times-Mail* advised, for example, "Keep your eye on Coach Jim Jones' Springs Valley Blackhawks in this high school basketball business. Last night the Hawks, playing at Salem, clobbered the Lions for an impressive 17-2 record."

The Blackhawks faced one last game before the Paoli sectional, a tilt against Brownstown. The contest had absolutely no drama, the kind of game that offers little to the winning team to help them prepare for post-season play. Brownstown came into the game at 5-14 and found itself behind every quarter. The lackluster game was a 76-60 win for Springs Valley.

Tony Clark, however, put in another great effort, knocking down twenty-three. Bird, whose name was misspelled Byrd in the Seymour paper, hit for twenty, and Land had thirteen. One sports report also mentioned after the game that Larry Bird was "one of the best assist men to ever wear a Hawk uniform."

At the end of the regular season, sportswriter Harry Moore summed up the individual scoring that season for the three Orange County teams with competent preciseness: "Once again a junior led the county in scoring. Curt Gilstrap finished the season with a 20.2 average. Last year Steve Land was the leader, averaging 18.3." In the 1972–1973 season Land followed Gilstrap with an eighteen-point average, followed by Orleans' Steve McCracken with a 17.4 average. Next came Paoli's Tim Eubank with 16.6 and Larry Bird with a 15.6 average.

Valley players and Jim Jones had a week to catch their breath before the sectional tournament, a time to ponder their amazing regular season and ideally build upon it to win the first rung of state tournament action, a sectional championship. Looking back, it was easy to see that the season had been a time of living in rare air, the team achieving the second-best record in the school's history, 18-2. The record was also Jim Jones' best at Valley in his eleven years of coaching there. Only the 1958 undefeated Springs Valley team surpassed the 1973 squad in wins. Strangely, it did not feel like enough. The Valley tradition, set by the undefeated 1958 team, was a heavy shadow. The 1972–1973 squad was also the team Jones told a Seymour sports reporter contained "the finest group of shooters we've ever had." Thus, much was expected. Then came the Corydon and Loogootee defeats. But all that was water under the bridge. For the regular season Land had averaged over eighteen points a game and fifteen rebounds. Bird had averaged almost sixteen points and was a close second in rebounding. Clark was a close third to Land and Bird in points with a fourteen-point average, and Danny King and Beezer Carnes both averaged ten points a contest. The team's shooting percentages, both in field goals and at the free-throw line, had often been spectacular, and the team rarely had an off-shooting night. The highly skilled team members also played together beautifully, and few would dare to believe that Valley would ever again produce such a fantastic group of players.

It was a dream regular season and team, the kind of team Jones knew could go deep into state tournament play.

The Forgotten Season

The week before and during Indiana high school sectional play was a time of great excitement for an Indiana school and its community, along with a time of high anxiety for coaches, players, and fans. Springs Valley was no exception to this phenomenon. One Valley native, Ron Prosser, a junior high student during Larry Bird's reign at Springs Valley, recalled that "listening to the sectional draw on radio or watching on a fuzzy Channel 4 from Indianapolis if conditions were perfect was the first phase of the frenzy. Local businesses all competed in a window decorating contest for sectional week." It was standard practice for school officials at Valley to "call students out of classes by grade level just to make sure every student had an opportunity to purchase a ticket. A car caravan of fans following the fan buses to both the sectional and regional were quite the sight. I am not sure how many cars were involved, but I remember being near the front and not being able to see the last car."

Hope was the overpowering feeling that burst forth at this time. Indiana communities, especially the smaller ones, put almost everything on hold during the week of sectional play. All regular season records, whether good, bad, or in between, were wiped away, and every team, worst to best, started over. In the heart of every Indiana high school basketball fan, it was deemed possible that a team with a poor regular season record, or a small-school team that had not played the bigger schools, would be fated to win a game over a much better team, and maybe even ride deep into tourney play. These were the key elements that made Hoosier Hysteria so exciting, such upsets staying in the memory of both winning and losing teams, perhaps in the memory of the entire state, for a long time. A few of these upsets gained the status of legend, and any teams playing in any level of state tournament competition were part of an archetypal experience.

Coach Jones had been made wise by his many years of varsity coaching, knowing each tournament game brought either exaltation or despair. Close games exhausted entire communities— both those at the gymnasiums and those with their ears literally next to a radio at home or their place of work. And the journey from heady joy, when winning a game, to complete shock and despair, at losing, was not like descending a stairway; it was a sudden plunge into a dark basement, a gallows' drop. Jim Jones had been through all these experiences. He had led a team with only five regular season wins deep into state tournament play. He had also experienced a bitter defeat to a weaker team in the sectionals, to archrival Paoli, when he had one of his top teams in 1970. He knew as much as anybody about how unpredictable Indiana high school basketball could be. But looking at the lay of the land in 1973, just before the start of sectional play, the situation could only have been reassuring for the Valley coach. All the teams in the upcoming Paoli sectional, save for Orleans at 15-4, were down, and Valley had soundly beaten Orleans earlier in the season. Milltown, Valley's first opponent, was 13-6 but played lesser competition in the regular season and did not figure to present much of a challenge. Other teams were so-so at best. English was 9-10, Leavenworth, 10-9, Marengo, 9-10, West Washington, 3-15, and host Paoli, 7-14.

One could bet there were several strong reasons why Jim Jones would have desperately wanted to win the 1973 Paoli sectional. As noted, when Valley was moved from Huntingburg to Paoli in 1970, he had told sports reporter Jerry Birge that the Blackhawks would dominate the Paoli sectional. But in the ensuing three years, Jones' teams had won only one trophy prize at Paoli, and that was in two squeakers where Mark Bird had stepped forward as the hero. Jones' 1973 team, however, was a powerful, well-balanced group, the best all-around group he had ever had. It would be devastating if they did not win.

If there was one thing that did bother Jones, it was the tournament draw. His team, clearly the favorite, and the only other team who could give Valley a game, Orleans, were in the same bracket. Valley, Jones went on to explain to *Courier Journal* sportswriter Pat Biggs, "will have three games as tough as anyone if we're going to win. We'll have to play them three nights in a row too."

But Jones could take solace in the knowledge he had great team depth. He would be able to rest the starting players while using other solid players as substitutes. In this regard alone, Valley was in better shape than any other team, the confident Valley coach telling a reporter he felt his team was "stronger than the others in terms of depth." Blackhawks fans took comfort too in the many sportswriters in the region who picked the Blackhawks to easily blow through the competition at Paoli. *Evansville Press* writer John Updike announced that at Paoli, "Springs Valley can't be touched." Jerry Birge at the *Jasper Herald* wrote that the winner at Paoli would be "Jim Jones and his Blackhawks," while another regional newspaper declared, "Springs Valley in a big way."

The *Evansville Press* was already looking ahead to the Washington regional, where they picked Jasper and Springs Valley as having the best chance of winning. The newspaper article went on to explain that Valley was an especially "good team, a lot better than some northern posters figure, though the Blackhawks haven't had much trouble convincing southern writers and coaches." Calling Steve Land "the major cog in the Hawks offense," the piece went on to emphasize that "Six-6 Steve Land, capable of scoring 25 points any night, is the key to this team, one that can score upwards 80 or 90 points on any given night and can play with anyone." The sports reporter added, after praising Land, "Tony Clark, Dan King, and company will just go out, do their job, and provide the balance necessary to win." This latter observation was understandable. The Valley team was now more than just the superb Steve Land, having come together in a dynamic way. By the end of the regular season, all five starters had been leading scorers in a game at least twice, Danny King had developed into the squad's "floor general," and Larry Bird was scoring, rebounding, and making passes that amazed the crowds at a rate that suggested he would be a player to contend with the next season.

But Harry Moore at the *Paoli Republican* was the one writer who sounded an alarm. "If the Hawks aren't careful, that 18-2

Junior Larry Bird and senior Tony Clark were photographed for an Evansville newspaper article about the Blackhawks on the eve of 1973 sectional play.

record can go right out the window. Practice is over; the big games are ready to commence. And in tournament play, it takes only one game." Moore did concede that "Coach Jones has had a lot of success in tourney play. This year's edition seems to be what Coach Jones has been waiting for. Eight lettermen make up this year's roster. Each one of the lettermen has been a starter." In listing and analyzing the main players, Moore started with Steve Land. Then he discussed Tony Clark and Dan King. Larry Bird was fourth in the discussion, a player who Moore explained "had many good games," an indication that Larry at this point was good, but not yet great.

Many years later, Coach Jones noted in an interview that he was "sure we would win the sectional. I knew we were in good shape. We were ready."

When the Valley bus carrying the Blackhawk players arrived at the Paoli gymnasium for their first game with Milltown, the players and the Valley fans were in for a not-so-good surprise. Although the Blackhawks and the Rams would play each other only if both teams made it to the final game, some of the Paoli students had placed a large display in a glass case in the hallway to the gym that featured a huge paper Sesame Street Big Bird with Steve Land's number on the front.

Steve Land thought it was funny, but his family was upset.

Despite the Big Bird episode, the game with Milltown seemingly electrified Jim Jones' team. "The Hawks ran the Millers 'out of the gym' in a runaway victory," reported the Bedford *Times-Mail*. Slender Tony Clark hit six of eight tries in the first half, but Dan King captured scoring honors with eighteen when the final horn sounded. Land was second in scoring with fourteen points, followed by Clark with thirteen and Bird with nine. Of the twelve Valley players, only two did not score. Valley ended up winning 78-47, a thirty-one-point spread. Even more important, the Blackhawks had shot an amazing 63 percent in the win. Orleans did well too in the first tournament game they played, almost breaking the hundred-point mark and clobbering Marengo 99-74 and shooting almost as well as Valley.

Springs Valley was rolling now, possessing a shining 19-2 record. And they prepared to meet county rival Orleans in a semifinal round with the knowledge they had soundly whipped the Bulldogs earlier in the season, 60-47. In that game, Steve Land had easily outdueled Curt Gilstrap, scoring twenty-eight points to Curt's eighteen. Looking ahead, Valley fans figured they would be playing Paoli in the final game. Excitement was sky high in the Valley.

It was ironic that Orleans Coach Charles Denbo had grown up in West Baden, although few in southern Indiana during state tournament time probably thought much about abstract concepts such as irony. Denbo certainly saw things differently from Valley supporters before the Bulldogs' semifinal sectional game with Springs Valley. And with good reason. After losing three of their first eight games, the Bulldogs lost only one contest the rest of the regular season, and that loss involved a close 46-42 contest with powerhouse Loogootee.

Assessing his team for the Louisville *Courier Journal* in an aw-shucks manner, Denbo argued, "We really don't have any weaknesses that someone can get at. We play decent defense, our offense is good, everyone can score, we have pretty fair speed and quickness and we've done a good job on rebounding, despite the fact that we're smaller by far than most of the teams we've played." In the game against Marengo, the Bulldogs shot almost 60 percent. Of course, it helped greatly that Orleans had one of the best big men around, hardnosed Curt Gilstrap. A junior, Curt had performed well in his sophomore year and was on his way to breaking several Orleans scoring records. Coming into the sectional, he had twenty-one-point and seventeen-rebound averages. Steve McCracken, a senior, scored at a seventeen-point clip for the Bulldogs, and junior Mike McClintic could quickly turn a game around with his clutch shooting and never-say-die attitude. Like the Blackhawks, the Bulldogs played intense, disciplined basketball. And they were the last team you would want to stack up a big lead on you out of the gate.

It probably hurt the Blackhawks that they had few if any

One astute sports reporter noted Orleans players Mike McClintic and Curt Gilstrap could do almost anything with a basketball.

games in the regular season where they had to struggle back from behind to win. The Blackhawks were staggered in the very first quarter after the Bulldogs took an unexpected 23-15 lead. Orleans never looked back. They were never behind and were "in total control throughout the process," explained the *Courier-Journal* the next day, "winning in stunning ease." Orleans could hardly miss, hitting at a 56 percent clip. Curt Gilstrap made 11-19 baskets and was 8-8 from the foul line for thirty points. Valley, meanwhile, hit only 36 percent from the field.

The box scores tell the complete story of Valley's horrible shooting from the field. Larry Bird was 6-22, Steve Land, 5-15, and Danny King, 6-16.

Despite the lopsided outcome, 81-65, the game was fierce, the desperate Blackhawks firing away to the very end, pushing to get at rebounds, hoping to close the gap, and the Bulldogs never hitting a bad patch. The intensity of that game was captured in a Bedford newspaper report the next day that noted, "Mike McClintic, starting forward for the Bulldogs, was hit in the throat in the opening period and had to leave the game. Oxygen was used to revive him, and he came back in the second half to finish

Beezer Carnes scores a layup against Milltown in the first game of the 1973 Paoli sectional.

Junior Larry Bird and other Blackhawk players are caught flat-footed in Valley's loss to Orleans in 1973 sectional tournament play. Big Curt Gilstrap looks on from the right.

with 12 points." In Indiana high school basketball there are few excuses for staying out of a game, even after an injury, especially in tournament play, and Mike McClintic was as tough a player as they come.

After the surprising upset came the post-mortem assessments. Harry Moore at the *Republican* pointed out that "The ball took crazy bounces for the Hawks, and it was just the opposite for the Bulldogs. For them it took crazy bounces but fell through the hoop." The Bulldogs, according to Moore, also "played like a championship team. Coach Charles Denbo had them ready. They jumped out early and were never headed." Moore, however, praised the game played by Blackhawk Danny King. "Dan King played one whale of a game. He was all over the floor on defense and held Bulldog ace Steve McCracken to 11 points." Moore also noted, "Curt Gilstrap was superb."

With this game, junior year player Curt Gilstrap established himself as the premier big man in the county and the region. Now approaching six eight and weighing in at nearly two hundred pounds, he dominated under the basket in both the scoring and rebounding categories. Curt possessed another important skill. Two years later, Coach Denny Crum at the University of Louisville would call Gilstrap "my best interior passer." More importantly from Valley's viewpoint, Larry Bird, also a junior, while skilled at shooting, rebounding, and passing, would probably be at a disadvantage at six three when playing against Curt in the next season.

The unexpected end of the 1972–1973 season for Valley verged on tragedy. The hometown newspaper spoke of the game and its impact on the season as if they were speaking of a death. "This has been a long week for Hawk fans and players trying to relive the game and find out what went wrong. These boys gave everything they had but one night can ruin a good year for everyone. This has been a good year for Coach Jones and the Hawks, finishing with the second-best record in Hawk history, but the big one got away."

Coach Jim Jones was devastated. "I didn't talk to anyone after the game," he recalled. This was the best Valley team Jones would ever have—balanced, skillful, and dynamic in play. Without a sectional victory, however, the sterling 18-2 record, the second-best regular season record ever accomplished by a Springs Valley boys' basketball team, would be all but forgotten, never enshrined in the Springs Valley gymnasium with a large team photo hanging on the wall, the team's hard work and great success cast into the dust bin of time. Also to be forgotten were the other great records, the scoring feats of Steve Land and of the Springs Valley team, and of Land and Bird making the all-conference first team.

If there was one winner to be found as the dust settled on the disheartening season, however, it was junior Larry Bird. By playing with a cast of awesome seniors—Steve Land, Danny King, Tony Clark—Bird had been able to play with less pressure, leaving him to develop at a more comfortable pace with his scoring, rebounding, and passing. If Bird had been carrying more of the load, especially as a six-three forward, the pressure

One of Larry Bird's toughest high school rivals, Curt Gilstrap, scores two.

might have had an adverse effect. Instead, he and the Blackhawk team received great support from the fans and sportswriters, the kind of adoration that lifted Bird to play his best
basketball. And since Bird had one more year, the sense of a
ruined season at the very end might not have touched him as
deeply as it did Coach Jones and the graduating seniors.

Another interesting event involving Larry that year is a story not well understood in all the other Larry Bird narratives.
Some books give the strong impression that Larry was not being looked at by college scouts until his breakout senior year
during the '73–'74 season. This research, however, discovered
a 1979 article appearing in the Terre Haute magazine *Spectator*, which suggested Steve Land's record-setting efforts helped
introduce Larry to the college world. A college scout coming to
see Steve play also noticed Larry. In the *Spectator* piece, Mike
McCormick wrote how he remembered the first time he heard
the name Larry Bird in 1973. Gordon Stauffer was ISU's head
basketball coach at the time, and he told McCormick of a solid
player who was a junior, a player other schools had yet to notice. "His name is Larry Bird," Coach Stauffer told McCormick.

Later, Indiana State did get Larry, but not when Coach Stauffer had hoped. Larry, in his own story, explained, "The first whiff of recruiting I got was during my junior year when some scouts came to look over my teammate, Steve Land. But after seeing us play, they started showing a little interest in me."

Big brother Mark Bird was also trying to help Larry get a college scholarship around this time. One story floating around was that as a student at Oakland City College who played basketball for the Mighty Oaks, Mark approached the Oakland City College coach after Larry's junior season and told him about his little brother. The coach asked Mark, "Is he great?" Mark said no, "But he's good." The coach responded, "We've got good. We need great."

All the college stuff, however, did not matter. Larry later told how he was not interested in thinking about college after his junior year. He just wanted to be the best high school basketball player he could possibly be in his upcoming senior year, especially after the team failed to win the sectional title his junior year.

The saddest casualty of the unexpected and heartbreaking end to the season, Steve Land, spent the Saturday night Orleans played and beat Paoli for the 1973 sectional championship at the local French Lick Springs Theater. He sat slumped down near the back of the cavernous theater room, crying in the darkness, wondering how his team could lose only two games all year and not be either conference or sectional champions. Not even his tremendous accomplishments brought relief. By the end of his senior year Steve owned the school's all-time scoring record, as well as the single-game scoring record and the record for most field goals scored in a game. Steve was also Valley's all-time leading rebounder. He held the Blue Chip Conference single-game scoring record, the record for most field goals scored in a game, and the rebound record, gained in his junior year. In 1973, he was a unanimous choice for the all-conference first team and the leading scorer in the Blue Chip Conference that year with a 25.7-point average.

Steve could not have known that the next year, Larry Bird as a senior, working with a lesser cast and playing in every game, would be completely unleashed, breaking all Steve Land's astounding records and casting Land's accomplishments to the wind. To add insult to injury, an *Indianapolis Star* article in June 1974 about Larry Bird, after it was announced Bird had made the Indiana All-Star team, incorrectly claimed Larry had broken the school records that had been set by Mark Bird. Another source stated that Larry had broken Marv Pruett's records. The 1972–1973 year, once so full of promise, came to be the Blackhawks' forgotten season, and the season of the forgotten Blackhawk, Steve Land.

The forgotten Blackhawk.

Reset

Larry Bird was not untouched by the bitter ending to his junior year season. For all of his disconnection from the world around him and his singular obsession with improving his game, he was still aware of how local basketball fans, the so-called drugstore coaches in the valley, made their thoughts known. Larry remembered critical locals sitting around places like the barbershops to "talk about last night's game. The day after the game, someone will always come up to the players or the coaches and say, 'You should have done this or that.'" But after the 1973 loss at the Paoli sectional, Larry likely saw that fans were more than discontented: their hopes for a deep plunge into the state tournament, ideally reminiscent of the 1958 team's successes, had been shattered. The disappointing ending of the 1972–1973 season made Larry Bird more determined than ever to become the best basketball player possible and help recapture the faith of the fans and the team's confidence. This level of dedication became clear early on.

When Springs Valley High School held its basketball sports banquet in 1973, Coach Jones was stunned when he realized Larry wasn't there. Knowing Larry, Jones quickly jumped into his car and drove to Larry's favorite outdoor basketball court, where he found Bird playing in a pickup game. Jones persuaded Larry to come to the event and receive his awards.

During those few months before school was out, and on into the summer, Larry spent almost every free minute training to get better, constantly shooting around, playing fierce pickup games, and experimenting with new passing moves. He also started a weightlifting routine.

Many athletes dreaded working out with weights, finding it painful, but Larry was totally committed to do whatever it took to pick up some needed bulk and strength. Working out in the Springs Valley gym in the close, sultry heat of an Indiana summer on a universal weight training machine, Larry huffed and puffed his way to a new level of physical power. While never bulky, Larry's lifting clearly gave him more size and strength, gains that increased both his rebounding abilities and the distance from which he could shoot.

Still, no one was ready for an unexpected phenomenon, an event that did touch upon magic in that it had nothing to do with effort. It was an amazing gift, coming on its own accord.

Mark Shaw, in his book *Larry Legend*, noted that after the disastrous ending of the 1973 season, "No one who saw Larry play in 1973 could imagine the greatness in store for him. Most expected he would become a small-college player like his brother Mark, who attended Oakland City College." Assistant coach Gary Holland assessed, "Larry was a good player, but not a great one. I never thought he could be that good." Of course, Indiana State was apparently looking at Larry, but they saw him as a six-three guard. What changed all this was the unexpected circumstance of Larry's astonishing growth spurt. Holland was the first to notice the change just before school was out for the summer. The team was photographed one more time wearing the pin stripe warmups Coach Jones had gotten for them for going undefeated in the first part of the season, a way to celebrate the year even though it wasn't what they hoped it would be. At first Holland thought Larry was wearing his hair a different way, making him looked taller. Then Holland saw him standing next to six-five Steve Land, and saw Larry was now taller than Steve. Larry had been growing almost before their very eyes, a visual manifestation of Larry surpassing Steve Land.

By the time school rolled around the next fall, Bird had grown four full inches, now standing at six seven and still growing. He would stop at six nine by the time he graduated from college. Just as amazing, Larry's high-level skills were not affected by the rapid growth, neither his coordination nor his ball-handling skills. He was now a six-seven center who could still play like a six-three guard. Larry later noted that one of the main things that changed his entire game "was my growth in height. There is no question my height has made a big difference." One could add this sudden increase in height to the list of the ultimate

This was the photo event at the end of the 1973 school year when Springs Valley coaches first became aware of Larry Bird's incredible growth spurt.

things that made Larry develop into such a great player, along with the influences of Mark Bird and Jim Jones, and Larry's own hard work and determination.

Larry's older brothers, Mike and Mark, likely got the first glimpses of Larry's amazing metamorphosis. The two were working that summer in Gary, Indiana, and Larry and a friend drove up there to see them a few times. This was after Mark's first year of playing basketball at Oakland City College. Mark reported of his younger brother, "Suddenly he's up to six-six and he's put on some weight."

Mark asked Larry if he would like to play some basketball at an outdoor court with him and Mike against some of the local high school kids. Larry smiled and nodded yes. The Bird brothers dominated all comers. After those games, Mark walked over to Larry and said, "Man, have you improved." When Mark went on to ask him if he had been practicing much, Larry answered, "Every day, all day."

That same hot, sultry summer, Milltown's six-eight center Dave Smith spent many days driving around to different towns looking for good pickup basketball games. He was told there was one where many top players showed up at Sprudel Hall gym in West Baden. "I got there and began talking to one of the Carnes guys who asked me if I had seen Larry Bird lately. 'He's

really grown. You won't recognize him.' Sure enough, he came
walking in. He was about as tall as me. And boy, could he play."

As the 1973 school year wound down in May and Larry Bird's
growth spurt and hard work were beginning to bring about extraordinary improvements, enhancements that would eventually
lead to an unforeseen golden future, Coach Jim Jones was assessing the next year's season and his own future as coach at Springs
Valley High School. Jones had several issues to consider.

It was true Larry Bird would be back, and he was certainly
good, but he was not yet great. Further, the other returners were
not like the ones that Jones had just lost to graduation from the
18-2 team—record-setting and scholarly Steve Land, along with
Tony Clark and Danny King. These three seniors had been quiet, hardworking sports companions since their Biddy Ball days,
and had come together their senior year to forge a dynamic,
highly functioning unit. In the upcoming season, besides Larry,
only senior starters Beezer Carnes and John Carnes would be
left. This was a bit of a rough-edged crew, Bird, for example,
having given the finger to the Corydon crowd his junior year.

Competition from opponents looked to be solid too. Jasper
would be returning with six-eight Mike Luegers and a strong
supporting cast. Orleans still had six-eight Curt Gilstrap and
gutsy Mike McClintic, one sportswriter noting, "You could
write a book on what Curt and Mike can do with a basketball."
Loogootee, a Blue Chip Conference foe, was said to be even better than the year before with Bill Butcher now leading the Lion
squad. And even Paoli, who had seen four coaches in four years
and had struggled with consistency, had a rugged six-eight center in Tim Eubank and two other fine players, Don Cook and
Brad Tuell. Blue Chip Conference teams, besides Loogootee,
looked to be tougher too, including South Knox and Mitchell.

Jones knew that any new coach would be cut slack, and that
twelve or so regular season wins might be okay for a newbie,
but Jim's reputation was that of getting much more from what
looked like a so-so team, a challenge at which he had certainly excelled. After the crushing, bitter end to the previous 19-3

season, however, Jones may not have felt up to another round.

There was one final consideration. The better high school basketball coaches in Indiana typically used good records to move on to bigger schools. Jones' accomplishments were far ahead of the few disappointments in coaching he had experienced, and thus he was a prime candidate for any opening at larger schools. But he would have to move fast. A coach's successes could quickly become yesterday's news in the world of Indiana high school basketball.

After just over a decade of success at the helm of the Springs Valley Blackhawks, Jones knew he was ready for a new challenge. Yet he did not share this decision for several weeks. When he did, the news hit the region and the Valley basketball world like a bomb.

State and regional newspapers carried the story, every article mentioning Jones had quit after ringing up a 19-3 year, probably causing most readers to suspect he was going to another school with a larger enrollment. Jerry Birge at the *Jasper Herald* gave the most in-depth and personal report about Jones' decision. Among other items, Birge reported, "Jones enjoyed tremendous success in the Huntingburg sectional before his team was moved to the Paoli sectional in 1970. His teams won the Huntingburg sectional in 1964, 1965, 1966, and 1969. The Hawks advanced to the semi-state in 1964. During his eleven-year tenure as coach of the Blackhawks, he earned quite a reputation as a coach, and Valley became an area threat every season. He did his job well."

Gary Holland remembered Coach Jones calling all the coaches to a meeting around the third week in June and abruptly announcing his resignation. "Jim then walked over to me, put one hand on my chest, leaned over and said into my ear, 'They're all yours.'" Holland was dumbfounded, having never coached at the varsity level before and with only a few years under his belt doing junior varsity coaching. He later told Dave Koerner at the Louisville *Courier-Journal*, "I never gave this coaching position much thought. Jim's stepping down left me breathless."

The community was just as shocked, perhaps even more so. The man who for eleven years had "wound them up and let them go" had simply stepped off the stage, keeping his position as athletic director. No group was as shocked as the players, including Larry Bird. Larry remembered being at the local bowling alley with his friend Mike Cox when Coach Jones walked up to them and said, "I'm getting out." Larry could not believe his ears. "We loved the man. He had taught us all we knew." Then and there, the two Blackhawk players "almost broke down and cried."

Of course, the remaining Valley coaches got together to try to make sense of Jim's decision, the consensus being he was likely looking at a coaching job at a bigger school, and although he stayed that next year, causing them to then believe he had simply been burnt out after the loss at the Paoli sectional, they were, in fact, correct. Jim Jones explained in a later interview that he had begun taking interviews for a coaching position in 1973 before school was out, talking to folks at New Albany, Jeffersonville, and Princeton. The last school ended up offering him a job, but his family talked him into waiting. A year later, Jim took over at Princeton. There, and later at Terre Haute North, Jones would continue a fine coaching career, ending up in the Indiana Basketball Hall of Fame.

Meanwhile, hopes dimmed among fans in the Valley concerning the next basketball season. Several "drugstore coaches" told Coach Holland he would be lucky to win half his games. Holland was a little more optimistic, looking down at the schedule and surmising his team might possibly win fourteen games. One thing seemed for certain: there would not be the glory of the last season. Instead, the Blackhawks would no doubt be hard-pressed to pack the gym like the season before, when things had gone along like a fairy tale until they didn't.

Little is Expected of Valley this Season

Gary Holland was only twenty-six when he took the reins of the Springs Valley basketball team. Not only was he relatively young, but this would be his first job as head coach. He did have some advantages going for him. Unlike Jim Jones, who had been sixth man on the Oolitic High School team in the mid-1950s, Gary was a highly recruited high school basketball player who started on a solid basketball team at Paoli in the mid-1960s. Holland had a twenty-four-point scoring average his senior year, one newspaper account telling how he copped a total of twenty-seven points in one game, "hitting from out in front, from the corners and driving under for his two pointers." His big game, however, was at Corydon, where he set a gym record of forty-three points, all but one point on field goals made from all over the floor. One coach noted Gary Holland was "a tremendous shooter, has good speed and is the best jumper on the team. He can play any position."

Several colleges sought his services in basketball, but the University of Louisville won the recruiting battle. Holland was on his way to becoming an important part of the Cardinal program until his sophomore year when a collision with future NBA star Wes Unseld tore up one of Gary's knees. After extensive surgery, he came back to make the starting five on several occasions, playing with both Unseld and another future NBA star, Butch Beard, but he never achieved what he hoped to while playing college basketball.

The meticulous twenty-six-year-old Holland immediately dived into his new job, but doubters remained. One sportswriter captured the concern of some Valley fans, noting the lack of older coaches in the system, especially with the absence of Jim Jones. "Valley undoubtedly has one of the youngest coaching staffs in the state. Eighth grade coach Butch Emmons is the se-

Gary Holland, on the right, broke several Paoli High School records when he played there. Later, Holland's family business was vandalized when Gary became an assistant coach at rival Springs Valley.

nior at 28, while freshman coach John Fountain is 26, reserve coach Jerry Denbo 25 and seventh grade's Trent Magner is 24."

As Gary Holland began planning his head coaching approach for the 1973–1974 season, Larry Bird, despite the shock of Coach Jones' retiring, torqued up his training to an even higher level. "I'd get up in the morning and the first thing on my mind would be playing ball. I'd go right to the gym." Larry also trekked to the gym to shoot around any time in the school day when he was free. Returning home from school, he would always go to the nearby outdoor courts and shoot or play intense pickup games, the sounds of the players' grunting efforts rolling down the street. "I never wanted to leave the court until I got everything just right," Larry remembered. "I would practice different moves for hours on end and work hard to make my left hand as strong as my right." And when school was out, "it was no different."

Coach Holland, as Coach Jones had done, made the team practice an hour every morning before school. This was fol-

Gary Holland with his University of Louisville teammates in the mid-1960s, front row on the left. A laid-back high school coach, Holland often shot around with his players in practice.

lowed by a three-hour practice every evening after school. Then there were always several "get-up games" at night in the school gym, sometimes until midnight. Even with all this, Larry would often sneak into the gymnasium to practice more. Coach Holland remembered, "We couldn't keep Larry out of the gym."

All these kinds of exceptional commitments and expectations had occurred under Coach Jones, but there would still be a new atmosphere created by the difference in how Jones and Holland operated.

While Jim Jones had been a kind of stern but caring father figure, Holland had a gentler side. Jim was methodical, emphasizing a controlled pace, complete teamwork, and the idea that no one player could win or lose a game. Conversely, Gary was organic, more apt to let things work out in their own way. Slender and a bit over six feet tall, Holland occasionally shot around and scrimmaged with his varsity players. "He was a great shot," one of his players remembered, "cranking them into the basket from all over the floor sometimes when we were warming up for practice." Holland also kept up his physical basketball sharpness by playing local independent basketball.

Gary's relaxed playfulness was captured in an incident in one of his PE classes. It also indicated how sensational of a shot Larry had become. Tom Roach, a junior high student at the time, remembered seeing Larry Bird sitting in the middle of a trampoline at half-court as his PE class walked into the gym for one of their classes. Usually, the session began with the students running ten laps around the gym. "This time Mr. Holland said that Larry was going to shoot ten shots as he jumped on the trampoline. For every shot he made, we would run one less lap. He hit seven out of ten. It was simply amazing seeing a tall, skinny Larry Bird hit those shots so far out while bouncing up and down."

As it turned out, Gary Holland was literally the luckiest high school basketball coach ever, having Larry Bird as a player his very first year of coaching. Larry was lucky too. Soft-spoken, Holland was more likely to let his squad play freestyle, an approach that perfectly fit Larry Bird's personality, much in the same manner Bill Hodges' style would be at Indiana State. Coach Holland probably hoped too that low fan expectations would place a yet-to-jell team under less pressure, allowing him and his players some room to make a few mistakes while getting to a solid level of performance. As one newspaper had phrased it, "Little is expected of Valley this season."

Meanwhile, Jim Jones' unexpected exit from coaching had surely rocked Larry Bird's world at its very foundation. Bird would not have much time to mentally digest the sudden change. It could be said, however, if Mark Bird had presented a model and laid down the initial path for Larry to follow, and Coach Jones had been the firm but caring father-figure who, in a tight cage, trained Larry hard in the fundamentals of basketball, Gary Holland was destined to be the gentle coach who uncaged Larry and let him fly.

At the beginning of the season, there seemed to be little expectation or excitement among the Blackhawk fans. Jim Jones, the coach whose known quality was his ability to get teams ready for state tourney play, was no longer coaching. Fans did not know what to expect, leaving a dull "wait and see" situation. Meanwhile, a few local newspapers gave their assessments of the upcoming basketball campaign and the likely outcomes. Not much out of the ordinary was said about the Valley team or Larry Bird. The Bedford newspaper noted that "except for Larry Bird, James Carnes, John Carnes, and Brad Bledsoe, Valley's varsity squad players have no varsity experience." The hometown paper now featured a sportswriter with a column and a byline: Hawks Nest by Arnold Bledsoe. In Bledsoe's first article, he spoke in a neutral manner of the Blackhawks' chances under the headline "Hawks Get Ready," noting, "Coach Gary Holland will have four boys back from last year's squad who have had two years' experience each. Coaches Holland and Denbo, along with the members of the basketball teams, are working very hard these days. They are trying to get everything going for the big season coming up."

The beginning of official practices brought some new surprises. Brad Bledsoe recalled being stunned by both Larry Bird's astounding growth and "that somehow, he had become an even better shooter. He hardly missed." Those on the team now began to have inklings of how good a squad the Blackhawks might become, despite some low expectations by the general public and by sportswriters.

Brad Bledsoe picked up on another singular trait of Larry's when Coach Holland took the team on a scouting mission to see another team play. "It was early in the season, and we had a space between games, so Coach took us to see a team we would likely meet in the sectional— Milltown—although we did not play them in the regular season. They had a good team and a great six-eight center named Dave Smith." What caught Bledsoe's attention was how Larry zoned in on Smith, blocking out everything else around, "his eyes locked on every move Smith made. You could almost see Larry's brain working, calculating how he would play against this adversary."

In the beginning, the great unknown factor for the coach and the team involved the degree to which the squad might come together and who would step forward as the team leader. Gary Holland knew, however, that whatever effective playing dynamic the team might develop would have to be earned and would most likely emerge organically. Larry Bird recalled his new coach pulling him aside that summer and "explaining what he had in mind." This respectful, egalitarian approach made Bird happy, Larry pointing out that he and the team "never had any problem" with their new coach. "He was a young fellow, just in his early or mid-twenties, and his personality was completely different than Coach Jones. Jones ran a pretty tight ship. Under Holland we had more offensive freedom. Holland knew what kind of talent he had, and he basically turned us loose."

The situation was a bit more complicated in the beginning. Senior player Beezer Carnes, a five-eight guard, took for granted he would be the "floor leader" of the team, much in the fashion of the previous year's Danny King. This made sense, because Larry Bird, now at six seven, would surely play just the center position. Others were not so sure. Time and game playing would dictate the answer.

It was all but automatic that the three seniors, Larry Bird, James Beezer Carnes, and Beezer's cousin John Carnes would be the heart of the team, having had solid varsity experiences from the year before. Two solid juniors, Brad Bledsoe and Doug Conrad, filled out the initial starting five squad that year, along with sixth-man junior Mike Cox. Later in the season, sophomore Chester Allen would break into the starting lineup. But the three seniors, Valley's three musketeers, consistently made up the core leadership of that season's team.

In an early game that year, Beezer tied Larry for scoring honors, tossing in twenty-six points in a blaze of accurate shooting. At this point, he and Larry were the top scorers in the Blue Chip Conference, before Beezer's scoring production slowed down. It may have been the only time Beezer's name came before Larry Bird's in a sports piece. Al Brewster at the Bedford newspaper wrote, "The 8-team Blue Chip Conference has several top scorers according to stats released for league games through Jan.

5. The leaders happen to be starters for Springs Valley—James Carnes and Larry Bird."

Friends since childhood, Beezer and Larry had their own dynamic going that senior year season. Sports reporters caught it occasionally, how Beezer would take off tearing down court as Larry went up for a defensive rebound. Junior high schooler Tom Roach recalled, "It took your breath away when Larry grabbed a rebound on the defensive end and in one motion threw a baseball-type pass down court to Beezer for an easy layup. Sometimes Beezer didn't even have to take a dribble, the pass was that long and perfect."

It would have been impossible to say what the rest of the season would hold even after the Blackhawks easily won their first game, an away match at Pekin Eastern. If nothing else, the fans came to see what they had been hearing about since the school year began: Larry Bird magically growing into a giant, at least in height. What they witnessed was the unexpected hatching of perhaps the best Indiana high school basketball player in history. There were, as with any hatchling, a few mistakes that would be made before this great bird would majestically fly.

To the fans' delight, the Valley squad played well, especially on offense, and Arnold Bledsoe's headline in the Hawks Nest the next day declared the team had "Come out Smokin'." Perhaps it was prophetic too that Larry Bird got the first basket. The Blackhawks were never behind Pekin Eastern, ending up pounding their foe 95-71. The three seniors carried the bulk of the offensive show, as they would for the rest of the season. Larry, however, was not the leading scorer, although he hit 13-25 field goals and ended up with twenty-seven points. John Carnes took top scoring honors, producing twenty-eight points. His cousin Beezer Carnes scored eighteen. One devoted Blackhawk fan, seventh grader Todd Marshall, was sitting next to a high school coach from another school who was scouting the Blackhawk team. Todd recalled, "Larry took a shot deep from the side and made it after making that fake with the ball he did over a defensive player's head before pulling up and taking the shot. I happened to look down as the scout was writing something in

From left to right, the heart of the 1973-1974 Blackhawk squad, John Carnes, Larry Bird, and Beezer Carnes.

his notebook—'Showboat.'"

Coach Holland was both shocked and pleased that his team was able to "score that many points in the first game." Brad Bledsoe, a junior starter, recalled how he and his teammates loved the suddenly less restrictive play, the atmosphere looser than under Coach Jones. Some fans, however, were not pleased with Valley's defense.

The next game was at home against the Washington Hatchets. Arnold Bledsoe wrote, "The game was played with all the gusto of a barn burner. Neither team showed any sign of quitting during the game." And what a game. Harry Moore reported that on the very first play of the contest, "Bird received thunderous applause from the Hawks fans when he blocked a Hatchet shot and passed to John Carnes. Carnes was fouled and made one of two." At the beginning of the next quarter, "Bird blocked another shot, took the ball down the court and banked in a left-handed shot."

But then Washington's Joe Collison got a hot hand, keeping his team in the game and leading all scorers with thirty-four points. Bird would tally twenty-seven points, including 13-14 free throws. What may have frustrated Blackhawk fans the most was that it looked as if Valley would take a hard-won victory until the last seconds of regulation play, when Valley took some bad shots and Washington came back to tie the game. This was also true in the first overtime. Bird had grabbed a rebound with forty seconds to go and his team was up by two points. "Hawks fans sensed a victory, but it was not so," reported Harry Moore. The Hatchets stole the ball and with three seconds remaining knotted the score. In the second overtime, Washington prevailed, 80-72.

The news was not all bad. Harry Moore at the Paoli newspaper believed "even in defeat Valley looked good. They actually had won the game, both in regulation play and in the first overtime. But they let victory slip by." Moore went on to say, "Larry Bird did his best to win. He grabbed 17 rebounds, blocked eight shots, had eight assists, and scored 27 points." The Valley squad, Moore continued, "has the makings of a fine team. Had they been a little more patient we believe they would have won. They took a couple of bad shots against a veteran team; you just can't do that."

After the Washington contest, some Springs Valley fans grew critical of what they thought was sloppy play and very poor defense. Missing too was the ball control, the take-only-the-good-shots strategy of Coach Jones. And although the team played well at times, there also seemed to be a lack of dynamic interaction among the squad members. It was enough to quicken the drugstore coaches.

Arnold Bledsoe took on these negative murmurs in the next Hawks Nest column. "The Hawks ran into a hard pressing Hatchet outfit Saturday night and fell in a double overtime 80-72. Washington has one of the better defensive teams the Hawks will face all year. The fans should be proud of the coaches and the ball players for the spirit shown by these kids in this game." Noting there were a few close calls that could have gone either way, but that all the players "hung in there and gave it their all, trying to pull it out," the local sportswriter argued, "I think that we as fans should maybe take a better look at ourselves and ask if we could do better in the same situation and instead of criticizing, offer a pat on the back for a job well done. Let's show the team we're behind them and try to applaud their good doing as well as always criticizing them in their mistakes."

Players saw and felt the fans' displeasure as well, one Valley team member recalling the fans "just shaking their head at the

Larry Bird scored the first basket of the season against Pekin Eastern in his sensational senior year.

first few games when they saw something that displeased them."

Coach Holland and his Blackhawks were now facing what loomed as a must-win game in the next contest if they hoped to have a credible season. It was a tough assignment. The Orleans Bulldogs, an old county rival with two top-notch players, big Curt Gilstrap and Mike McClintic back for their last year, were coming to town. At this point, Orleans was undefeated with three wins. Nevertheless, most Valley folks thought the Blackhawks, with the home court advantage, would get the job done. The outcome shocked a few sports gurus and all the Valley fans. Harry Moore wrote, "Springs Valley entertained county rival

Orleans in a basketball game Friday night and after the smoke had cleared the talented Bulldogs put it all together for a 77-71 win." Sportswriters, like Moore, thought Valley would be victorious. "We have to admit," the Paoli sportswriter noted after the game, "we thought Valley would beat Orleans."

Larry Bird gets the tip against Washington but the Hatchets win the game in a grueling double overtime.

Moore summed up Valley's weakness by observing, "Hawk defense left something to be desired. Tim Wheeler, smallest man on the floor, and Greg McCoy, a reserve forward, put the scoring whammy on the Hawks. Tim pumped in 16 points, many from long range, and Greg scored 14, unmolested." The game was a close struggle in the first quarter, but in the second quarter it was all Bulldogs. Moore noted, "Gilstrap controlled the tip, Mike McClintic hit a basket and Orleans was off." Indeed, Curt hit a soft hook shot over Larry "that brought a standing ovation from Bulldogs fans." Moore pointed out too that it did look for a while in the third period that Valley might yet pull out the game with Larry Bird taking charge. "Valley made their move. Bird, Bird, Bird, Bird! Four Larry buckets around a Bulldog basket left Valley down by four, 43-39. An Orleans time out and then a McCoy bucket put them up by six. Beezer hit from a mile away and Bird's two-fer brought Hawk fans to their feet." But Coach Denbo then called a time-out and settled his troops, who went on to establish a six-point lead at the end of the third quarter. The final quarter was Bulldog glory, the fans of the victor streaming out on the floor after beating their county rival, the celebration almost at the same level of a sectional championship win. Valley, meanwhile, seemed destined to endure a long season.

The one thing that did salvage a bit of joy for Blackhawk fans was the amazing shooting and scoring of Larry Bird. His long, beautiful jump shots from the corners and his soft put-back shots underneath were "breathtaking," remembered Coach Holland. In the Orleans contest, Bird broke Steve Land's recent single-game scoring record by two points, scoring forty-three, the last two points coming with eight seconds left in the game. Moore called the feat "one of the most brilliant performances we have seen from a high school player."

But Gilstrap had a big night too, scoring thirty-one markers and out-rebounding Larry. Leaving the Springs Valley gym, resigned Blackhawk fans may have figured if the season wins would not be up to par, they would at least have an exciting scorer to watch, a player who would bring recognition to the team and to the community. Adding to this angle of excitement, after the Orleans game, Larry was the leading scorer in the state. Interestingly, later Larry Bird narratives presented the Orleans/Valley game as a breakthrough event in Larry's scoring prowess. But, in real time, the Valley team, coaches, and fans felt the loss to the Bulldogs and the 1-3 record as a bummer.

There was another subtle slant to this game, one easily missed. Unnoticed by most players, coaches, and fans at the Valley/Orleans contest was a sudden change in how Larry played the game, a change that would have monumental consequences. Mike McClintic, at six one, was perhaps the first victim of Larry's sudden change in playing style, an adjustment probably dictated by hulky Curt Gilstrap playing beneath the basket. Many years later Mike recalled, "I had guarded Larry the year before when he was six three. Now he's six seven but suddenly coming out to play all over the floor. Curt was a force that night under the basket, and I don't think Larry wanted to come in and slug it out with Curt, so he went outside. Of course, it ended up he could hit outside shots as easily as inside ones. Me guarding Larry that night was a joke. No one later in the NBA could guard him either when he was on."

Larry observed in *Drive* that the Orleans game was pivotal to him for another reason. "Springs Valley won our first game

The 1973-1974 Orleans Bulldogs, one of Valley's rugged Orange County rivals, were a tough team to beat.

and then we lost two in a row." After the Orleans contest, Larry recalled, "I had only scored something like twenty-five and twenty-eight points in those two losses, but I got forty-three on him [Curt Gilstrap]. From then on, everything just seemed to come easily for me. It seemed I could do whatever I wanted to do in a basketball game."

The hatchling had become a young eagle.

The Orleans game settled another important issue. According to Lee Levine's book, because of the team's poor efforts in the first three games, Larry took over the leadership of the team. Up until then, Beezer Carnes "figured Gary Holland wanted me to be the leader." This made sense, because Carnes was the point guard. But with Larry suddenly realizing he could use the entire floor, including bringing the ball down court like a guard, Larry naturally began directing the team out on the floor. "After the second or third game, it became clear who our leader was," Beezer recalled. "He would come down on you out there [in a game]. Larry might say to a loafing player, 'Why aren't you working, helping us to win?'" Coach Holland also noted how Larry started leading by example, always giving beyond one hundred percent and teasingly chiding any player who showed signs of not giving his all.

Ironically, Larry, who loved how Coach Holland let his team just play, was now channeling the voice of his old stricter coach, Jim Jones, getting after anyone who wasn't giving their very best effort. It was part of a dynamic that was about to lead to a long winning streak and regional recognition.

Valley next played a weak North Daviess team that would eventually end up with a 3-21 record. The Blackhawks beat

Larry and Orleans' big man Curt Gilstrap fight for a tip.

them easily, Larry and Beezer both knocking down twenty-eight points, and the three other starters all hitting double figures. The only unusual aspect about the game was Bird's name being spelled Byrd in the next day's Bedford *Times-Mail* newspaper, a sign perhaps that Larry's sudden exceptional basketball skills had yet to be recognized outside Orange County. No matter. Coach Holland and his crew now faced one of their toughest games on the schedule. The Jasper Wildcats were coming to the Valley.

Larry Bird shoots a foul shot. Perfect form.

Glory

While Springs Valley was having its troubles early in the season, the Jasper Wildcats were riding high with a 3-1 record and a high state ranking. Rich in tradition, Jasper basketball teams were almost always a leading contender in the region. The Cats had won a state championship and had also reached the semi-state level ten times in the school's history, capturing twenty-two sectional championships in the process. Jasper teams, coaches, players, and fans wanted and expected victories, especially over rivals like small-school Springs Valley. Jerry Birge, the local Jasper newspaper sports reporter, wrote that Coach Ed Schultheis would be especially motivated to direct his team to a victory over the Blackhawks in the early part of the 1973-1974 season.

Ed Schultheis wasn't the most popular man in Jasper in February of 1969. In his second year as head coach of the Jasper Wildcats his team had just been beaten by Springs Valley at the Huntingburg sectional and his first two years as boss of the Cats had produced 22 wins, 20 losses and two disappointments in the sectional. Ed, and most Jasper fans, knew that the pressure was building up in the community where basketball boosters don't like to lose. His future as the Wildcat coach was shaky to say the least. But in the following four seasons his teams reeled off records of 18-4, 19-6, 16-10, and 20-6, produced one SIAC Championship, three sectional crowns, and two regional titles. Suddenly, Ed Schultheis is right near the top when it comes to Jasper coaches. He will be shooting for his 100th victory.

The Jasper coach certainly had the horses to pull the load. The Wildcats, wrote Jerry Birge, featured "Mr. Inside," six-eight, 220-pound Mike Luegers, and "Mr. Outside," sharpshooter Mike Keusch. In the second game of the season, Luegers scored thirty-one points, making thirteen of sixteen shots against Harrison, a large Evansville school team. Luegers, a senior, would continue to put up big scoring numbers, eventually breaking the single-game scoring record held by his older brother Robert "Chesty" Luegers.

There had been one bump in the road for the Wildcats at the beginning of the season, a two-point loss to another highly ranked team, Evansville Memorial, just before the Valley contest. The Wildcats led almost the entire game, but then blew a thirteen-point lead in the fourth quarter and ended up losing by a single heartbreaking basket in the last eight seconds of the contest. Even in that game, Jasper played superb basketball, leaving "many Jasper fans wondering if the Cats could be beaten at all this season," until that question was rudely settled in the last second of the game. Mike Luegers had turned in another stupendous effort, scoring twenty-five points, half of the Jasper total, and pulling down twenty rebounds, and all this against Memorial's six-nine Jeff Fehn.

After the loss to Memorial, Coach Schultheis hoped his team could get back on track by beating Valley, a tough assignment, given it was a day after a disappointing defeat. Then again, scouting reports had labeled the Springs Valley team as only decent. Unknown to both teams, the game would mark the beginning of Larry's recognition as an exceptional high school basketball player. As Mark Shaw noted in *Larry Legend*, it would be this contest that woke up many "pundits and fans alike" to Larry Bird's greatness, while becoming a nightmare for the Wildcat squad.

The game at Springs Valley offered a surreal vibe for the Jasper team from the very beginning. "The place was packed, and the Valley fans were rowdy from the moment we walked out on the floor," recalled Mike Luegers. To add to the charged atmosphere, Larry Bird's unexpected growth caught Luegers and the Wildcat team off guard. Mike noted that "Larry was still thin, but it looked as if someone had just stretched him several

The Jasper Wildcats were led by six-eight Mike Luegers, shown here scoring in a game against Memorial of Evansville.

inches, like in a cartoon. The season before, it had been Steve Land who led Valley in their win against us. At six three, Bird had hardly been a factor in the game, and I easily kept him from coming underneath the basket."

Now Luegers watched as a much different Larry glided around the court during the pre-game warm-ups, hitting soft jump shots from everywhere on the court. "It was as if I was looking at a completely different person. Larry's transformation seemed unbelievable."

Mike was not the only one astounded by Larry's metamorphosis. Coach Ed Schultheis kept saying, "That can't be the same guy," as he watched Bird warm up. Two weeks later the Jasper coach was still puzzled by what he had seen, telling *Evansville Courier* writer Chip Draper, in an article titled "Big Bird 'grows up' to stardom," how he was taken aback by Larry Bird's sudden changes from the year before. Besides being markedly taller, Coach Schultheis said, "he looked quicker and more agile than last year. I couldn't believe it was the same kid."

The Paoli newspaper narrative, captioned "Hawks upset Jasper Again," set the stage for the game. "The P. A. announcer stated Jasper's starting lineup was 6-6 and 6-3 forwards, 6-8 center, and 6-2 and 6-1 guards. It didn't impress the Hawks."

The Valley team, in the words of another sportswriter, "played the best game ever seen in the Springs Valley gym." Paoli's Harry Moore noted that the Hawks outrebounded Jasper 36-21 and on two occasions one of the Carnes' hands "was above the rim to snare the rebound." Moore also declared, "Bird tore Mike Luegers to shreds. Time after time Larry would cram a shot down Luegers' throat and the big boy just wasn't used to that kind of treatment."

Jasper did manage to stay in the game during the first quarter, the lead shifting back and forth several times until Valley began to pull away and take the lead. Just as Jasper made a comeback bid in the opening minutes of the second quarter, drawing close at 26-22, Larry Bird "made a beautiful hook shot then blocked a shot by Mike Luegers and made a long down court pass to James Carnes for an easy Valley basket." The most devastating blow, according to one sportswriter, came when Bird blocked a shot, kept the ball, and "drove down the floor and scored." Of course, the Valley fans went crazy.

The Blackhawks' overall team play was just as amazing. Once the contest started, Valley players were hitting shots "from all over the place." A few times Bird did one of his favorite fakes, the one he had learned on the West Baden playground when he was a boy, taking the ball in both hands and putting it over the defender's head like he was passing it. When the defender turned to see where the pass went, Bird pulled the ball back to shoot.

Swish. Another basket.

No one on the Jasper team was more aware of the carnage than Mike Luegers. "Early in the game I was about five feet from the basket, starting to raise the ball up for an easy shot when Larry came up behind me and easily blocked the attempt. Then he said to me, 'How did you like that, Luegers.' That's when I knew Larry Bird was for real."

All the while, the Springs Valley crowd kept up a constant wall of sound, wildly cheering from the minute the players got on the floor. Luegers found the ear splitting noise especially disorienting. "From the beginning, the crowd was going crazy, and

Jasper's players and coaches hardly recognized the much taller Larry Bird when the team played Valley in the early part of the '73-'74 season.

the Valley team had us down by twenty points at the end of the first half. It was very humbling."

The Springs Valley gymnasium could not have held another ounce of energy. At every Valley time-out, explained Arnold Bledsoe in the Springs Valley paper, "the Hawks fans, adults as well as students, gave the Hawks a standing ovation." The fans had much to be happy about. The team was finally playing great defense, a defense that according to Harry Moore, "left the Wildcats dumbfounded. They pounced on the Wildcats and stuck like glue."

Valley also shot the lights out with Bird hitting thirty points. But it was not just Larry Bird doing the scoring and rebounding damage. The Blackhawks were finally working together as a solid unit on both offense and defense. One after-game assessment noted, "Cousins John and James Carnes were steady performers for Valley. John is playing much better defensively, rebounding well and averaging 18 points per game. James, or 'Beezer,' is a nifty little guard, a whiz on defense and averaging 16.2 points." Brad Bledsoe and Doug Conrad, the other starters, "were instrumental in the Jasper win. Brad had his best game. He was a demon on defense and had six assists, three steals, and scored six points. Doug hauled down seven rebounds and had seven points."

Arnold Bledsoe, at the local paper, the *Springs Valley Herald*, was especially ecstatic. Under "Hawks Claw Cats," Bledsoe told how "Gary Holland's crew started to work in the first quarter finishing off the Wildcats with a shooting display that left the fans limber in their seats." Bledsoe added, "Larry was blocking shots and snatching the ball away to throw to a streaking Hawk on five occasions for the night." Other regional newspapers chimed in. The Louisville newspaper headlined "Bird Flyin' High At Springs Valley With added Muscle." Al Brewster, sports editor at the Bedford paper, in a similar vein, headed his column "SV's Bird Flying High" and observed of the slender six-seven Bird, "College scouts wouldn't be wasting their time by keeping a close watch on Bird. He's going strong this season and is capable of playing either center, forward or guard."

Larry Bird blocks a Mike Luegers shot.

The *Evansville Press* poked a little fun at Jasper, observing, "Springs Valley's Blackhawks gave Jasper an anniversary celebration Saturday night. A reenactment of an upset for the second straight year. If it keeps up much longer, they'll stop calling it an upset."

Jerry Birge's caption in the Jasper paper, however, won the prize for capturing the essence of the Jasper/Valley contest: "Valley Gives Cats The Bird."

After the Jasper/Valley battle was over, Mike Luegers had one more reminder of how awful the game had been for him and for his team, although he had been the Wildcats' leading scorer with twenty-one points. "I had returned home and was trying to wind down from the horrible game, my parents and

I discussing what went wrong, when our phone rang. My mom answered and then turned to me and said, 'Larry Bird's on the phone and wants to talk to you.' Of course, I was very surprised. I had really never conversed with him before, except for his short bit of trash talk after he blocked my first shot. At the other end of the call, I could hear a group of people laughing and talking. I wasn't sure who it was, but then the caller said, 'This is Larry Bird.' The conversation was very short, and he kidded me about how badly they beat us a few hours earlier at Springs Valley. I never forgot that phone call and always wondered if it was Larry calling or some of his friends." As it turned out, it was Larry on the phone, Brad Bledsoe recalling a party after the game where Larry not only called a Jasper player but the Jasper coach, giving them a hard time.

Coach Jim Jones had said, shortly after his coming to Springs Valley in the early 1960s, that a win against Jasper always made for a great season. Now Coach Holland basked in the glow of such a triumph. In truth, the victory over Jasper was electrifying, a stupendous blessing for the Springs Valley squad and a real morale booster after their 2-2 start. (When the two teams did meet again in the Washington regional that season, both Valley and Jasper players were rested and the contest was a thriller, with the game decided by a single basket.) The overpowering victory suggested to Blackhawk fans that the

Page 12   The Dubois County DAILY HERALD, Jasper, Ind.

Valley Gives Cats The Bird;

A humorous sports headline in the *Jasper Herald* after Springs Valley's stunning victory over the Jasper Wildcats.

team had the makings of a squad equal to the top-notch team from the year before. But it remained to be seen if the dynamic play of the Valley team against Jasper would stand as a permanent fixture. Springs Valley's next two games, to be played in the Paoli Holiday Tournament, would certainly help basketball "experts" gauge the true capabilities of the Valley team.

With Jasper out of the way, Springs Valley, now with a more credible 3-2 record, faced a rematch in the first game of the Paoli Holiday Tournament, a grudge contest with still undefeated Orleans. Although the next day the Bedford Daily *Times-Mail* reported Springs Valley's "stunning 84-68 victory over the Bulldogs," the first quarter of the tilt suggested Valley was in for trouble, the lead changing hands several times before the Bulldogs took a 16-15 lead at the end of the period. But the rest of the game was all Springs Valley. The Paoli newspaper reporter astutely noted a more specific aspect of the contest, a change in the dynamics of how the Blackhawks operated as a team. Harry Moore wrote that in the first meeting with Orleans, "It was all Larry Bird, but in the tourney game Larry had plenty of help." And Larry certainly helped his teammates. About this time, Coach Holland noticed Bird's increasingly unselfish playing style, his love of passing for an assist, "his joy in seeing another teammate score."

Newspapers were also suddenly full of admiring comments about Bird's breathtaking full-court passes, often made after blocking a shot, stealing the ball away, and passing to a Blackhawk player streaking down the court for easy baskets. "Even in high school, he made an average player great," said Coach Holland.

Along with his many assists in the Orleans game, Bird kept up his own torrid scoring pace, exploding for thirty-eight points and grabbing twenty-one rebounds while Orleans' big man, Curt Gilstrap, clocked thirty-one points and picked off twenty rebounds. The Blackhawks were now in the championship game, where they faced their other county rival, Paoli. The Rams had won an even easier victory, led by six-eight Tim Eubank, who knocked in thirty points, including "10 straight baskets during one stretch of the game," besting Forest Park in their first holiday tournament game.

The championship tussle was a rugged battle with both Bird and Eubank fouling out of the contest, leaving it to the other players to bring about the exciting finish. Harry Moore wrote that the high-pressure tilt between the two county rivals had a sectional championship game feel from the very start, with the Rams' resurgence at the very end leaving everyone—players, coaches, and fans—exhausted. It was the kind of game Hoosier high school fans lived for. Paoli's Don Cook shared the scoring honors with Valley's John Carnes, both grabbing twenty-six points, while the Rams' Brad Tuell followed close behind with twenty-four. Both Cook and Tuell were perfect from the foul line, Cook getting eight and Tuell canning nine. The contest was tied at the end of the first quarter, and Paoli led by two at halftime. Things stayed tense through the third period, the scoring locked up in a tie at three different junctures. Valley, however, managed to claw out a tenuous three-point lead when the quarter ended.

Larry Bird is caught flat-footed for a change, watching Orlean's Curt Gilstrap lay in a basket.

The fourth quarter was a doozy. The Blackhawks surged to a ten-point lead, but with just two minutes left, the Rams came roaring back, "causing the Hawks to hold on for dear life," in the words of Harry Moore. With foul-plagued Larry Bird limited to a little over half of his average scoring pace, it was left to other Blackhawk players to save the day. And save the day they did. "For Valley fans enough cannot be said of the sparkling play of Brad Bledsoe," noted Harry Moore. "Brad was a demon all night, and with 15 seconds left, stole a Rams' pass that preserved a Hawk victory. Reserve Mike Cox also added greatly to the win. He spelled Bird and came through with five points. On one occasion, Mike completed a three-point play, and it was a big one." Altogether, four Valley players were in double figures in the close 84-78 win. Rams' Tim Eubank's foul situation limited him to nine points, but as noted, Rams players Don Cook and Brad Tuell carried the scoring load for the disappointed Paoli squad. Eubank, however, would do dramatically better in the two teams' next matchups.

Larry Bird gets a shot off over Paoli rival big Tim Eubank.

Meanwhile, Larry Bird was beginning to get on the regional sports radar. Just before the 1973 Christmas break, sportswriter Tom Tuley at the *Evansville Press* noted, "The word is out that the finest big man in southern Indiana high school basketball—and there are quite a few big ones—may be 6-7 Larry Bird at Springs Valley High School."

A new atmosphere of excitement descended on the Springs Valley school after the Christmas break. Student Ron Prosser remembered that on game day at school, "There were periodic announcements about sign-ups for a student fan bus for away games. Upperclassmen, too cool to ride a bus, would network passing notes to arrange rides to the game." At home games the crowd included a large, well-organized, and energetic student cheer block. Meanwhile, the adult portion of the crowd "was positioned in an unofficial pecking order. I can't remember if there were assigned seats for the adults, but it was clear where the longtime fans were going to sit."

As the 1973–1974 season progressed and the crowds grew, Friday night games in the valley turned into "a frenzied blur of factory workers trying to get off work, get to the bank, clean up, grab some supper, and get to the game in time to get a good seat. Getting to the game late not only meant the possibility of standing for the entire game but also meant finding a parking space on a side street in the nearby neighborhoods."

The team's bus rides to away games were a mixed bag, Brad Bledsoe recalling, "We were always quiet on the team bus going and noisy coming back, as we almost always won." Larry Bird, however, was never the center of attention. "His shyness took over, but you could tell he was happy that everyone was in a good mood. He was most who he was on the basketball floor— confident and in charge, a team player who hated to lose."

But not all aspects of the season were fun for Larry. After

Springs Valley won the Paoli Holiday Tournament, a problem emerged in the form of a herd of college scouts showing up one-at-a-time at his door. Up until

Valley's three musketeers, (l to r) Larry, Beezer, and John, stand with the 1974 Paoli Holiday Tourney Championship trophy.

this, Larry had been contacted only by Coach Stauffer at Indiana State, and that was the season before, when Stauffer was after Steve Land. Of course, Larry, while a solid player, had been just a six-three guard during his junior year. Fast-forward a year, and now everyone was watching him improve with each game, a six-seven player who had the skills that allowed him to play any position on the court.

Gary Holland believed Larry's hyper-shyness and his total concentration on high school basketball made Bird not want to deal with college coaches and their offers. Indeed, Bob Kelley, after interviewing Bird in September 1974, reported in the *Evansville Press*, "As a junior in high school, Larry Bird had no intention of going to college." College just wasn't on Bird's radar at that time and even into his senior year. "I wasn't a fan of college basketball," Larry himself recalled. "I knew next to nothing about it." But after he started performing so well, the scouts came, like a few drops of rain at first, and then in a downpour as Larry just kept getting better.

Not counting Stauffer, Coach Bob Knight at Indiana University was likely one of the first coaches to come in person to see Larry play.

Bob Knight had left West Point and come to Bloomington to coach in the 1971–1972 season. By Larry's senior year, the Hoosier coach was putting together a squad that would lose only one game in two seasons and cop a national championship in an undefeated year in 1975–1976. It was this fantastic group of players that Knight wished Larry to join.

A newspaper account found in this research showed Knight traveling to Bird's next game after Valley had taken the holiday crown at Paoli. This would have been Valley's eighth contest of the season, a tilt at Springs Valley with the Blackhawks playing Shoals. The Jug Rox were a solid 7-4 club at that time but had little height, and Valley pulled away in the second half, winning 78-54. The *Vincennes Sun-Commercial* observed the next day that "Indiana University Coach Bobby Knight attended the Springs Valley-Shoals game Friday night for the purpose of inspecting Bird in action. The Hoosier coach's interest is easy to

Perfect form!

understand."

Coach Knight had to be pleased with what he saw. In the game Larry knocked down thirty-two points and swept the boards as usual for rebounds. One Shoals player, however, apparently tried a new tactic to stop Larry from scoring. "He pulled bits of hair off Larry's legs every time Larry went up for a shot," a Valley player recalled, "until Bird stopped and took a swing at him. The guy was so much shorter, Larry's swing missed wide, and the ref did not catch it." Meanwhile, after the game, Knight told IU player Quinn Bucker that the Valley senior was "a special player, one of the best." Altogether, Knight, or his assistants, would make several visits to see Larry, all the while watching as Bird just kept getting better. "Each time," said Knight, "we were more impressed."

That Bob Knight would make the trek down from Bloomington to see Larry and his Valley squad play Shoals makes sense given that the only long article during the regular season about Larry Bird in the *Indianapolis Star*, the state's leading newspaper, had appeared the morning before the Shoals game. The piece was in Bob Williams' noteworthy sports page column, Shootin' the Stars. The article, headlined "Valley Of The Giants," focused on the big men in the upcoming Paoli sectional—Tim Eubank, Larry Bird, Curt Gilstrap, and Dave Smith. In part, Williams wrote, "Bird is averaging 30.4 points a game and

Shootin' The Stars ━━━━━━

Paoli Sectional Valley Of Giants

━━━ By Bob Williams ━━━

This was the only sports report in the state's largest newspaper during the regular season about Larry Bird. The next night, Coach Bob Knight of Indiana went south to see Larry play.

19 rebounds per-game for first-year Springs Valley coach Gary Holland, shooting 50.3 from the field and 75.9 from the charity stripe." Quoting a down-state coach, Williams also said that both Bird and Gilstrap "should play college ball somewhere." Knight may have wondered, after reading the piece, if that place might be IU. About this same time, however, Jim Plump, sportswriter for the Seymour newspaper, believed "The University of Louisville appears to have the inside track on Springs Valley's Larry Bird. The 6-7 Bird is coached by former U. of L. performer Gary Holland, who played for John Dromo's squad during the days of Wes Unseld and Butch Bread."

The list of coaches interested in Larry only grew longer as the season progressed.

Valley's next victory, over North Knox, was a cakewalk, both coaches emptying their benches after the Blackhawks built up an impossible lead. "The Warriors were unable to cope with Bird's aggressive play under the boards," explained the *Vincennes Sun-Commercial* the next day. Bird, playing just over half the game, still managed to capture twenty-eight points. As it turned out, Bird's best games were just over the horizon.

The Blackhawks traveled to West Washington on a Friday night and had such a hot hand shooting, the gym surely came close to being set on fire. Brad Bledsoe made six of his first seven shots, several "from a mile away," and ended up with twenty points, but Larry was the star, ending up with forty-two points. Moore at the *Paoli Republican* reported that Larry "dazzled the crowd with his basket shooting, passing, and rebounding. He broke a record in the rebounding department with 27. The old record of 25 was set last year by Steve Land." Valley won 98-45 as Larry did whatever he wished on the floor that night, the game under his complete control, a Titan among mere mortals.

Larry had lots of help in his senior year play from teammate number 30, Brad Bledsoe, a junior.

The game against Corydon, played at Springs Valley the very next night, witnessed a hot, over packed gym full of Blackhawk fans geared up to see their team take revenge for the embarrassing upset defeat of the year before, a defeat that was their first loss of that season and one that led to a terrible tailspin.

Valley fans were more than delighted at the game's end. Harry Moore wrote, "The Valley gym sounded like an atomic bomb had exploded as Larry walked to the bench." And for good reasons. His performance was one of complete mastery. "Bird scored Valley's first 10 points. They came on an assortment of shots—hooks, tips, and 20-footers." He obliterated two records, "his own and that of an Orange County record. Rex Hudleson of Paoli scored 47 points to set a county record. Saturday night Bird scored 55 points. Larry's record came on 22 of 33 attempts and 11 of 17 free throws." Larry also had twenty-four rebounds, six assists, three steals, and two blocked shots.

Larry came out of the game with two minutes to play, his teammates gathering to meet him as every Valley fan rose to give him a standing ovation. The final score was 99-73. Corydon coach Jim Stewart was simply staggered by Larry's domination of his Corydon team, telling a Louisville reporter after the one-sided game, "We played a couple of big boys before, and they usually stay inside and muscle around. But Bird goes from corner to corner and even brings the ball down the floor. He plays more like a guard." Coach Stewart believed Larry was so dominating for a couple of reasons: "the shooting range he has and his ability to go with the ball. He has all the attributes of a guard. He can shoot from the bleachers or take the ball from 25 feet out and with a fake or two go in like a guard."

Somewhere in the amazing scoring barrages Larry achieved in these two contests were two awesome passes Bird made that astounded everyone. Harry Moore pointed out how, in the Corydon game, that Larry made "one of the neatest passes to [Doug] Conrad we have ever seen. He faked the defender, flipped a good hard two-handed pass behind his back. Doug was all alone under the basket for two." Several biographies also related another unbelievable pass that game. Levine called the innovation "a redirected pass, with a flick or tap of the hand." It would be "popularized by Larry and is now known as the 'touch pass.'" Larry had been sprinting down court when John Carnes threw a pass toward him from the other side of the court. The pass was slightly behind Larry, "but instead of slowing down and waiting to catch the ball, Larry continued his sprint and reached behind his back to redirect the flight of the pass with his left hand." The redirected pass, after one bounce, went into the hands of a Blackhawk player who finished the act with an easy layup.

After these two incredible games, Larry was scoring at a 33.6 clip, and the Springs Valley team suddenly found themselves at 9-2. More than a few Valley fans now believed that the

Corydon players watch helplessly as Larry
Bird sets a new scoring record.

Blackhawk team would not only tie Jim Jones' crew's winning record from the season before but also capture the Blue Chip Conference and take back the Paoli sectional title. The *Evansville Courier* thought Springs Valley was pretty good too, listing them as the third-best team in southwest Indiana after undefeated Loogootee and 11-1 Evansville Memorial. Sportswriter Dave Koerner, at the *Courier Journal*, across the river in Louisville, did a nice piece on the team at this time, under the banner "Springs Valley Is Flyin' High—Just Like A Bird!" In the article, a confident Larry Bird said he felt he was "twice the ballplayer I was last year," although he added he wished to improve on his dribbling skills. Coach Holland, however, could find no weakness in Larry's play, saying, "He's more effective in the post now, but still has a fine touch from out. Often, he'll even be the lead man on our fast break, and believe me it sure looks odd for a 6-7 kid to lead a fast break. He has very quick movement for a 6-7 guy. He has big hands, excellent ball control and shoots real well from the corners."

Holland's only concern, as Larry kept getting better, was the sometime tendency of the other Valley players to stop in awe and watch as Larry took one of his deep jump shots. But Holland could also be a sometime victim of distraction when watching Larry play, telling an *Evansville Courier* reporter, "We always knew he was going to be a good shooter and we knew he was going to be tough this year. But we never knew he would score like this, and it just thrills me each time I see him play."

At this time too, Jasper sportswriter Jerry Birge became one of Larry's biggest fans among the newspaper sports reporters in southern Indiana. In his column, Keeping Score, under the title "High Flying Blackhawk," Birge penned a super write-up in mid-January about Larry and the Springs Valley team. In part, Birge asserted, "One only needs to check the results of area high school basketball games to discover the hottest team on the hardwoods heading into the last half of the season, and, without a doubt, the most exciting—if not the most talented— individual player of the year." After losing two of their first three games, the Blackhawks, noted Birge, "have done a complete

KEEPING SCORE

With Jerry Birge

HIGH-FLYING BLACKHAWK

One needs only to check the results of area high school basketball games to discover the hottest team on the hardwoods heading into the last half of the season and, without a doubt, the most exciting—if not the most talented—individual player of the year.

The Springs Valley Blackhawks, after defeating Pekin Eastern (95-71) in their season opener, dropped back-to-back decisions to Washington (80-72) and Orleans (77-71) the first week of December. The Hawks were 1-2 after three games, but since then they have been rolling through Southern Indiana like Larry Csonka rolled through the Minnesota defense in the Super Bowl. The Hawks of coach Gary Holland have done a complete reversal, winning their last eight outings, most of them by impressive scores.

And there's good reason for the sudden success of the young men from French Lick—a 6-7 senior lad named Larry Bird who is suddenly the most-sought after cager in Southern Indiana.

97 POINT WEEKEND

The Blackhawks steamrolled over West Washington (98-45) and Corydon (99-73) this past weekend and in the process the high-flying Bird left the nets limp in the West Washington and Springs Valley gyms. They were still smoking yesterday morning after Bird touched them for 42 points Friday night (at West Washington) and an incredible 55 points Saturday night at Valley. In that Saturday display of offensive talent, Bird tossed in 22 of 33 field goal attempts, one of the finest shooting exhibitions ever staged in Indiana basketball.

For the weekend Bird scored 97 points in two games, running his season total to 370 points in 11 games, an average of 33.6 points per outing.

OTHER BIG GAMES

His 55 point count Saturday night was quite a feat but it came as no surprise to anyone who has seen Bird play. He has been over 40 points twice (the 42 against West Washington and 43 against

Larry Bird
High-Flying Blackhawk

Jasper Herald sportswriter Jerry Birge was instrumental in letting the region and state know about Larry Bird's great performances in Larry's senior year.

reversal, winning their last eight outings, most of them by impressive scores. The Blackhawks steamrolled over West Washington (98-45) and Corydon (99-73) this past weekend and in the process, the high-flying Bird left the nets limp in the West Washington and Springs Valley gyms. They were still smoking yesterday morning after Bird touched them for 42 points Friday night (at West Washington) and an incredible 55 points Saturday night at Valley." Birge ended the article arguing that "area coaches will face quite a task when they meet the Hawks in tournament time."

Valley players, coaches, and fans could read all the positive newspaper accounts they wished. The big game with Loogootee, the heartbreaker team from the year before, would soon be coming up, a game that would be the ultimate test in the regular season of how good the Blackhawks really were. The Lions were undefeated and playing methodic, solid basketball in the second half of the season. As usual, the winner of the Valley/Loogootee contest would likely take the conference champion crown.

Jack Butcher, the Loogootee coach, certainly seemed confident about his undefeated squad. Two weeks before the big

Calmly coming out of the huddle.

Valley/Loogootee showdown, Jack told Dave Koerner at the *Courier-Journal*, "The idea of going undefeated is fine, I guess, but you can't point to it. We went undefeated in 1963 but lost in the sectional. That loss in the sectional is a tragedy in this town." Then Jack added, "I haven't really been frightened by the second half of the season yet this year. We feel our two guards are two of the strongest in the southern part of the state." After singing the praises of his son, junior guard Bill Butcher, and Bill's senior sidekick, Alan Crane, Butcher mentioned a lesser-known player, Wayne Flick, a senior who had put the kibosh on Steve Land in Loogootee's upset of Valley the year before. Flick had undergone two knee operations and missed much of his two previous varsity seasons. Butcher explained, however, that Wayne was "a very important ball player. The number of points he scores doesn't indicate how much. He is more important from the standpoint of leadership, defense, rebounds, and just all-around ability."

Larry Bird would soon find out how accurate Coach Butcher was about Mr. Flick.

As Loogootee waited in the wings, the pressure on the Springs Valley team and its young coach was building for another reason. Coach Holland could certainly not afford to look past the regular season scheduled game with county rival Paoli. In the holiday tourney, Valley had squeaked by with a six-point win, as the Rams' big center, Tim Eubank, had been plagued by fouls. Valley's next game with the Rams would be a complete restart, and Paoli, now with a decent record of 6-7, had nothing to lose. It helped Paoli too that the game would be played in their gym, the place packed with Ram fans. Meanwhile, many loyal Blackhawk fans remembered what had happened about the same time the year before, how one defeat had sent the Valley team into a tailspin. Arnold Bledsoe in the Hawks Nest column sounded his own warning. "The Hawks can't overlook Paoli as they will be ready to play. They're still smarting from the last time we met in the Holiday Tournament."

Valley took first possession in the battle, and Bird hit a swisher from the deep corner. Things went downhill from there. Two

Valley players, Brad Bledsoe and Beezer Carnes, quickly ran into foul trouble. By the end of the first quarter, the pumped-up Rams led 18-14, thanks to the scoring of Eubank.

Eubank got the tip from Bird at the beginning of the second quarter and then scored a basket that put Paoli up by six. Valley fought back, taking the lead until a hook shot by Eubank over Bird "brought Rams fans to their feet." At halftime, Valley was up 38-36, the tight contest leaving Blackhawk fans worried and Paoli fans hopeful. Gary Holland, however, did not panic.

The day after the game, an astute Harry Moore noted the nature of the strategic change the Blackhawk coach made. "Coach Holland switched defense to a zone in the third period and it hurt Paoli." Meanwhile, at one pivotal juncture, Larry Bird scored ten points in a row in a big Valley third quarter, using his nifty head fakes and bombing in long, arching twenty-five-footers that made

The sharp shooting of Loogootee guard Bill Butcher would put a crimp in Springs Valley's '73-'74 season.

even the Paoli fans place their hands on their hearts. Springs Valley mascot Lisa Stackhouse also added to the excitement, keeping Blackhawk fans on task with her entertaining tumbling across the court during time-outs, to the point that Harry Moore reported, "Isn't she something to see tumbling across the floor."

The final score was almost a carbon copy of the match the two teams played in the holiday tournament, 82-74 to Valley's advantage. The intensity of the game, however, may have been best captured toward the end of the battle when Bird and Eubank got twisted up and both fell to the floor, fists flying. Future Purdue football team captain Tim Eubank was on top, but the two players were quickly separated. Despite that altercation, even Paoli fans were cheering for Larry when Bird left the floor at the end of the game, both his arms lifted in the air in jubilation.

Paoli's center, big Tim Eubank, pulled no punches when he played against Larry Bird.

The next day the *Courier-Journal* reported, "In a rare occurrence, Springs Valley's Larry Bird was outscored by a rival center last night. Bird, whose averaging 33.6, got 35, while Paoli's Tim Eubank collected 38." But while Valley fans left the gym happy with a victory, sports reporter Harry Moore posted a warning. "The Hawks will have their work cut out for them Tuesday night when they entertain No. 17 state ranked Loogootee. The Lions come roaring into town undefeated in 12 outings. It will take another Jasper game or maybe better for Valley to win. The Hawks will have to be at their best on defense."

The upcoming Valley/Loogootee tilt caught the eye of sports fans across the region. Russ Brown, the *Courier-Journal* sports editor for the paper's Indiana section, visited both coaches to see what their plans were to win what was likely to be an epic basketball contest. Holland noted that the Lions were "a guard-oriented club. They're quick and have great outside shooters. I feel like our guards will have to play super defense if we are going to win. We've got to contain [Bill] Butcher: he's the one we've really got to concentrate on. We'll have to make him do things he doesn't ordinarily do."

Coach Butcher dropped a surprise in his interview. When asked how the Lions would stop Larry Bird, Jack said, "We'll just play him straightaway, let him get his points and hope we do an adequate job on the rest of their players. I don't think you can stop him. He's too mobile and too good an outside shot. We'll probably end up using a half-dozen players on him."

As it turned out, for the inside play, it took only one player to counter Bird in this contest: Steve Land's old nemesis, Wayne Flick.

Larry grabs a hard-fought rebound in a game against Paoli.

We'll Get Them in the Regional

By the time the Valley/Loogootee contest rolled around, interest in the game was at a fever pitch. The upcoming face-off between the two great basketball traditions was being headlined in the area as the premier high school game of the season. State-ranked Loogootee was undefeated, and Springs Valley had Larry Bird, who was the second-leading scorer in the state and one of the state's leading rebounders. Valley also had a nine-game win streak going. College scouts were sure to be in abundance at the contest. Many believed Loogootee would be a true test of just how good Valley and Bird really were. In his autobiography, Bird concurred. "We were playing well, and Loogootee High came into our gym for what they were saying

Coach Holland gives his players a pep talk before a game. Bird is sitting next to last on the bench, with his head bent down.

was the biggest regular season game we'd had in ten or fifteen years."

Meanwhile, Coach Holland had begun to fret that a loss to Loogootee might put the Blackhawks in the same kind of psychological tailspin the loss to Corydon had the year before, when Jim Jones had his best Valley team ever and still lost the Blue Chip Conference title and was knocked out of the state tournament in the sectional round of play. It did not help that Holland was young and in his initial year of his first head coaching job, and that he possessed a quiet, inward-turned personality that often absorbed more responsibility than was healthy. In short, Coach Holland was a worrier, and the previous year's shocking ending now hung over him like a raised sword.

Even the weather seemed to understand the game was unusual in its importance, warm winds coming up from the south and making for an abnormally warm day and evening, with small dark clouds occasionally scudding low across the sky. The spring-like weather also made the drive from Loogootee to French Lick a pleasant trip for both those riding on the team bus and those on the fan bus, one Loogootee high school fan remembering the hilly wooded landscape flashing by the bus windows on curvy Highway 56 until the waning daylight morphed the hills into something a bit more sinister in the gathering darkness. Older driving fans, however, had concerns that may have made them miss the pleasant weather and scenery. In one of the cars poking along in the Loogootee caravan, the driver, looking straight ahead to handle the curves, announced, "Be ready for a crowd like you've never seen before and plenty of big-name college coaches." He was on the mark on both counts.

Things were also unusually busy in the valley that afternoon. Long before local folks started driving to the game after work, a crowd was already forming before Springs Valley High School had finished their school day. Valley student Ron Prosser remembered the curious circumstances. "After eating lunch, we would go to the gym, which was in another building, to hang out and play pickup basketball. As I was going to the gym, I noticed several adults sitting in lawn chairs outside the main

entrance to the gym. Some were retirees but several were locals that had taken the day off to ensure that they would get
in." Standing in the Valley gym during his last class of the day,
Blackhawk player Brad Bledsoe noticed a crowd of people "already lined up outside the gym door and portable bleachers being brought in from the baseball field."

Those adult fans who arrived at what would normally have
been considered early, during the junior varsity game, were
shocked to find the gym already loaded with a crowd that was
beyond capacity. "The crowd that night was simply unbelievable," Ron Prosser noted. "The concrete area that encircles the
bleachers was standing room only and several more limber fans
had hoisted themselves up into the girders for a better view."

Long before the junior varsity game, the place was beyond
packed. Among the throng was none other than Bobby Knight
and at least five other college coaches. All of them—fans, players, and scouts—an estimated assembly of 4,000 people, had
somehow been shoehorned into a gym made to seat 2,700.
In a sports page photo in one newspaper showing the packed
gymnasium, the caption read, "Fans jammed the aisles, sat on
the floor, sat on windowsills and actually climbed on the raf-
ters." People were also sitting on others' laps in many instances,

Not a seat was left for the big Springs Valley/Loogootee game at the Blackhawk gym.

and the crowd noise was deafening. On top of the overflowing crowd, the unseasonably warm weather soon turned the gym into a sauna.

Jasper sportswriter Jerry Birge was in that overflowing crowd, twisting and turning to get out the little notebook he carried in one of his pockets. Once the game began, those around him must have wondered what he was up to as he scribbled away in his own personal shorthand only he could read. The next day in the *Jasper Herald*, under the heading "Standing Room Only," Birge rendered a colorful narrative of the festive atmosphere as he saw it. "A circus-like atmosphere filled the air Tuesday night as a Springs Valley record crowd jammed into the Springs Valley gym for the high school basketball clash between the host Blackhawks and the undefeated Loogootee Lions. The big crowd was lined three-to-four persons deep in the area behind the 2,700 seats in the Valley gym. All the seats were filled before halftime of the junior varsity game. The varsity game developed into the Indiana basketball classic expected."

It was a state-tournament-like atmosphere, the excessive crowd like a volcano, rumbling and ready to explode. That energy spilled over into the junior varsity contest, a nail-biting battle won by a last-second shot made by Valley's Kevin Mills, a childhood friend of Larry Bird's. Brad Bledsoe remembered the news of the junior varsity's victory arriving down in the locker room where the varsity was getting ready for the next game. When the junior varsity came into the room, "Larry suddenly grabbed Kevin Mills and shouted, 'Way to go!' Then Bird literally shook Kevin, getting us all pumped up to take on Loogootee."

Although several sports articles before the game had emphasized the play of Lion guards Bill Butcher and Alan Crane, Valley fans watching the Loogootee team step out on the court were surely impressed by some of the other players. Senior Mike Mattingly, while just under six feet tall, had the physical build and aggressive attitude of a football player. Mattingly had exceptional leaping abilities, his legs working like two large pistons. Mike was also the third-leading scorer on the squad.

Then there was six-three Loogootee center Mike Walls, a wide-body player who looked as if he knew how to use his bulk under the basket for maximum effect. Perhaps the most underrated player on the Lions' team was Wayne Flick. As his teammates shot around, Wayne carried on light chatter, laughing and keeping everyone loose. All the Loogootee players easily lofted arching jump shots as they warmed up, making the net dance.

Loogootee's muscular Mike Mattingly, seen here scoring in white, knocked Larry Bird out of the Lions/Blackhawks tilt for a few minutes, and the time-out Valley had to take proved pivotal.

Local sports reporters and those from the larger region filled their next day sports pages with detailed accounts of this epic Indiana high school basketball struggle. Both teams looked focused and ready to play at the tip-off. Hardcore sports fans watching the game, however, noticed from the start the difference in the teams' approaches. Loogootee players were constantly in motion, making precise moves—the point guard throwing a quick, crisp pass to one side, the forward holding the ball for an instant, looking for an open man as Loogootee players set screens to get a player open, then the ball whipping back out to the front where it was then passed to the other side to repeat the process. Conversely, Valley tended to come more quickly down the court, making fewer passes, confident in their shooting. Of course, they had Larry Bird, who was a deadly shooter from any distance or angle.

The fans were constantly on their feet, the contest turning into a war of back-and-forth jump shots, most of them from what would now be the three-point range. Larry was certainly hot in the first quarter, knocking down five baskets from way out. John Carnes helped Valley's cause by adding two baskets. But Loogootee was hotter. Coach Jack Butcher explained to Russ Brown at the Louisville *Courier Journal* after the game how he decided when the contest began "to go to Bill [Butcher] more than usual. We were trying to get our people to screen exclusively for Bill." The coach's son came through. Brown reported how the unfettered Bill Butcher "in Valley's steamy 2,700-seat gymnasium," made basket after basket "with uncanny accuracy from distances up to 25 feet."

At the beginning of the second quarter, Jack Butcher made another strategic move. He had Wayne Flick to front Larry on defense while Mike Walls played behind Larry when Bird was under the basket. Larry scored only two goals in the second period, and the Lions' methodic emphasis on passing slowed the game down a bit, though the ball was whizzing around the court with sharp passes. Brad Bledsoe and the Carnes cousins also scored that quarter for Springs Valley, keeping the game close. Halftime witnessed Loogootee up by five, 32-27.

Several impacting events occurred in the third quarter. Bill Butcher's shooting went cold, probably from his being fatigued. He made only one of six attempts. This allowed Valley to chip away at what had been a five-point halftime lead and to go ahead of the Lions. Jerry Birge mentioned two other events, however, that worked against Valley, happenings that turned out to be pivotal.

The first incident is mentioned in every Bird biography, although these accounts are not completely accurate. Still, the story is one of the most repeated of Larry Bird's high school basketball legends. Levine, in *The Making of an American Sports Legend*, for example, noted that "with 2:55 left in the third quarter there was a jump ball at the top of the Loogootee free-throw circle, and Larry grabbed the tip. Incredibly, Larry then wheeled around and dropped the ball into the Loogootee basket, thus scoring for the Lions. To make matters worse, Larry's mistaken basket proved to be the margin of difference." Jerry Birge, who was there, explained otherwise in his next-day newspaper report. "With 2:55 remaining in the third quarter the Hawks controlled a jump ball at the Loogootee free throw circle. Bird took the tip and went immediately to score—in the Loogootee basket! The 'wrong way'

Loogootee's Alan Crane scores against Springs Valley as Larry Bird looks on.

move by Bird was nullified, however, as he was called for traveling just before he made the basket. Valley was fortunate the basket didn't count, but it did give the ball back to Loogootee after the Hawks had controlled the tip."

But Birge also pointed out that "A much bigger play occurred with only 10 seconds left in the third quarter. Bird caught a perfectly placed elbow in the third quarter on a rebound battle and sagged to the floor in pain. The injury led to a Valley time out with only 10 seconds on the clock in the third quarter, a precious timeout when one notes that the lack of a timeout with seven seconds remaining in the game was the most critical play of the evening."

The elbow came from the built-for-football Loogootee player Mike Mattingly.

In the end, Larry Bird played superbly, but, as the Louisville newspaper reported, "While he was blazing away Bird was also having problems trying to shake free of Loogootee forward Wayne Flick." Flick was the unsung hero that evening, his success in keeping Bird from scoring underneath made more amazing by the seven or so inches he had to give up in height while guarding Larry. Still, Bird "often went to the corner to drill 25-footers. He led fast breaks, worked the offensive boards effectively, fed his team with pinpoint accuracy and turned in a steady performance even though Loogootee did an excellent job keeping him away from the ball."

The next-to-the-last nail in the Valley coffin was the deadly shooting of Bill Butcher in the final quarter. He made six of seven shots during the fourth quarter, including the decisive goal, "driving to the baseline and putting up a 15-foot jumper that bounced off the back of the rim and dropped through the basket." The basket put Loogootee up 64-63.

One last, dreadful for Valley, act ended the game. After Butcher's basket, the Blackhawks still had time to pull out the win. But John Carnes missed a shot, and then Loogootee's Alan Crane was fouled. Crane missed the first of a one-and-one at-

tempt, and in the fight for the rebound, the ball went to Valley with nine seconds left. When Valley threw the ball into play, Beezer Carnes, surrounded by Loogootee players, was unable to get it to another Valley man. In panic, he called a time-out, not realizing that his team had no more time-outs to use, having spent one when Bird was hurt in the third quarter. The referee quickly called a technical foul.

One of Bird's teammates, John Carnes, leads the team onto the Springs Valley gym floor.

Bill Butcher missed

the technical shot, but on the inbounds play, Crane was fouled and hit both shots for the final score of 66-63.

The writer for the *Springs Valley Herald*, Arnold Bledsoe, perhaps shell shocked, wrote only a very short, terse piece about the contest the next day. The report ended with "This was the first loss for Valley in the Blue Chip Conference and just about wrapped up the crown for Loogootee." The next day, the Louisville *Courier Journal* carried a much longer narrative headlined "Bill Butcher puts ax to Springs Valley." Russ Brown reported, "Butcher stole the show. He hit 14 of 22 shots, including seven of nine in the first half, and got sixteen of Loogootee's 24 points in the hectic final quarter." Valley, Brown also pointed out, had problems controlling Loogootee's other top-notch guard, Alan Crane, who tallied sixteen points and scored key baskets. A disappointed Coach Holland shared in the article what he believed was the key to Loogootee's win. "We just couldn't stop Butcher. His range is too good and one of our guards was too little and the other too slow. We just had to hope he missed." That, of course, did not happen.

Larry scores from the side, keeping Valley in the contest against Loogootee. Number 35, Bill Butcher, looks on.

While Larry Bird had tallied a more than respectable twenty-eight points, Butcher had garnered thirty-six. As Jerry Birge put it in the Jasper newspaper, "Bird was rating the headlines before the game, but those headlines belonged to Loogootee's Bill Butcher Wednesday morning." Perhaps Birge, his little notebook now jammed full of nearly illegible scribblings, summed up the epic basketball clash best when he finished his *Jasper Herald* sports article by writing, "Bill Butcher and Larry Bird treated the overflow crowd to a pair of great individual basketball performances. The two teams treated the fans to an exciting, close game the way Indiana cage fans love it. Loogootee fans were thrilled, and Valley fans were disappointed. But they got what they wanted to see: a whale of a basketball game."

The southern Indiana blockbuster game even caught the eye of Indianapolis sportswriter Bob William, who marveled, "Bill Butcher stole some of Bird's thunder in the Springs Valley contest." Coach Butcher, however, heaped only praise on the Blackhawk team and Coach Holland in the Indy article, calling Larry Bird "the best senior I've seen all year. Most of our fans told me later Bird lived up to everything we'd heard about him." Indeed, the 1974 Springs Valley/Loogootee game was destined to become a part of Indiana high school basketball legend.

And if everyone had been in the gym who claimed so later, the gym would not have had room for the players on the floor.

Jack Butcher's praise meant little or nothing to Valley players, coaches, and fans. Brad Bledsoe recalled the bleak atmosphere in the locker room after the game. "We were heartbroken, not so much that we had lost, but how we lost. We felt we hadn't played our game and that we were the better team. And we felt sorry for Larry with all those college coaches in the crowd." Bledsoe thought Larry "was torn up about it. He just hated to lose."

The community was devastated, especially given the game's ending on such a horrible mistake, Beezer Carnes' calling for a time-out when the team had none left and the act drawing a technical foul. Coach Holland, however, graciously stepped in and took the blame, telling a reporter, "Jim (Beezer) called the time out, but it was my fault. I just forgot to tell him we didn't have any more time outs left. He was really hurt about it; I hope it doesn't get him down too much."

In Larry's autobiography fifteen years later, Larry indicated the sting of the loss had stayed with him, perhaps one of the few games Larry may have wished to do over. "It gets to be a real close game and one or the other of us is up by one. We've got the ball and the coach calls for a time-out. The first thing

Larry Bird, soaring to score in the team's epic battle against Loogootee.

he says when we get into the huddle is: 'We have no more time-outs.' Then he goes: 'Try to get the ball to Larry . . . work it around.' We take the ball out and throw it in to Beezer. He takes two or three dribbles and then can't find anybody for a second, so what does he do? He calls time out." Beezer recalled however that just after the game Larry "didn't criticize me. He just said, 'We'll get them in the regional.'" This became the battle cry for the remainder of the season, to do well going into the sectional, to win the sectional, and then beat Loogootee at the Washington regional.

One more recollection touches upon Larry's frustrations with the loss to Loogootee. After the game, as the Loogootee fan bus waited in the Springs Valley High School parking lot for all the riders to get on board, a high school fan remembered seeing Larry Bird come out a back door. "When he saw the bus, he gave the finger. Of course, we had been hollering at him about our win."

The day after the Tuesday night loss was a time of reckoning in the valley. Gone was the hope of Coach Holland and his team tying Jim Jones' best regular season record of just two losses. Gone too was the likely possibility of winning the conference championship.

While these two losses brought profound sadness, another

pressing concern brought great anxiety. Coach Holland, and likely every Valley fan and player, now fretted that the team would go into a tailspin like the season before, when Loogootee beat the Blackhawks and took the conference title and the Valley team never seemed to get its momentum back, losing to county rival Orleans in the sectional. It did help, however, that they hoped to get revenge for the Loogootee loss if they went on to win the sectional, since Loogootee would likely be an opponent in regional play. In this regard, Coach Holland told a *Courier Journal* reporter, "The kids DO want to get back at Loogootee. They don't think they played well in that first game."

A new specter now haunted the Blackhawks—what if Valley did not win the sectional? It would be a nightmare. No one felt this concern more deeply than Coach Holland. After the Loogootee loss, the already slender Blackhawk coach began to lose weight rapidly, having "to walk around with my fist down the back of my pants to hold them up." Holland later told a sports reporter about the issue, and how he noticed "A few days after the Loogootee game that I had to take my belt up a notch." While the young first-year coach lost physical weight, he also began to feel he carried an invisible psychological weight on his back. "I started worrying about the sectional. Are we going to be ready? Are we going to be healthy? Are we going to shoot well? Things that aren't coachable. You work hard all year, then it could be shot in one night."

Of course, Coach Jim Jones could have told Holland about all of that and more.

Who Is That Guy?

One of the things that emerges from giving a close read to old newspaper accounts of Larry Bird's high school senior year is just how grinding some of these contests were and how, despite Larry's amazing skills, teams managed to beat the Valley team, or at least take them to the wire several times. That grind got rougher after the Loogootee loss. Springs Valley was 10-3 after the contest with Loogootee and faced seven more teams before sectional play started. They needed to win every game in this last stretch to have the momentum necessary to go deep into state tournament play. It could be argued, however, that the Blackhawks' next game against Southridge, a consolidation of Huntingburg and Holland, was one of the most essential contests of the remaining season. A second straight let-down loss, this one against a solid Southbridge team that stood at 8-7, would likely have been devastating for Gary Holland's club, causing the Valley team to lose its confidence. The Southridge Raiders, on the other hand, had nothing to lose, playing on their own court in the cavernous Huntingburg gymnasium and having just won two recent games against good competition.

It was also a perfect situation to cause the local Valley drugstore coaches to start complaining. Bird biographers also seemed critical. Levine, in the part of his Bird biography that briefly covers Larry's senior year, noted that "the Blackhawks weren't the most disciplined group, and Coach Holland was inexperienced. . . . Valley also had the tendency to stand around and watch Larry as he played." Newspaper accounts, however, showed that Coach Holland clearly perceived a need to shake up the lineup after the bitter Loogootee loss and did so. The Raiders had a couple of tall, wide-bodied players named Joe Mundy and Dave Schmett, just the kind of guys who could knock around opponents and clear rebounds. Holland adjusted to this specific problem by starting little-used junior Mike Cox,

Opponents always struggled to stop Larry from scoring during his senior year. Here, Larry gets set for a shot.

who ended up grabbing thirteen rebounds in the game. Coach Holland would also make another major change later in the contest, one, as it turned out, any previously complaining fan would have surely approved.

The next day, *Springs Valley Herald's* Arnold Bledsoe began his narrative about the make-or-break contest by observing that the Raiders "were a strong test for the Hawks after dropping the heartbreaker to Loogootee on Tuesday night. This game had all the earmarks of trouble for the Hawks from the start. The boys of Gary Holland couldn't seem to get rolling, but the rebounding and defense kept them in the game."

Holland surely lost more weight as the Southridge game progressed. Both teams struggled with offense, Larry Bird, for example, missing most of his shots in the first half. *Jasper Herald* sports reporter Denny Spinner's account captured the closeness of the match, the piece also suggesting the game was not a thing of beauty. "The game was close all the way as Southridge led at the first stop 17-16 and at the half 33-31." Fortunately for Valley, Beezer Carnes, perhaps trying to atone for his last-second mistake in the Loogootee game, garnered eight points in the first period to keep the Blackhawks close. Then John Carnes picked up the slack in the second quarter to continue to keep the Blackhawks in the game.

Looking at the scoreboard and seeing the Raiders up by a

Larry's long arms and his height made him a devastating shot blocker.

point at halftime made for disgruntled and fidgety Valley fans, the memory of the last season's up and down second half and bitter ending suddenly hanging in the air. Fortunately, something good was about to happen, a coaching move that brought great dividends.

When the second half began, Valley supporters were surprised by a change in the lineup. Coach Holland was sending in another little-used player, Chester Allen. Harry Moore later reported, "Coach Holland liked what he saw in Allen and left him in the remainder of the contest. Chester played a dandy game. In fact, it seemed as if he sparked the Hawks." Other Valley players did better in the third quarter, especially John Carnes. But so did the Raiders. A reporter noted, "With 1:51 remaining in the third stanza, the score was tied 43 all, but John Carnes put the Hawks ahead on a free throw. Eric Olinger put Southridge ahead with 38 seconds to go, but Larry Bird made the score 46-45 with 34 seconds left. Husky Dave Schmett connected with 19 seconds left." Larry Bird then made a long shot with ten seconds showing on the clock to leave the third quarter 48-47 Valley. The basket was an important boost for the team from French Lick.

To the Valley crowd's great relief, Bird finally got hot in the fourth quarter, scoring twelve of Valley's first fourteen points, and Valley pulled away at the very end to achieve a 66-58 victory. And although both teams had a hard time hitting the basket, Valley took down an amazing fifty-eight rebounds to the Raiders' thirty. Larry Bird grabbed twenty-six of Valley's total rebounds and racked up twenty-five points, five or so points below his average. Big Joe Mundy was the high point man for the Raiders with nineteen.

Valley fans were grateful for the win, but unsure about the degree to which the Blackhawks were back on track. Harry Moore at the *Paoli Republican*, however, thought the Blackhawks' slow start against the Southridge team in the first three quarters and the ensuing victory indicated resilience, "the ingredient of a good team." Looking at how the entire game had played out, Moore saw the win as the kind of hard-earned victory that might

lay a foundation for a new win streak. The Hawks wouldn't have to wait long to see if the sports reporter knew what he was talking about. The next game, a home contest against Bloomfield and its veteran coach, Guy Glover, would let the Valley basketball community know if Larry Bird and the rest of the team would be firing again on all cylinders as they had earlier in the season.

Bird did not hesitate to rumble if he got pushed around.

The Valley gym was packed when the Cardinal and Black-hawk teams came out on the floor for the varsity game. Like Southridge, Bloomfield had a break-even record and nothing to lose. They were another tall team, and once more, Gary Holland worried about a rebounding disadvantage. The pressure only incresed when Bob Knight walked into the gym with his no-nonsense posture and took a seat in the bleachers. It was the third time that he personally showed up to see Larry play.

Bird and the Valley team did not disappoint anyone but the Cardinal team and their fans. Hitting almost 50 percent of their shots, the Blackhawks played one of their best regular season games as a team, and Larry Bird was as dazzling as he had been in the earlier West Washington and Corydon contests, hitting shots inside and out, tearing down rebounds, making amazing passes, and blocking shots. Harry Moore wrote in the next issue of the Paoli newspaper, "It was another record shattering game for Hawk Larry Bird. Larry hauled down 34 rebounds, surpass-ing his old record of 28, set Jan. 18 against West Washington. For good measure, Bird also tossed in 34 points." John Carnes added twenty-eight and his cousin Beezer chipped in fifteen.

Knight left the building impressed, but he wasn't the only major college coach interested in Larry. Dave Schellhase, then a graduate assistant basketball coach at Purdue, remembered how Coach George King at Purdue and a friend of Schellhase's took the long trip down to southern Indiana to watch Larry Bird play. "When I saw my friend the next day, he told me, 'I saw the best high school basketball player I've ever seen. His name is Larry Bird.'"

While all seemed back to normal for the Blackhawks after the Bloomfield contest, Coach Holland was now concerned that his team would be playing three games in five days. In the next match, the next night after the Bloomfield contest, Valley played South Knox. So hot now was a Larry Bird playing ap-pearance in the area, the game was moved to the larger Adams Coliseum in Vincennes to accommodate all the interested fans. South Knox was a tough Blue Chip Conference foe who had earned a 9-6 record. That the two teams were both in the hunt

Bird brings down a rebound with authority.

for second place in the conference only added to the tension.

The next day, the Springs Valley paper carried the sports headline "South Knox—Ugh." Reporter Arnold Bledsoe wrote, "It was cold outside, it was cold in the Spartan goalry and the Hawks were ice cold. Valley's 32 per cent was by far the poorest of the year. It's bound to happen to any team, and Saturday it happened to Valley—the shooting percentage we mean. For the first time this season the Hawks were outrebounded, 31-22." Happily, the reporter was able to add, "But the big factor was, the Hawks overcame several obstacles and won. They could have given up any time, but they didn't."

South Knox methodically carried out a sound game plan, slowing down the contest by holding the ball and taking only good shots. Larry had only four points in the first quarter, and the Spartans led 9-6. The half ended 23-19 with Valley ahead, after a lucky Blackhawk player got a tip-in off an offensive rebound as the horn sounded, an official signaling it was good. The South Knox crowd broke out in an ear-shattering chorus of boos.

Nevertheless, the Spartan fans had much to be happy about as the teams went to their dressing rooms. South Knox's Jim Wyatt had been especially effective in the second period, hitting Bird-like corner shots with dead-eye accuracy, frustrating Valley fans, who were used to seeing Larry carry out such displays.

The third period ended at 35-31 with Valley ahead, although the Blackhawks had possessed a ten-point lead at one juncture. The final quarter was an Indiana high school basketball nail-bitter with every fan standing and the noise so loud, players were unable to hear any directions coming from the benches. It may have been freezing outside, but everyone was sweating inside the Vincennes gymnasium. In this quarter, Ed Vieck lit up the goal for South Knox.

Springs Valley, behind Larry's shooting, kept the lead until 3:26 left in the game, when South Knox crept ahead by a point. One spectator recalled that because of the contest's intensity, the riveting excitement of the large roaring crowd in the packed gymnasium, the last few minutes seemed to run in slow motion. Valley failed to score on the next possession, and the Spartans held the ball, taking only one shot. It went in.

South Knox was up by three with just under two minutes left in the game.

Adams Coliseum rocked with noise, South Knox fans chanting "Upset, upset." But just when the lights seemed to go out for Springs Valley, things jelled for the Blackhawks. Valley got their hands on the ball, and John Carnes put back an offensive rebound, bringing Valley within one. Playing hard-core defense, Valley got the ball back again and Bird hit a shot, giving the Blackhawks a one-point lead with twenty seconds remaining.

Basketball games often turn on a single play, and Larry's basket has been seen as the winning act. But Harry Moore at the *Paoli Republican* captured another angle, now forgotten, reporting that South Knox had the ball and a chance for a major upset when junior Brad Bledsoe somehow managed to tie up a South Knox player and won the tip. With one second left, John Carnes cashed in on a foul shot, leaving the score 50-48 in favor of Springs Valley. The next day the *Vincennes Sun-Commercial* headlined "South Knox Loses Heartbreaker" and added in the subhead, "Bird Held to 19." The report also offered insight into the pivotal part of the game. "With less than two minutes in the game remaining in the final period, the Spartans led 48-45, but the Blackhawks used a desperation defense and sharp rebounding to score five unanswered points and salvage victory." Ed Vieck and Jim Wyant were the "almost heroes" for South Knox, being just seconds away from becoming Indiana high school basketball legends, almost to have been able to say what few would, that they beat Larry Bird.

It just did not feel like a clean victory, being forced into a close game by a team Valley should had easily whipped. As the Vincennes newspaper had reported, Larry Bird had only scored nineteen points, shooting a surprisingly poor 9-26 from the field. However, Harry Moore at the *Republican* may have offered the most interesting, practical, and wisest take on the contest's results. "We were glad to see a team throw a stall game against the Hawks. Sooner or later, it was bound to happen. With the Hawk defense, had they hit anything, they would have routed South Knox."

The hair's-breath closeness of the South Knox battle brought Coach Holland a continuing rise in his level of anxiety. He wasn't going to be gaining weight any time soon. The tense Southridge and South Knox contests had also exhausted Valley fans, but they showed up hopefully at Barr Reeve High School for the Blackhawks' third game in five nights and were happy to see Valley easily take out the Vikings, 86-65, with Bird hitting for thirty-four points. Everyone knew, however, that Valley would now face a tough Mitchell squad at Mitchell four days later. Gary Holland was still trying to fine-tune his troops, searching for the best possible combination.

Valley fans may have been a bit surprised to see sophomore Chester Allen replacing Beezer Carnes when the Valley team came out of the huddle at the beginning of the Mitchell game.

The next day Arnold Bledsoe wrote that the Mitchell contest "left the Hawk fans screaming and holding on to their seats as the clock ran out." It did not start out that way. The Blackhawks zoomed out to a big lead. In the third period, Larry Bird canned seven of ten shots from all angles and by the beginning of the fourth quarter, Valley led Mitchell 65-51. Brad Bledsoe put

Valley up by sixteen at the beginning of the last quarter before Mitchell came roaring back on six straight Valley errors, their efforts lifted even higher by the roaring Mitchell crowd, who felt in their very bones an upset in the making. With just a minute to play, the Bluejackets were three points down and had the ball. Then Bird stole a pass that led to a basket by Beezer Carnes and an eventual 79-74 victory.

Chester Allen drew the most accolades after the game, however, as one reporter wrote, "Hawk Chester Allen, a sophomore, was instrumental in Valley's win over Mitchell. Chet won a starting berth and came through in grand style." Another article was even more specific. "To say that Chet played well is putting it mildly. He scored 12 points, passed out nine assists, high for the team, and hauled down three rebounds."

Besides the closeness of several games for the Blackhawks, another disturbing event occurred as sectional time drew near. That same night that Springs Valley squeaked by Mitchell, Orleans clobbered undefeated Loogootee on the Lions' floor, a feat that was headlined in all the next-day sports reports. The story of that game would be long remembered in Orleans basketball history, an Indiana high school basketball gem. Writing about the battle the next day, Harry Moore believed the Bulldogs' defense played a great part in the upset. "Mike McClintic did a great job on Bill Butcher, holding him to six points and the Bull Dogs came out growling. Before the Lions knew what hit them, Orleans was on top 22-6." Even after Loogootee put on its famous press, "McClintic found himself open for 11 points in the first frame." Meanwhile, Curt Gilstrap was clearing the boards and starting effective fast breaks. When Gilstrap went out of the game on fouls with five minutes remaining and McClintic soon followed, Loogootee crept back into the contest. With his two top guys out, Coach Denbo called a time-out. McClintic remembered Denbo being almost beside himself, beseeching his players, "Whatever you do, don't let these guys come back on you!" The Bulldogs held on, winning 55-49. In the end, Moore reported, "Gilstrap and McClintic with their combined 31 points wrecked the Lions."

The news that Orleans had clipped Loogootee was a mixed bag for Valley fans, who were still stinging from the late-January defeat at home against the Lions. Although Loogootee had been beaten and knocked out of the possibility of an undefeated season, Orleans' victory portended its own trouble for Valley. As Harry Moore pointed out in his column, "This was a big win for Orleans and with it, they will undoubtedly be the favorite in the upcoming sectional. They now have a shiny 17-1 record."

Springs Valley's last home game that year would be against Salem, a squad that had won but three games. The few days leading up to the home gym battle quickly grew to take on a festive spirit, with school officials announcing they were hiring a band to play for the student body after the game. Coach Holland, however, faced a dilemma. Although the contest against Salem would most likely be an easy victory, promising a chance for everyone to play, someone pointed out that Larry Bird had

Bird goes up for a rebound against the always tough Mitchell Bluejackets.

a chance of breaking Steve Land's all-time scoring record. Now all the players were begging Coach Holland to turn Larry loose. In fact, the team thought a give-it-all-you-got blowout game would be an exciting way to end the home season, keeping the fans hyped up for the upcoming sectional.

But Holland feared Larry might get injured in such a circumstance, the kind of dreaded possibility that caused the Valley coach to continue to lose weight and have nightmares. One fan recalled Coach Holland had grown so nervous in posture that he looked "as if he might break." In the end, Holland turned Larry and the team loose, later telling one Louisville *Courier-Journal* sports reporter, "If this hadn't been the last night for seniors to play at home, I probably would have taken him out instead of letting him play all the way. I was just gritting my teeth, hoping he wouldn't get hurt." Jim Jones, now the school's athletic director, did his part to add to the circus-like atmosphere, keeping the two officials for the game talking in the locker room while Larry Bird entertained the crowd with awesome and artistic dunks during his team's warm-ups, an act that would have drawn a technical foul to start the game had the referees known.

Awed Salem players stopped their warm-up shooting to watch Larry's thunderous dunks. It would truly be Larry's night.

The Louisville paper reported that the result of Holland's decision to turn Bird loose "was devastating. Bird, a 6-foot-7 center, collected 54 points and 38 rebounds, and handed out eight assists as Valley breezed to a 94-46 win." Larry hit twenty-five of forty-two field goal attempts from all over the floor.

Oddly, Larry's ongoing emergence as one of the best Indiana high school basketball players continued to go unnoticed in most of the state toward the end of the 1973–1974 regular basketball season. A case in point involved the band hired to play that night after the contest with Salem.

The band, called Justice, came from Jasonville, Indiana, a small coal mining town toward Terre Haute. The group was led by two brothers, Bo and Jeff McNabb, both excellent high school basketball players who loved the game and prided themselves on keeping tabs on the better players in the state. Bo, the oldest, was then a freshman basketball player at Franklin College, while Jeff was the leading scorer for the Shakamak High School Lakers and was solid enough that a sportswriter from the Greene County region had called him "one of the best players in our area." Jeff eventually ended up at Indiana State, where he would play for a short while with Bird. That night, however, Jeff and his brother had yet to hear of Larry Bird or of his "magical" basketball skills. That would soon change.

As Jeff McNabb worked to prepare for the band's performance, Bo wandered to the gym to watch the game. He quickly returned, telling his brother he needed to hurry up and come see something.

Jeff recalled how his brother took his arm and said, "This guy just got knocked down hard at the top of the key, then popped up and scored. The damn thing went in and he was fouled and made the foul shot."

Jeff McNabb, possessing his share of Indiana high school basketball player ego, replied, "Probably just luck." That perspective quickly changed.

Jeff and Bo McNabb watched the rest of the game, a contest where Larry scored a mind-blowing fifty-four points and grabbed thirty-eight rebounds. The two brothers witnessed Bird hitting put-backs under the basket and long, arching jump shots, the smooth rotation of the ball leaving the nets dancing. But Bird did more than just shoot and sweep the backboard for rebounds; he made beautiful, pinpoint passes and dished out several keen assists.

Just before the game ended, Jeff McNabb remembered his brother turning to him and saying in astonishment, "Who *is* that guy?"

Jeff McNabb, of Shakamak High School, seen grabbing a rebound in this photo, never forgot witnessing Larry Bird breaking a single-game scoring and rebounding record toward the end of Bird's senior year.

Maybe it was because it was the last regular season high

school basketball game that Larry Bird and two other Springs Valley seniors—John Carnes and Beezer Carnes—would ever play that this trio came together and performed as they had the first half of the season. The contest occurred on February 22, 1974, in a game at Brownstown Central High School.

Jim Plump, a sportswriter for a Seymour, Indiana, newspaper, wrote a colorful narrative the next day about the Blackhawk senior trio and the game. "Tick . . . tick . . . tick. It was like a bomb. Springs Valley was ready to explode, but Brownstown kept blowing on the fuse. Finally, midway through the final period, the bomb went off." With Joe Hall, head coach at the University of Kentucky, and scouts from Western Kentucky and the University of Alabama in Huntsville looking on, "the Carnes boys, James (Beezer) and John, and the ever-present Larry Bird took control of the game, hitting 13 of 20 shots in the fourth period stanza." Jim Plumb went on to point out that "It was John Carnes who broke Brownstown's back, however. His seven of 10 shooting in the second half, four of four in the final period, put the Braves away."

As the Springs Valley team bus drove the long road back to French Lick, full of cheerful players who grew quieter as the bus's headlights continued to cut through the darkness, Coach Gary Holland likely breathed a sigh of relief. The team had ended the regular season on a strong note. Now Holland could completely turn his attention to the sectional tournament.

The next day, Harry Moore summed up Valley's regular season accomplishments by putting the story in its earliest perspective. "The Hawks have a new coach in Gary Holland. And what a job this young man has done. Not one Valley fan dared hope for an even season much less a 17-3 slate. But Coach Holland and his Hawks have now spoiled the Valley fans." Moore noted too how the Hawks were "an explosive outfit. They scored in the 90-point bracket six times and hit 80+ points four times. However, it isn't the offense the Hawks are proud of—it is their defense. And this defense, in the late goings, has really paid off." Moore also recognized the dynamic of the three seniors, Larry Bird, John Carnes, and James "Beezer" Carnes, who had carried much of the scoring load. Of course, Larry received the highest praise. "Larry Bird—what a performer he has been. He has broken every record imaginable." Bird and the Springs Valley Blackhawks had accomplished an essential task, finishing out their season after the brutal Loogootee defeat with a long win streak going into sectional play.

Larry Bird now seemed to be able walk on water, and younger Springs Valley school kids adored Larry, Coach Gary Holland recalling, "Kids really looked up to him, wanting to be like him." Larry was good about being aware of these Bird worshippers, often going out of his way to talk to the junior high boys who thought Larry was a god. Tom Roach remembered tossing his shirt in the air while running the gym stairs in a PE class and the shirt ending up hanging on a rafter. "I didn't know what to do. I couldn't reach my shirt. Then I saw Larry Bird walking through the gym and asked him if he could get it down for me. He shook his head and laughed and went up the stairs to get it for me. I was so thankful."

Redemption

In mid-February of 1974, the blind bracket draws had been announced for each Indiana high school sectional. For the Springs Valley Blackhawks, it was a so-so outcome, a three-rung ladder to win the championship and move on to the regional round in Washington High School's spacious gymnasium. Gary Holland's crew would have to play host school Paoli in the first game of the sectional tournament, and, if they won, would likely face a solid Leavenworth squad. If they won that contest, Valley no doubt would have to beat their sectional nemesis from the year before, the Orleans Bulldogs, in the championship game.

Drug store coaches from every Indiana community offered their views about the possible outcome of each game to anyone who would listen. At this time too, a sportswriter penned an unusual editorial in an Orange County paper, explaining his concern about the overheated fan support in the Paoli sectional. "Every year at this time," the reporter explained, "the charge is raised that high school basketball in Indiana is over-emphasized. It is sad to see a rooting section toss debris upon a playing floor. It is sad to hear adult fans vile-mouth a referee for every unfavorable call." The writer called on local fans "to put a rein upon our emotions. Let us all unite in good will to the survivor of the eight contenders, whichever it turns out to be."

Despite the editor's wishes, the beat went on. Coach Ron Ferguson of Milltown High School told one sports reporter that he believed the tournament would turn into a dogfight, with Springs Valley, Paoli, Orleans, and Milltown having an equal chance at taking the title. Coach Ferguson also thought the Paoli sectional tourney would be "a recruiter's dream. You'll see four of the best ball players in southern Indiana. Each night there will be an action-packed game." Coach Ferguson's comments were on the mark. Larry Bird held a thirty-two-point a game average, second highest in the state, while Paoli's Tim

Eubank was clocking twenty-five points a contest. Dave Smith of Milltown was not far behind Eubank, with a twenty-three-point average, followed by rugged Curt Gilstrap, who averaged twenty-two. All four of these players would start their college careers at Division I universities.

Gary Holland was not optimistic when he talked to a reporter from Louisville. "We kinda wanted to see us and three of the weakest teams in the same bracket." There was good reason for Holland's wish. Although the Blackhawks had beaten Paoli in two close games during the regular season, in the Indiana coaching culture, winning a third game against the same team in a basketball season was thought to be very difficult to accomplish, as if a jinx had been activated. Meanwhile, Paoli coach Woody Neel was guardedly optimistic in an interview with Dave Koerner at the Louisville *Courier Journal.* "Both times we played Valley, we were ahead or at least close around halftime. We just

DAVE SMITH
Averages 23.5 points

Milltown's Dave Smith led the Millers in their upset victory over a 19-2 Orleans team in the semifinals of the 1974 sectional at Paoli.

played three quarters the first time and that has been our trouble all year, inconsistency." Neel added that he believed his team "matches Valley to a tee," especially with center Tim Eubank, who had outscored Larry Bird in one of the teams' encounters that year. Neel planned to have his troops "work the ball and work it, make them (Valley) play some defense. In practice," the Paoli coach added, "we look like all-Americans doing it."

Conversely, Coach Holland, a Paoli native himself, explained to another reporter that his team "was really keyed up." Referring to the pressure that came from trying to beat the same team three times in the same playing year, Holland said he knew it was going to be hard to beat the Rams "after only beating them by six and eight points before. Besides, we have an awful lot of respect for them, especially Tim Eubank."

Of course, sportswriters had their own picks. A Bedford *Times-Mail* writer figured the Paoli tourney turning out this way: "Springs Valley over Paoli by eight; Marengo over English by one; Orleans over Milltown by two; Leavenworth over West Washington by three; Springs Valley over Leavenworth by 26; Orleans over Marengo by 20 and Springs Valley in the championship game, over Orleans by four." Interestingly, the same paper also pointed out, "The Orleans Bulldogs, defending Paoli champions, will be waving a blistering 19-1 record at the field in next week's tourney and it's possible they might be back in the Washington regional." In the Bulldogs' final regular season game victory, their big man, Curt Gilstrap, finished with thirty-two points and thirty rebounds, certainly a Larry Bird level of play.

Finally, nut cracking time rolled around. On February 27, 1974, a Bedford sports headline announced "Paoli vs. Springs Valley" and followed with a short summary. "Action opens tonight in the Paoli sectional and it's a big one. The Blackhawks and Rams are long-time hardwood rivals and one can expect tonight's match to be a give-and-take battle." Up until the contest started, Coach Neel kept talking about the third-game jinx, as if the adage had magical powers.

The next day, after the smoke had cleared, Woody Neel told a

Louisville *Courier Journal* reporter, "It was unreal. Three times in one year." And the game hadn't even been close, 81-60. As expected, Bird and Eubank were the keys, and both had solid games. Tim hit for twenty-four points and grabbed fourteen rebounds. Bird was just a bit better in those departments, scoring twenty-six points and getting sixteen rebounds. But Larry had sparked "a sizzling second quarter that allowed Springs Valley to break open the game," hitting "four of five shots in that span." A frustrated and disappointed Coach Neel explained, "We couldn't shoot, and we couldn't rebound with them. We wanted to work the ball, make them play some defense." In practice, Neel said, his team had been perfect in their execution, but then his team went out during the game "and threw caution to the wind."

Coach Holland and his Springs Valley team had successfully climbed the first rung of the sectional ladder, easily getting past the three-game jinx. They would now face Leavenworth in the next contest. Meanwhile, the biggest upset in that year's Paoli sectional play occurred in one of the next night's battles. Powerful Orleans, having lost but one contest in the regular season, and conquering highly ranked Loogootee in a dazzling performance, fell to Milltown. "The Orleans offense lost most of its direction when Mike McClintic, a three-year-starter at guard, fouled out with 5:36 to play," reported the *Courier Journal*. "Orleans then lost its inside strength with 4:08 to go when Gilstrap got his fifth foul." Dave Smith did a job on Curt Gilstrap, his defensive play causing Curt to make only five out of fourteen attempts. Meanwhile Smith was pouring in twenty-four points to lead his team to an unexpected and easy 72-53 win. Tony Poe was also an important scorer for the Milltown squad. In the semifinal games the next evening, Springs Valley had an easy time with Leavenworth as well, winning 88-62, while Milltown spanked Marengo 64-44. The stage was now set for the championship battle.

The Paoli gymnasium strained to hold the 4,400 fans who came in from a cold, dark winter night to see the championship contest. Many of the Springs Valley fans arrived early, traveling in a long, snakelike motorcade that traversed the ten or so miles of curvy road that linked French Lick to Paoli. The excitement and energy as Valley fans organized to leave for Paoli reminded several Valley old-timers of the undefeated 1958 team when it traveled to the state finals. In fact, many fans carried small signs that said, "To The State in '58- Goin' For More In '74."

Those who had managed to get a ticket and walk inside the Paoli gym got a super blast of Hoosier Hysteria. The packed Milltown cheering section, constantly in chants, had a large sign hoisted by their fans—"Bye, bye Birdie!" Other Milltown fans were tossing a rubber chicken around, one that substituted for a Blackhawk, fans screaming in delight as it was thrown from one set of hands to another. The Springs Valley section was just as rowdy and noisy, a large Valley sign proclaiming "We're No. 1."

On paper, Milltown looked to be a prime contender, and Valley coach Gary Holland, knowing that his team could easily meet the awful fate experienced by Jim Jones and the Blackhawks the year before, was at the height of his anxiety. Holland had watched the Millers easily take down Orleans, a team that had split with Valley in the regular season. All things considered, the two squads looked evenly matched. The Millers had a fourteen-game win streak going and stood at 18-4. Valley had a nine-game streak and a 19-3 record. Anxious fans, along with general appreciators of Indiana high school basketball, could hardly wait for the Larry Bird/Dave Smith matchup. What many folks did not know, however, was the degree of scouting the Valley coaching team had been carrying out. Five different Springs Valley scouts had watched Milltown play several times in the regular season. Holland later told sports reporter Dave Koerner, "We just put our notes on a table and went with what we had seen." That insight involved noticing how other teams had been using a box-in-one to concentrate on Dave Smith but without much success. Holland, however, decided on going with a man-to-man defense. "We knew we had to keep Smith off the boards, and we knew Mark Walton was a good shooter against the zone. So, we felt a man-to-man was the thing." This

Dave Smith tries to block a Larry Bird shot.

turned out to be a perfect strategy.

The atmosphere at the game was awesome. "The tension was mounting at least 30 minutes before the tip-off as the Valley and Milltown yell sections started whooping it up," reported a *Springs Valley Herald* sportswriter. "You could feel the tension rising as the tip-off started when the Valley and Milltown fans seemed to rise as one unit and continued to stand throughout the game." At halftime, Valley held a slight lead, 28-23, and the fans "had a chance to sit down and rest a bit but were back up starting the third quarter." That period was "the best quarter of basketball in Valley history," the reporter claimed. *Courier Journal*'s Dave Koerner pointed out that "Once Valley strode to a comfortable lead, it was able to allow Bird to play the high post, direct the offense, and draw Smith from the basket." Larry Bird was now totally in his element—shooting, passing, rebounding, and in general, making his team into a perfect playing machine.

Almost fifty years later Dave Smith recalled the game. "I was a six-eight center, suddenly finding myself having to go outside to guard Larry Bird. Larry was already doing that head and body fake stuff where he kept faking this way and that, until he'd see a patch of daylight and go blasting around you for a quick jump shot or a move to the basket." Like so many other Larry Bird opponents, Smith got the full treatment. "The toughest fake he made, the most humiliating, was when he'd put the ball behind my head, like he was passing, and I'd turn to look. He'd go up for a perfect jump shot."

It was a hopeless situation for Milltown. Springs Valley easily won 63-46. Larry, however, was not the leading scorer. That honor went to John Carnes, who knocked down twenty-six points to Larry's sixteen. Milltown's Tony Poe had twenty-three points.

When the horn sounded ending the game, jubilant Valley players hoisted the twenty-seven-year-old Gary Holland on their shoulders and carried him out into the middle of the gym. One observer, Russ Brown at the *Courier Journal*, believed Holland's success had "exacted a nerve-wracking toll on the quiet, unassuming former University of Louisville guard," the most visible being the weight Holland had started losing after the Loogootee game. But now everything was the way Holland had hoped for. "This is the thing you always dream about," the Valley coach told Brown. Indeed, the reporter witnessed the dramatic release of all the pressure of the entire season and of the sectional on the Blackhawk coach. Brown wrote, "The usually reserved Holland surprised even himself with his display of emotion. 'I generally don't show any excitement. But when we won, the kids picked me up and paraded me around the floor, and I didn't just sit there—I had my fists clenched in the air. I never thought I'd do anything like that.'" Holland also revealed his escape from the tremendous pale of disappointments for the team and fans from the season before. "I'm still nervous, but it's a different kind of nervousness. At least if we foul up now, we've already gained something."

Holland had one last thought about his team, a thought that touched on the bitter loss to Loogootee earlier in the season. Thanks to the proliferation of transistor radios among the fans in the hot Paoli gym, many knew who the other three teams were going to be at the Washington regional—Bedford was lined up to play Loogootee in the second game, and Springs Valley would go up against Jasper in the first bout. This knowledge prompted Coach Holland to say to the Louisville reporter, "My players want to get back at Loogootee. They don't think they

Larry, to the left, watches with joy as his teammates come to get the sectional trophy.

played well in that first game." The next day Holland continued this theme, telling Jerry Birge at the *Jasper Herald* that he and the team wanted another shot at Loogootee. "We made too many mental errors the last time we played them." Of course, Larry Bird himself had promised Beezer Carnes and the team they "would get back at Loogootee in the regional" after Valley's late-January loss.

Every Valley fan leaving the Paoli gym that evening likely had the same thought—a deep run in the Indiana high school basketball state tournament now looked possible, a run that could bring the Blackhawks and Larry Bird the notice and respectability they deserved in their basketball-loving state. A few of these Valley fans lingered in the gym until a janitor turned off some of the main lights and began sweeping. And as these fans left the building to go back to Valley for a big celebration, more than one took pleasure in stepping on one of the "Bye, bye Birdie" signs lying crumpled at the edge of the gym floor.

Come On, Mr. Quarterback

It is hard to say which was the more exciting aspect of Indiana high school basketball in the 1970s—watching a close, thrilling game or speculating earlier about who might win. State tournament time witnessed plenty of the latter, these talks, sometimes volatile but always packed with animation and energy, taking place at all the local gathering places.

Prognosticators could easily tie themselves up in knots trying to figure who the winners would be.

The week before the Washington regional, one sportswriter dived in, pointing out Jasper had easily beaten Bedford, Springs Valley had beaten Jasper, and Loogootee had beaten Springs Valley and Bedford, the Lions besting the latter by eighteen points. It would seem then that Loogootee would be the favored team.

But another writer noted Loogootee had lost its last two games at the end of the regular season, one to Orleans, a team Springs Valley had bested one time out of two, and that the Lions had only squeaked by the Washington Hatchets in the sectional in the last seconds of the championship game, 35-34. Meanwhile, Jasper had easily handled the Hatchets in two regular season games.

Then there was the matter of another jinx situation.

On the cusp of regional play, Coach Jack Butcher explained to Jerry Birge, "It has proved to usually be a disadvantage when you've beaten a regional team during the regular season. Mitchell beat us in a holiday tournament in 1970 but we beat Mitchell in the regional. We beat Jasper during the regular season in 1972 and Jasper beat us in the regional. Last year we beat Bedford during the season, but they reversed it on us in the regional." Then Jack, perhaps trying to dispel any jinx, added, "Bedford has been up and down all year, and it appears they are playing real good ball right now. But we feel we are a little better." Looking ahead at playing either Valley or Jasper in the final round, Coach Butcher finally noted, "We will have to worry about defending a good big man inside, Larry Bird or Mike Luegers and some good outside shooting. Our main problem in the final game will be defense."

While basketball fans, sportswriters, and other Hoosier folks tried to read the tea leaves, Springs Valley High School spent the week before the regional in quasi-celebration mode, teachers and administrators realizing students would be too hyped up to do much studying. At some point before regional play, Gary Holland received a letter from Indiana University coach Bob Knight, a note he shared with his players, the school, and the community. The brief message said, "Dear Gary, Congratu-

Valley's three main players, in a photo taken by the Louisville Courier-Journal the week before Valley's upcoming regional tournament play.

lations to you and your players on your fine victory over Mill-town and your winning the Paoli sectional. Best of luck in the regional and throughout the state tournament." The short message was signed, "Sincerely, Bob Knight, Indiana University basketball coaches, and Players."

It was enough to make the Valley community feel they had died and gone to heaven, and there was surely more to come.

In the middle of the pre-regional week, a reporter and a photographer from the Louisville *Courier Journal* came to the school and did a full-page feature about the Blackhawk team. There were individual shots of Brad Bledsoe and Mike Conrad, and another, the largest, of the three seniors, Beezer and John Carnes and Larry Bird. The latter photo was taken in the school library.

It is an interesting pose. John Carnes stands in the forefront, at a table, staring deeply into the distance, an open newspaper in his hands. Beezer sits in a chair to John's left, holding a book but looking up at his cousin. Larry is at the back, standing by a tall library shelf full of books, an open book in his hand, looking shyly up toward the camera.

The three Blackhawk players surely hooted and hollered when they saw the photo in the newspaper the next day, the caption reading, "Basketball doesn't occupy all the time of John Carnes, Larry Bird, and James (Beezer) Carnes, who spend some leisure time in the Springs Valley High School library."

It would be difficult for an outsider to grasp the excitement, energy, and tension of an Indiana high school regional tournament in 1974. At this time the state tourney was still a one-class affair and included 411 schools. By the regional round at sixteen sites, only sixty-four schools were left standing, and those games were usually played in coliseum-like gymnasiums. Boasting fifteen of the top sixteen largest high school gyms in the country, these Indiana gyms are sometimes called "Hoosier shrines." The Washington, Indiana, gymnasium where Springs Valley would play in the regional round was built in 1967 and held over seven thousand fans.

The regional winners advanced to the level old-timers considered the final stage of state tournament play, the so-called Sweet Sixteen, these contests played at four different sites throughout the state. This was the level Coach Holland and his team now hoped to at least achieve by winning the Washington regional, a level that would bring them local basketball immortality, like the famous 1958 Springs Valley squad.

On the Saturday morning of regional play, Valley student manager Kevin Smith traveled on the team bus with the players and coaches to the Black Oak Motel, just east of Washington, where the Valley team would headquarter after their first game with longtime archrival Jasper.

Larry Bird in a thoughtful pose a week before Valley played Jasper in the first game of the Washington regional.

Smith recalled how "the opportunity to take part in the 1974 semi-state at Evansville's Roberts Stadium seemed inevitable. Roberts was a shrine of Indiana basketball lore, especially in southern Indiana."

On March 9, 1974, Springs Valley faced Jasper in the first game of the Washington regional. This clash would immediately be followed by Loogootee battling Bedford. That evening the two winners would play for the championship. Long before the Valley/Jasper contest began, however, every section of the spacious gym, including the rolled-out bleachers down on the floor, were crammed with people, most of them ready to stand for the entire game, a cauldron of chanting, shouting, cheering, sweating fans.

When the contest started, Jasper coach Ed Schultheis unveiled an interesting strategy to shut down Larry Bird; Wildcat guard Jeff Bawel always hounded Bird out on the floor when the Blackhawks had the ball. When Larry went underneath, six-eight Mike Luegers would join Bawel in trying to stop the Blackhawk star.

At first, the tactic seemed not to work, the game quickly tilting Valley's way.

Luegers remembered Larry playing in top form during the tight contest. "His jump shot had gotten even better than when they played us and beat us earlier in the season. He had a lightning-quick release." Mike Luegers watched as Larry "shot jumpers from the corners with his feet almost on the out-of-bounds line, which illustrates how far out he could shoot. If pressured out front, he would drive to the basket or flip a no-look pass to a teammate."

Jasper guard Jeff Bawel, the Wildcat quarterback in football and an all-around athlete, had his hands full guarding Larry Bird in Jasper's box-and-one defense. Nevertheless, he stuck to Larry like a shadow, following Bird wherever he went on the floor. The amazing thing that Bawel discovered, as Mike Luegers described, was that Bird could shoot from anywhere—from deep out on the front of the floor or clear back to the out-of-bounds lines on the sides, the almost certain outcome of his

Jasper Wildcat coaching came up with a strategy they hoped would limit Larry's scoring.

perfect-form jumpers being a loud swish of the nets. Jeff also endured the humiliation of Bird's famous step-back jump shot during the first half, Larry moving the basketball over the defender's head with both hands, then stepping back with the ball and releasing one of his long-range jump shots.

Larry talked trash too. Several times when Bird was far out on the court, he would say to Jeff Bawel, "Come on, Mr. Quarterback. See if you can guard me."

Jasper sportswriter Jerry Birge, stopping to sit down only when he hurriedly scribbled in his little notebook, also described the battle in the first half, the aftermath witnessing a solid 36-23 lead for Valley. "The Hawks from Orange County hit 10-18 in the first quarter and 8 of 19 in the second frame, mostly from long range. Bird knocked in 14 first half points, Carnes tallied a dozen and Bledsoe six from long range. Jasper, meanwhile, couldn't find the range."

During halftime, Valley fans buzzed with noise and excitement while the Jasper crowd was subdued. But down in the Wildcat locker room, Coach Schultheis encouraged his team to keep working. The Wildcat coach had been around Indiana high school basketball long enough to know a game was never over until the final horn sounded. He also realized the two players on Larry Bird tactic was beginning to pay off. The Jasper coach was correct, the turn of events causing the crowd in the stands to go from standing flat-footed to standing on their toes throughout the second half, and often keeping Jerry Birge in his seat, furiously scribbling.

Jasper's Terry Tucker "cracked in three field goals and Mike Keusch two field goals and a free throw" in the first four and a half minutes of the third stanza to Valley's single goal, that one by Bird. Jasper had pulled within four points, 38-34.

Then the Blackhawks resurged. When Larry nailed a bucket ten seconds into the fourth quarter, Valley was back up 50-40. Then Jasper came back again, Jeff Bawel's defensive work taking its toll. Bird, after scoring seven field goals in the first half, managed to hit only three in the second half. With 1:06 remaining, Mike Luegers hit two underneath to make it 58-56, pulling Jasper within a single basket. With thirty-three seconds left, Bird whipped a behind-the-back pass to Beezer Carnes, who made a clutch basket. Wildcat Terry Tucker put back a rebound that made it 60-58 with seventeen seconds on the clock. The gym was rocking.

After a Valley player missed the front end of a one-and-one, Jasper got the ball back. The Wildcats came roaring down the floor. Many fans had their hands on their heads, mouths wide open. But three quick shots under the Jasper basket all failed to go in before the horn sounded. The Blackhawks had held on, but just barely.

Larry Bird was the leading scorer of the game with twenty-five, but the box-and-one defense held Bird to seven or so points below his average. Mike Keusch had

Mike Luegers scores over Bird in a down-to-the-wire game.

nineteen for Jasper. As the two tired teams walked off the floor, the crowd relaxed. Immediately after the game, as the Springs Valley team walked back to their dressing room, several in the crowd could hear the word Loogootee being repeated among them. Getting back at Loogootee, as Larry Bird had told the team they would after the tough late-January loss to the Lions, continued to loom large in every Blackhawk player's mind.

One Valley team member, Brad Bledsoe, recalled how rough the game against Jasper had been and wondered if it would affect the Blackhawks in the championship contest. Bledsoe, for example, had taken "an elbow to my nose from big Mike Luegers. But somehow, we fought and clawed and pulled out the win by two points, but I was a little worried that the win had come at a cost."

Between the first and second first-round games, most fans sat back down while others made a quick trip to a restroom or concession stand. Then the second contest started. It was an unexpected drama.

Loogootee, a 23-2 team that fed off a methodical, ball-control rhythm, was unable to find its groove against the 12-11 Bedford Stonecutters. The Bedford team had some height in stocky six-five Mark Robins and six-six Jim Pentzer. Ken Hutchinson and Rick Brown also started. But the spark plug of the team was the coach's son, a short, skinny, scrappy kid named Kelly Masterson.

Ironically, Bedford played Loogootee-style basketball, getting a small lead, then slowing down the tempo. The Stonecutters led by 9-8 after the first quarter and 26-23 at halftime. Loogootee stayed within a basket until the last seconds and ended up losing 49-43 in an upset. Hot shooting guard Bill Butcher was only 1-10 from the field, and his sidekick, Alan Crane, shot 6-15.

It brought no pleasure to Coach Butcher that he had been correct about the regional jinx.

The stage was now set for 21-3 Springs Valley and the surprising 13-11 Bedford squad to battle it out in the evening game for the regional championship and a trip to the Sweet Sixteen.

Valley followers were cautiously optimistic, believing their

biggest obstacles, Jasper and Loogootee, had been safely routed. One Valley fan leaving the gym predicted the Blackhawk
team would likely be in prime contention for the coveted "People's Choice" label after they won the regional, an honor last be-
stowed on a Valley team that completed the undefeated 1958
season.

As much as he liked Larry Bird, Jerry Birge was not so sure
about Springs Valley's chances against Bedford, earlier label-
ing the Stonecutters "the top underdog among the 64 regional
contenders." Birge had warned the week before, "It's easy to see
how the Stonecutters finished under .500 during the regular
season. Their difficult schedule included the likes of powerful Columbus East, New Albany (twice), Madison, Columbus
North, Loogootee, Terre Haute South, and Jasper." Bookies and
other prognosticators, however, believed the Washington regional was a toss-up among every team "but Bedford," a club
that had lost more than half their games. One scout from Evans-
ville, charting Springs Valley "because I thought they would win it," told an Evansville writer, "To be honest about it, just look-ing at Bedford Saturday afternoon (against Loo-gootee), you had to think they were the worst team there."

Larry tries to stop a Wildcat.

As the second morning game moved toward its unforeseen ending, Valley players had a few hours back at the Black Oak Motel to get something to eat and to rest. Then came the stunning news about the Loogootee defeat. For the Valley players it was a surprisingly disturbing letdown, not having a chance to show the Lions and the Valley fans, and the rest of the state that the Blackhawks were the better team. All the talk and excitement about playing Loogootee on the bus ride now seemed for naught, leaving a strange void. Then, student manager Kevin Smith noticed an interesting attitude as the players' bus loaded up to make the short trip from the Black Oak Motel to the Hatchet House. "I overheard comments downplaying the opponent Springs Valley was about to take on for the regional title. Looking back on it, I wonder if the Hawks lost their focus due to underestimating Bedford, not totally, but just enough." On the other hand, most Valley fans were happy, thinking Bedford would be an easier foe.

While the Valley team digested the results of the second morning game, Coach Holland worried about another issue: Jasper's rough play had been brutal on the Valley players, es-

Jasper's Jeff Bawel, trying to guard Larry Bird in the Washington regional when Bird wasn't beneath the basket.

pecially their double-teaming of Larry Bird. Too, at the back of many basketball pundits' minds were the twin thoughts that Bedford was on a roll, an always formidable aspect at tournament time, and that the Stonecutters had nothing to lose. And it probably helped the Stonecutters' chances that the season would be the last for Bedford High School, as it would be consolidating into the North Lawrence school system in the coming year. And, of course, there was yet another basketball jinx hanging in the air.

As with any Indiana high school team with a long tradition of successful basketball, old ghosts also lingered. Harry Moore, at the *Paoli Republican*, for example, felt few Hawk fans had forgotten regional play in 1969, when the Blackhawks defeated a good New Albany team and Bedford edged Paoli in the morning games. Valley had thought they would be playing against Paoli, and some fans believed this thinking threw them off in the next contest. In the championship battle, Bedford defeated Valley by ten points. Before the 1974 final contest, Moore feared history would repeat itself, especially when Valley players were so keyed up to play Loogootee. But Moore's opinion was a minority one. One sports reporter, listening to the talk of Valley fans just before the final game started, noted, "Hawk fans felt sure Valley could defeat Bedford. The Cutters had defeated Loogootee earlier but played bad in doing so."

When the championship contest began, some of the Valley fans were surprised to see Bedford employ a slow pattern offense, as they had with Loogootee. It worked. Bedford led by four at the end of the first quarter, leaving Valley fans biting their nails. Larry had made just a single basket, but Brad Bledsoe and Beezer Carnes had made up for that deficit, keeping the Blackhawks in the game. Kelly Masterson and Jim Pentzer carried the load for the Stonecutters with six points each. At some point, John Carnes twisted an ankle, but continued to play.

Later, an observer from Evansville at the game, scouting for the Evansville Bosse team, noted Bedford's rugged play. "Bedford doesn't quit. They do things with confidence and are deliberate in their attack, a very physical ball club. They have a boy at forward who is well over 200 pounds and 6-7 at center." Most of Bedford's aggressive attention was focused on Larry Bird.

In the second quarter, Bird, still reasonably fresh, exploded for nine points, including a three-point play that brought Valley their first lead and brought Blackhawk fans to their feet. The Blackhawks kept at it, moving out to a 26-18 lead. They were up 27-22 at halftime.

When the third quarter brought Valley a six-point lead, thanks in large part to Beezer Carnes' scoring, Jerry Birge began hearing Blackhawk fans "making plans for the trip to Evansville" and the Sweet Sixteen. "The plan looked like a good idea when Valley opened up a 52-44 lead with only 5:36 remaining in the game." This lead had not come easily.

Working hard and making three field goals against a fierce Bedford defense, John Carnes' shooting kept Valley in the game during much of the fourth quarter. Brad Bledsoe added another field goal, and sophomore Chester Allen contributed two free throws. Beezer Carnes had a point on a one-and-one situation. All that did not matter. The 5:36 moment marked the high point of Springs Valley's 1973–1974 basketball season. Jerry Birge later reported that the closing minutes of the game "produced one of the most dramatic come-from-behind victories in regional history."

During the entire game, Valley student manager Kevin Smith was dutifully keeping a shot chart on the Blackhawk bench. Smith recorded that Larry Bird, perhaps worn down from battling with the two big Bedford players, took only three shots and missed all of them in the fourth quarter. Two attempts had been taken under the basket and one from way out. Luckily, John Carnes knocked in three of five field goals while Brad Bledsoe was one for two. Meanwhile, several Bedford players were suddenly fruitful in their scoring. Kelly Masterson popped in a shot from fifteen feet with 5:18 on the clock. Shortly after that, Jim Pentzer scored to cut Valley's lead to four. John Carnes brought the Blackhawks' lead back to a more comfortable six points before Bedford retaliated with another field goal. Beezer was fouled and made one out of two, making the score 55-50 with 2:38 on the clock, making Valley fans breathe easier.

At this critical point, Bob Masterson, the Stonecutters' coach, quickly called a time-out to get his team centered for the last two minutes of play, telling his charges "to hang in there and not lose their poise." The short pep talk must have worked. No Blackhawk would score for the rest of the contest after this point.

Bedford's Hutchinson hit a twenty-footer to cut the Valley's now tenuous lead to three with 1:30 left. Then Masterson banged in a seventeen-footer. Bedford trailed by one.

Beezer Carnes was fouled and stepped up to the line for a one-and-one, the clock stopped at 1:21. He could put his team up by three if he made both baskets. The noise was deafening as the attempt left his hands.

The ball came off the rim and was grabbed by a Bedford player. Then, with 1:01 left, Larry Bird fouled Jim Pentzer, who made both baskets, giving the Stonecutters the lead again, this time by a single point, 56-55.

No one was sitting in their seat now, not even Jerry Birge, who grasped his little notebook to his side while tiptoeing with the rest of the hollering fans to catch a view of the final hectic seconds of the game. The Blackhawks had the ball, and if they could score again, they would be up a point with just a few seconds left.

Valley fans were shouting their heads off.

Then came perhaps the pivotal moment of the contest. Larry had yet to score in the fourth quarter, but everyone assumed the ball would come to him. With thirty-five seconds remaining, however, Jim Pentzer intercepted a Blackhawk pass. Valley was forced to foul, and with seventeen seconds on the clock, little Kelly Masterson sank two free throws. The Stonecutters now led by three, but as it turned out, Jim Pentzer's two points on the Larry Bird foul was the clincher. "The Hawks had three more tries at the basket in the closing seconds before the ball rolled to the opposite end of the floor following a missed shot and time ran out. It was a classic win for Bedford, a heartbreaking loss for Valley."

Those were Birge's last comments in his notebook for that game.

Larry Bird had been held to fifteen points, half his game average, and the Bedford coach explained nonchalantly, "Jimmy (Pentzer) is a pretty decent defensive player when he wants to be." For Valley, Beezer Carnes had thirteen, John Carnes eleven, and Brad Bledsoe ten. Little Kelly Masterson did the damage for the Stonecutters, striking for twenty-two points. Jim Pentzer had fifteen.

Besides the score-box information, there was another, more

visual sign of the game's intensity. So rough were the Bedford players in holding back Bird that Larry's upper legs were covered in ugly black and blue bruises from being pinched, bruises that stayed for several days, turning a repulsive yellow as they faded away.

When the final horn had sounded, Bedford team members, coaches, cheerleaders, and fans swept onto the floor, a flood of shrieking humanity, all this while Valley players, their heads hanging low, trudged off the floor, led by Larry. When Bird came to a thick rope draped in front of the hallway leading to the dressing room, he was so angry, he took the rope in both hands and threw it back behind his head. Brad Bledsoe recalled, "We were just devastated in the locker room after the game. We had so wanted to play at Roberts Stadium for the semi-state. Instead, it was just like we were a balloon, and someone had just poked a hole in us."

Many Valley players cried, with the entire locker room in disbelief. "I don't believe we were overconfident going into the game against Bedford," noted Bledsoe. "We just couldn't finish. Of course, all the way back home on the bus, I thought, Is there anything I could have done differently during the game? Second-guessing myself. As for the seniors, Larry, John, and Beezer, I could see their heads hanging down in the locker room after the game and all the way home on the bus. I couldn't believe our season was over, and I'm sure they felt the same way."

After the bitter ending to the final game, a shell-shocked Coach Holland told an *Evansville Courier* reporter, "We were just tired and a little leg weary. We feel like the best team didn't win the tourney." Then he added, "Masterson killed us. We just couldn't guard him one on one." Holland told a Louisville sportswriter much the same, saying his team was "physically weak after beating Jasper" and adding that Bird had an "off night."

The Evansville paper called Bedford's victory "the biggest upset in Washington regional history." This point was underscored at the handing out of the regional championship trophy, Valley student manager Kevin Smith remembering the announcer slipping and announcing "Springs Valley" as the winner before quickly correcting himself. "That's how surprised everyone was that Valley lost."

Valley fans would spend much time over the years ruminating over what had happened in the final minutes of the 1974 regional. The most popular narrative soon after the game involved Valley's excitement about playing and beating Loogootee in the final game, an event that did not happen, taking some of the air out of the Valley players. That thinking was then coupled with the possibility that Valley players lacked respect for the skills of the Bedford squad, a team that had the poorest record going into the tourney. Later narratives about the championship game, especially in Larry Bird biographies, seemingly lay blame for the loss totally on Beezer's missed foul shots in the fourth quarter. One account has Beezer missing three front ends of one-and-one situations toward the end of the contest. Newspapers accounts and the scorebook, however, show Beezer having only two one-and-one attempts in the fourth quarter and making one of those baskets. On the other hand, Beezer made only three of eight foul-shooting attempts for the entire game.

But there were other key elements that impacted the outcome.

Over a decade later, Bedford's Jim Pentzer shared his recollections of the iconic game with a local sportswriter from the Bedford *Times-Mail*, Jeff Bartlett. Pentzer had his own personal reasons to best Larry Bird after reading an early season *Indianapolis Star* article naming Bird and two others in southern Indiana as the best big men in that region. Pentzer was left off the list. "I put that article in my locker to remind that they didn't think that much of me. I was hoping to prove myself, to prove I belong among those players." Going up against Larry Bird offered Pentzer the chance to do so, and the Bedford player took advantage of the opportunity.

The sportswriter likened Pentzer's defense on Larry that night to the "equivalent of the man who gunned down Liberty Valance, largely because Pentzer neutralized Bird, limiting the Valley Star to 15 points." Pentzer shared the secret of his successful defense with the reporter, remembering how he had watched Larry in Valley's morning game against Jasper use his awesome fake move to score. It was Larry's go-to move. "He would take the ball, with the defender right up on him, and extend his arms so the defender couldn't see the ball anymore." When the defender turned around to find the ball, "Larry would pull it back and dribble around him or shoot an open shot."

Pentzer committed himself not to fall for the trick. Never giving in to Larry putting the ball behind his head, Pentzer just played intense defense on Bird "and didn't worry about anything else." Interestingly, Pentzer failed to mention anything to the reporter about the nasty looking pinching bruises on Larry Bird's legs that Bird received during the intense game.

But there were other events that plagued the Blackhawks in the bitter loss to Bedford. Valley was not a very deep team. The starting five had to play most of the game since the contest was close. The two games in one day circumstance would have made this situation worse. Then there was Bird's sudden lack of scoring in the last period, a rare occurrence happening at the worst of times. Also, Larry's fouling of a Bedford player in the last minute of play when Valley was up by one, the Bedford player hitting both foul shots and putting Bedford up by one. Finally, there was the interception of a Valley pass that kept the Blackhawks from scoring and going up by one point near the very end of the game, the Blackhawk thrower of that missed pass forever forgotten in the passing of time.

One other event was missed during the excitement of regional play that year, although only one spectator in the crowd caught it and shared it at the time. As the Jasper/Valley game unfolded, and Larry made a basket, Steve Land's father, Frank Land, reached over and tapped his son on the knee, telling him, "Larry just broke your all-time career scoring record."

Not even Larry Bird could stop the Stonecutters' amazing comeback.

The Lost Year

Springs Valley fans experienced a tremendous letdown after the 1973–1974 high school basketball season ended, but only until two related occurrences brought another round of excitement back to the community. The events involved a powerful interest in Larry Bird's struggle to gain state recognition for his amazing senior year's achievements and the question of where he would go to college. To begin with, Bird's amazing performances and stats during his senior year should have guaranteed his selection to the first team All-State list and to the Indiana All-Star team. The second group competed against the Kentucky All-Star team in a two game series each year. But it did not look like Larry would be part of it.

This issue, and the college question, quickly become supremely important to folks in the valley and the immediate region, as Larry's ongoing battles now seemed to have become one with those who had followed and rooted for the blond shooter during his high school playing days. Watching Larry do all those amazing things was addictive, and no one wanted the excitement to stop.

The issue of Larry, the second-leading scorer in the state, not making the All-State list and thus the Indiana boys' basketball All-Star team was the first hot topic, and sportswriter Jerry Birge would have much to say about the issue. In late March 1974, Birge penned a pithy column in the *Jasper Herald* titled "IT'S FOR THE BIRDS." In part, Birge complained,

> *We read in disbelief today when the Associated Press announced its All-State team, six players on the first team and nine on the second and didn't include Valley's Bird! It was a first-class rook job by those who voted for the team, but it wasn't anything new. Southern Indiana was again completely overlooked. I'd like to see all of the 15 players named ahead of*

*Bird. They must have been super players for some reason or
another since none of them came close to the accomplishments of the blond bomber from Valley.*

The *Springs Valley Herald* promptly reprinted Birge's entire
column in one of their issues, but Larry, then and later, seemed
oblivious to who exactly had saved the day, noting in his autobiography, "A writer in Jasper had written some articles about me
and sent them all around the state. The word was getting out
about me." Indeed, Birge, and others, got busy making sure that
Larry would make the select All-Star group.

Having finally gotten his well-deserved spot on the All-Star
team, the experience was hit-and-miss for Bird. Although the
focus for the Hoosier All-Star games involved two contests with
the Kentucky All-Star team, other games were played, too. Larry
was hungry to show basketball fans in places outside his region
that he was as good a player as those who had gotten more press
from the bigger up-state Hoosier newspapers. Bird started out
strong, leading the All-Star team in scoring in a game against
the state's Amateur Athletic Union (AAU) championship team
that year. Bird also did well in a warm-up game against a Soviet
Union junior squad but got much less playing time than he received in the AAU tilt. After a solid first game against the Kentucky team, Bird played little in the second matchup, a game
played at Market Square Arena in Indianapolis. He was so angry about not playing more early on that he refused to go back
into the game when there was very little time left.

During the high school season, and after, recruiters from all
over the country trekked to Larry's hometown, and the intense,
ongoing fight among major college basketball programs to sign
Larry Bird was followed closely by people in Springs Valley, becoming a hot topic in every place in French Lick and West Baden
where people gathered. It may have surprised Bird that people
in the community not only carried strong opinions about where
they thought he should go to college, but also that each believed
their particular pick was the absolutely right one. It seemed to
be another sign of how much Larry's story had become theirs.

Super Black Hawk ... Bird

With the help of Jasper sportswriter, Jerry Birge, Larry is finally chosen to be an Indiana All-Star.

Eventually, Larry sought to dispel the tremendous pressure of being recruited by choosing only a handful of schools to consider. Even with that, the process was torture for the seventeen-year-old youth.

The set narratives concerning Larry Bird's recruitment saga say that Indiana University was always the surest bet to get Larry. However, in a revealing article in the Bedford *Times Mail* by sportswriter Phil Bloom, who interviewed Larry in 1977, it was reported Indiana State, the first school to go after Larry to any degree in his junior year, was at the very top of the list until Larry got word that the Indiana State coach who had recruited him was likely going to be pushed out. Of course, hindsight suggested Larry should have gone ahead with Indiana State from the get-go. Whatever the reasons, Indiana University suddenly became the focal point of Larry's recruitment in the spring of 1974, and the valley was full of IU fans, including the Bird family. In *Drive*, Larry noted, "It seemed everyone wanted me to go to I.U. and they really made the decision for me. In a way, I just went along with what they felt was good for me. My mom was happy, my dad was happy, and Coach Jones was happy."

Lee Levine, in his book about Larry, noted, as well, "For the [Springs Valley] townspeople, attention from Knight was the most exciting thing that had happened since the 1958 state finals team. Around town, the implicit as well as the explicit pressure upon Larry to go to IU was unavoidable." Coach Gary Holland truly believed all the people in the valley "wanted him to go to IU," including Larry's essential mentor and father figure, Coach Jim Jones, who was an IU grad. Mark Bird pointed out his family felt the same way, as they "were all IU fans." This included Larry's mother's brother, Amon Kerns, an important male figure in Larry's life.

Coach Gary Holland, Larry Bird, and Coach Bob Knight at Springs Valley High School where Larry signed his IU letter of intent.

The entire town might as well have been decked out in crimson and cream colors when it came to where most folks hoped Larry would go to college. Still, there was great drama in the real-time recruiting.

Bob Knight certainly knew who Bird was and how well he could play, having, as noted, attended three of Larry's high school games, including the iconic Springs Valley/Loogootee battle. In fact, between Knight, some of his assistant coaches, and several of the IU players, a Bloomington entourage had watched Larry play ten times that year, "and each time we were more impressed," Knight had asserted.

Perhaps suspecting Larry had reservations about playing for him, Knight sent three of his players—Steve Green, John Laskowski, and Kent Benson—to the valley sometime before April. They met with Larry at the high school, Coach Holland providing pizza as Larry and his prospective fellow basketball colleagues talked. Bird explained that he was able "to ask some questions that I might have been scared to ask the coach, and it also showed me that somebody up there really wanted me." It probably helped Coach Knight's recruiting efforts too when he told sports reporters across the state, shortly before Larry signed on at IU, that Bird "has as good a pair of hands as we saw on anybody all year. He has a lot of varied skills."

Any understanding of Larry's difficult year after his triumphal high school experience must be framed by an essential bit of backstory, one that begins at an exciting high point in his life. Two photos of Bird capture these moments, the first taken toward the end of his senior year. In the first photo, snapped just before the Blackhawks were to face the Jasper Wildcats in Washington regional play in 1974, Larry is standing before a wall in the high school hallway decorated with signs wishing him and his teammates luck in the upcoming game against the "Krauts," as the Jasper team was sometimes called in those days. Larry is staring into the distance to his left, reflecting perhaps on the just passed regular season successes, on winning a sectional tourney, and on the hope of advancing deep into state tournament play.

The second photo was taken a couple of months later. In late April 1974, Bob Knight traveled from Bloomington to Springs Valley High School, and Larry officially signed papers to attend IU. Outsiders could only believe Bird was on top of the world, although in a newspaper picture of Coach Holland, Larry Bird, and Coach Knight after the signing, Larry's face reveals no emotion. However, a local sportswriter certainly captured the excitement of the community and their longing for Larry to continue to represent the towns of French Lick and West Baden with his exciting basketball skills. After listing Bird's many amazing accomplishments in just his two years of varsity play for the Blackhawks, the reporter noted, "Larry's signing at I.U. will give Valley fans a better opportunity to watch him play as he progresses in his career."

Larry in better days, signing his letter of intent to go to Indiana University.

Only two people knew how miserable Larry was the day before the signing: Larry and his mother. Lee Levine reported that like a groom getting cold feet the day before the wedding, Larry cried and told his mother the night before the signing, "I really don't want to go to IU. But I guess I'll let too many people down if I don't."

Since the Bird family lacked a car, Larry's uncle Amon Kerns drove Bird the fifty miles to Bloomington late that summer, leaving him in a dorm room with a quick and uncomfortable goodbye. Larry, an unsophisticated seventeen-year-old who was exceptionally shy around strangers, now found himself sitting in a small, unadorned room in a world that was as strange to him as another planet.

Larry lasted less than a month, walking out of his IU dorm room with his few possessions without telling a soul and then either hitchhiking home, as one version tells it, or calling his uncle to come pick him up. It's possible both occurred, because Larry tells in *Drive* that he hitchhiked down Route 37 to Mitchell, then found a way home from there. The latter ride likely occurred after Bird called Amon Kerns from a telephone in Mitchell. Mark Shaw's book about Larry describes how Bird called his uncle Amon, telling him, "Come and get me. I want to go home." Other local versions of this story have either Kevin Mills or Beezer Carnes bringing Larry back to the valley.

So why did Larry drop out? Various accounts speak to how the school's size, the huge classes, and the lack of comradery with the other IU players quickly overwhelmed the teenager from the tiny community of French Lick. Then, as Larry scrimmaged against the players already there, great stars in their own right like Scott May, he began to doubt his own abilities. He later recalled how he felt "there was no way I'd ever make that team." Later, Larry got into his playing groove and felt more confident playing with the other IU team members, but he remained mindful of the high-powered competition, knowing he would be playing second fiddle for a long while if he played there.

It did not help Larry's mood either that Bob Knight failed to move into the role of a surrogate father figure, a type of figure which Larry needed and had received from others before going to IU. As Larry put it to one sportswriter shortly after he left IU, "Coach Knight was not around much—of course he couldn't be when we were in practice—but the few times I did see him he always looked as if he had much to do." The reporter added, "So no matter how much one hears about the controversial Knight, he apparently was not responsible for driving Bird off. Then again, maybe he didn't work nearly as hard at keeping him as he did on recruiting him."

In Knight's defense, he did not treat Larry any differently than his other new recruits and players.

The official IU explanation for Larry's leaving was that Larry thought the classes would be too difficult. Larry's uncle Amon may have been at the root of this notion. The *Indianapolis News*, as did many other papers in the state, explained, "Coach

The Lost Year **247**

Bob Knight said yesterday Bird will not return. Knight said an uncle of the youth quoted Bird as saying the university was too big and the class work more than he wanted to do." Larry denied the latter point in another newspaper interview, telling a reporter schoolwork had "nothing to do with it." Meanwhile, newspaper sports headlines across the state ran from "Bird Flies the Coop" to "Bird decides to Leave I.U.," but the short articles failed to explain in any depth the reasons for Bird's abrupt decision, leaving everyone to wonder what in the world had happened.

A close analysis of Bird's own memory of the situation, offered a decade and a half after the event in his book *Drive*, suggested that money issues were also a major factor. "I had no money—and I mean no money. I had virtually no clothes." Larry noted that his roommate, Jim Wisman, "had a full wardrobe, while all I had was five or six pair of jeans, a couple of slacks, a few shirts, some T-shirts, and my gym shoes." Once away from home, Bird also became more fully aware that his mother worked three jobs to try to pay the bills, all the while with the family not having a car.

Perhaps the best real-time explanation for Bird's departure from Indiana University can be found in a detailed account in an interview taken by sportswriter Bob Kelley in the *Evansville Sunday Courier and Press*, "Bird's reasons not academic." Given just a week and a half after Bird's leaving IU, the piece is an important artifact because it represents Larry's voice in real time, rather than several years after the fact.

The biggest surprise Kelley revealed after talking to Larry "was not that Bird would leave Indiana but rather that he would have enrolled there to begin with." Larry told the reporter that "I don't know why I did it. I really didn't want to go there." Larry also explained he favored going to Indiana State all along but found himself signing a letter of intent to go to IU the first day possible, and said, "I was sorta pressured into it." Larry went on to exonerate both Coach Gary Holland and his uncle Amon Kerns, the latter a major family adviser to Larry, from being a part of that pressure.

Ultimately, the article revealed that a money issue was the final blow. The turning point came when Larry and the other IU athletes were told they would have to pay a nominal fee for a physical education class. Larry told the sportswriter, "They didn't tell us until we were enrolled in the class. I was supposed to be on a full scholarship, and they were making us pay for the class."

Although Larry said it was the principle of the matter, neither Larry nor his family probably had the money to pay.

Larry returned home to be greeted by a firestorm of disappointment and, in some cases, even anger. The French Lick/West Baden communities were completely unaware of their hero's struggles at Indiana University. Larry, always one to hold his cards close to his vest, didn't let anyone know he was coming home and just showed up unannounced, this only adding to the confusion. In *Drive*, Larry told how his family "was upset, and the townspeople were shocked." Part of the blow to his family and the community sprang from the feeling Larry had given up too soon. "It was considered a great honor to play for Indiana University," Larry recalled, and at first the community, thinking Bird had just made a rash decision, tried to talk him "into going back." A shaken Amon Kerns even offered to take his nephew back to Bloomington, but Larry responded with a defiant "No!" to the offer. As time passed, and with no explanation forthcoming from Larry about what had happened, locals grew more disgruntled. The rest of the state's sports world was just as confused.

While Larry's family and the community believed Larry was misguided and wrong about leaving school, Larry, before he left IU, felt he had worked hard to face uncomfortable realities about his personal and financial limitations and, in the process, gained an understanding of what needed to be done next. In short, the seventeen-year-old Bird, perhaps for the first time, was beginning to make important adult decisions based on his understanding of who he was and what he wanted to do with his life. As he noted about leaving Indiana University in his autobiography, "That was the first extremely important decision I had ever made for myself and I was sticking to it. I knew that everyone would be angry with me when I made it and that there would be a lot of pressure on me when I got back, but I didn't care."

Larry had not given up on playing college basketball, but he likely realized while at IU that a large flagship school such as Indiana was not the kind of place he would be most successful. He knew too that he still needed to figure out what he must do to operate in a college setting. Clearly, this meant going to a smaller school, likely Indiana State. Larry also came to understand that he needed to make some money so he would not be taking funds from his mother, money that could be used for other important family financial burdens. Larry explained in *Drive*, "I just knew it was going to help me—mentally and financially— to sit out that year."

Larry may have looked at this time off from playing college basketball as his "red shirt" year. Other writers have called it Larry's "lost year" and his "year off." However, there would be a definite bump in the road.

Larry's family continued to be disappointed and disrupted by his dropping out of college. Bird got a taste of their sore mood shortly after he returned from Bloomington to French Lick.

He and a friend decided to go and see Larry's brother Mark play in the first game of his senior year at Oakland City College. When Larry arrived at the gym in Oakland City, his parents were already there. "Dad started talking to me," Larry remembered, "but Mom wouldn't say a word." Georgia was so mad at her son, she barely talked to him for a month.

Even the local sportswriter, Harry Moore, joined the controversy, taking a wise, middle-of-the-road position.

The big news this week in the sports world, at least for Orange County basketball fans, is Larry Bird's withdrawing from Indiana University. We have heard much comment, both pro and con. A lot of people expressed their disappointment. Some were pleased they would still get to watch him in action. At first, we too were disappointed—disappointed that we

Larry went to see his brother Mark play in his first senior year game at Oakland City College just after Larry had left IU.

wouldn't get to see Larry play Big Ten ball. But like most fans, we were thinking only of ourselves and not of Bird. It is Larry's decision—he has his own life to live.

It was at this point that Larry's uncle Amon Kerns stepped back into the picture with a plan for getting Larry into a college again, playing basketball, and bringing peace between the valley community and the IU dropout. This time Larry complied, noting in *Drive*, "Despite leaving IU, I still needed to play basketball. I came back home, and people were after me to go to Northwood Institute, which was right there in West Baden. The next thing you know, I was enrolled there."

The Northwood ball had started rolling when Amon Kerns called a friend, Northwood basketball coach Larry Bledsoe, to see if Larry might be able to play for the Blue Devils. Kerns brought Larry to the campus, where the Northwood coach explained there wasn't any money at that point for a scholarship. Kerns insisted Larry wanted to play for the team anyway and that Larry could stay with his family. But Coach Bledsoe later recalled that the talk did not seem quite right, that the young man seemed uncomfortable, and that his uncle did all the talking. Bledsoe, for his part, was likely taken aback. The year before, the Blue Devils had achieved an unimpressive 11-16 record while playing smaller four-year schools like Oakland City College, where Mark Bird played. Furthermore, in the 1974–1975 school year, Northwood Institute would be moving from four-year status to becoming a two-year junior college and playing even lesser competition. Coach Bledsoe just figured the school's basketball program would not offer Bird enough competition. But of course, the coach still quickly said yes to the request.

Larry likely agreed to go to Northwood because he would be accomplishing several things by joining the Blue Devils—acclimating himself to college studies in a more manageable environment after being overwhelmed at IU, keeping his hand in basketball, and pleasing his family and the community after returning from Indiana University. Concerning the community aspect, Lee Levine, one of Bird's biographers, pointed out that the pressure on Larry was all but unbearable. "The valley had been living vicariously through Larry ever since he'd started to be a basketball success. When Bobby Knight had recruited Larry, it was almost as if he had been recruiting the community itself."

The news in Indiana papers of Larry's coming to Northwood Institute hit with a bit

Larry Bird

Larry Bird Enrolls At Northwood

of a pop, with almost every newspaper sports page in the state noting and discussing the event. Lafayette's *Journal and Courier* playfully headlined "Indiana Bird Finds New Nest," while the *Munster Times* declared "Bird Finds Home." The *Kokomo Tribune* captured an important feature involving Bird's decision in their headline, one that suggested why Larry chose this small, little-known school—"Bird to Attend Hometown College." The *Indianapolis News* emphasized how small Northwood was, having just two hundred students, but also pointed out Larry would be close to home. There was even an out-of-state report on the event, the Louisville *Courier-Journal* headlining, "All-Star Bird Boosts Northwood's Hopes."

Al Brewster, a sportswriter at the more local Bedford *Times-Herald*, may have offered the most astute assessment of Larry's surprising decision, asserting that with Larry's enrollment at Northwood, there would be "singing in the Valley." Harry Moore, at the *Paoli Republican*, certainly seemed happy. "Now Bird has enrolled at Northwood Institute and we think this was a wise decision. And again we are pleased that we will be able to watch him play. The Blue Devils, we think, have a fine coach in Larry Bledsoe; he has produced some fine players at Northwood. We believe county fans will turn out in full force to see his Blue Devils play."

Ironically, although Larry had lived all his life in the West Baden/French Lick communities, he likely knew very little about the goings-on in the former West Baden resort hotel that now housed the Northwood Institute. Students staying on campus were housed in converted hotel rooms of the first three stories of the historic hotel structure, the history and the sight of which was just short of breathtaking. The circular six-story, 388-room building, completed in 1902, possessed an incredible dome that was 208 feet in diameter with a 130-foot-high ceiling, said at the time to be the largest unsupported dome in the world. Visitors soon discovered that sights and sounds were distorted in the spectacular open area because of its immense size. The original promotor/owner dubbed the magnificent structure "the eighth wonder of the world," believing his place could outdo the nearby resort hotel in French Lick.

For the next three decades after it opened, wealthy folks from all over the nation and Europe flocked to take advantage of the properties of the spring water available at both hotels while enjoying the pastoral hills that surrounded the hotels' location in the long, narrow valley. Many, too, came to partake in the conventions and entertainment, which included celebrities

The only known photo of Larry Bird in a Northwood Institute uniform.

and politicians of all sorts. Some guests sneaked off to the illegal gambling joints in the area as well. There was a circus wintering there, sports figures and movie stars staying at most times, and even a few professional baseball teams carrying out spring training on the grounds. But there was also a strange dichotomy in the valley, where the local people, mostly folks of more meager means than the guests who came to the resorts, went about their quiet daily lives.

These good times at the West Baden resort would not last, its fortunes taking a quick nosedive when the stock market crashed in 1929. In 1933 the hotel's owner, Ed Ballard, sold the building to the Jesuits, who established a seminary there called West Baden College. After a run of more than forty years, the Jesuits left in 1965 because of declining enrollment. Good fortune saved the grand building when a Michigan couple bought the aging structure and donated it to Northwood Institute of Michigan to operate a four-year satellite college campus there in 1967. The school offered degrees in advertising, automotive marketing, business management, fashion merchandising, hotel and restaurant management, and retailing and marketing, among other programs. Many students who attended Northwood found the atmosphere created by the unusual dome and the old hotel grounds exotic and mystifying, hinting at events and ghosts from other eras. The strong sense of place also drew the community of students into a close-knit group. And, of course, Northwood also had a collegiate basketball team.

It was likely that second-year head coach Larry Bledsoe was thrown off kilter with Larry's coming. Michael Rubino, in his 2015 article about this period in Larry's life, believed Coach Bledsoe "was more concerned with the players in his own program as the season approached," although the writer went on to say, "he wasn't about to turn away a player of Bird's caliber." Of the returning squad, Bledsoe had five-five playmaker "miniguard" Glen Tow from Greenwood High School up by Indianapolis and several new local recruits like six-four Dave Early, who came from a solid basketball tradition at powerhouse Seymour High School, plus Mike McClintic from Orleans and Kent Hutchinson from Bedford, both of whom had been on high school teams that had beat the Springs Valley squad Larry played on the year before. Interestingly, one of Larry's high school teammates, John Carnes, was also on the roster, but dropped out before practice began.

Larry's coming to Northwood quickly brought attention, the athletic department's Basketball Press Book hopefully noting that with the addition of Bird, the season might be an exceptional one.

The 1974–75 basketball season will provide a mysterious and exciting voyage for the Blue Devils. Entering the first season as a two-year college, the Blue Devils will be faced with an entirely new schedule and many new faces on the basketball team. The biggest strength will be the depth the Blue

Devils will possess. There will not be a first five, but rather a starting five with many players seeing action. Although lacking in over-all size, the Blue Devils will have 6-8 Larry Bird, 6-5 John White, 6-4 David Early on the front line. Speed and quickness will be another asset, but inexperience could hurt the team in the early going.

The Paoli paper carried a full page ad just before the team's first game, a sketch titled "Shootin' For The Stars," with a drawing of the magnificent dome at the top and underneath, the fifteen players' pictures each framed by a star.

Of all of Coach Bledsoe's new recruits, before Larry came into the picture, Dave Early ended up being the nicest surprise, one of those basketball players who was a late bloomer, making a coach feel as if he had accomplished something after working with him. But this aspect would unfold after Larry Bird left the team. Meanwhile, the Seymour recruit recalled the complete surprise he and his other teammates experienced when Coach Bledsoe announced that the former Indiana high school All-Star player and once IU recruit would be showing up in practice. "I know I was excited, and when we started scrimmaging, Larry lived up to his reputation. He was great, playing at a whole other level."

Just after Larry joined the team, he and the other players had their pictures taken for the basketball sports program booklet, wearing their Blue Devil warm-ups, the distinctive pitchfork design on the jacket's left side catching one's eye. Larry looks lost and disconnected in his portrait, staring not at the camera but gazing up to one side instead, hoping, perhaps, to grasp some insight into what seemed an unfathomable future.

Although the Blue Devils played their home games at the local Springs Valley High School gym, they usually practiced in the old West Baden High School gymnasium called Sprudel Hall. Dave Early was surprised by how ancient the gym seemed, filled with the atmosphere of faded glory and a strong sense of resident ghosts. There were a few rows of bleachers on both sides at the floor and at the upper levels, a stage at one end and a brick wall at the other. "It was a very old, drafty place, with hardly any space between the out-of-bounds and the stage, wall, and bleachers." Still, Early and the other players were excited with Larry being in their midst.

Glen Tow was tasked by Coach Bledsoe to help Bird get his books for his classes and to assist with any other problems that might come up connected with Larry's schoolwork. They must have been an odd-looking pair, the five-five Tow and the six-eight Bird, walking together inside the Northwood atrium. An event, however, seemed to foreshadow what would soon follow. When Tow explained to Larry that he was ready to go to the bookstore to help him get his books for his classes, Larry just responded, "I won't be needing any books." Much later, assistant basketball coach Jack Johnson assessed that Larry was unsettled the entire time there, having "trouble attending class" and being "very undisciplined." In short, Larry was never totally there in body or in spirit.

Larry did come to every practice, and while his family lacked a vehicle, Bird found ways of getting there, showing up one memorable time in a squad car, having talked a local policeman into giving him a ride from French Lick to Sprudel Hall. After practice, all the players but Larry were eager to get back to the Northwood campus, as the culinary arts people often prepared the meals. "We had great food," Dave Early explained, "but Larry never went with us. Instead, we'd leave the lights on in the gym, and he would stay in there by himself, drop-kicking the ball or throwing it off the backboard or walls to grab and shoot basket after basket." A few times, while driving around late at night, Northwood team players saw the lights were still on in Sprudel Hall and realized Larry was still at it. Of course, this was always Larry's go-to response to pressure—shooting a basketball again and again, finding a rhythm, hearing the swooshing of the nets, shutting out an uncontrollable world.

When ticket sales for Northwood home games were announced in late September in local newspapers, Larry Bird's presence on the team was often emphasized, creating anticipation once more among folks in the valley that they would again see Bird doing amazing things on the basketball court while leading the Blue Devils to a great season. True, it wouldn't be at an IU level, but it would still be Larry.

By November 16, the Northwood team had played two tough scrimmage games, one against Bellarmine College from Louisville and another against Indiana Central College in Indianapolis. Both schools were four-year college division schools and had strong teams. The results indicated that Larry's heart may not have been in those games, but other Blue Devil players' hearts certainly were. One sportswriter observed that Dave Early was especially impressive for the Northwood Blue Devils. In comments to the reporter about the contest, Coach Bledsoe noted that he too was "particularly pleased with the play of David Early," who hit eleven of fifteen from the field in the contest with Bellarmine. Meanwhile, Larry Bird had a cold shooting night in that game, making only seven of twenty-two field goal attempts. Bird did better in the next game against Indiana Central, scoring twenty-two points, but the Blue Devils were beaten by the tough Indiana Central squad, and Coach Bledsoe chose to highlight Mike McClintic's solid play in the game when talking to a reporter.

It was at this point, in mid-November 1974, on the very cusp of the Blue Devils' first regular season game, that Larry Bird disappeared from the Northwood campus. As assistant coach Jack Johnson put it, "He just dropped out of sight." Some thought at the time that Larry became concerned about losing a year's eligibility if he played in even a single regular season game for Northwood. It's also possible that Larry was told this on one of the occasions when the Northwood team practiced before the four-year college scouts who typically watched him from the stands. Mike McClintic recognized one of the spectators as an assistant coach at the University of Louisville. "I knew who he was because the same guy had helped Coach Denny Crum recruit my high school teammate Curt Gilstrap."

McClintic, one of Larry's old Orleans High School rivals, may have also been the first to know in mid-November that Bird was leaving the Northwood program. "We were practicing in the

Springs Valley High School gym for a change, getting ready for our first regular season game, and suddenly Larry comes over to me and puts his hand on my back. 'I'm out of here,' he said, and he walked out of the gym."

While attending Northwood and thereafter, Larry lived with his grandmother Kerns, perhaps leaving Larry's mother out of the loop regarding information about her son. Not long after Bird's abrupt disappearance from the Northwood practice, Bird's mother called Bledsoe, asking him if he had seen Larry. Bledsoe told her he had not but asked her to tell her son to contact him. But the Northwood coach and Larry never spoke again.

The Paoli newspaper was quick to make a point on Larry's second college drop out. "We understand Larry Bird has withdrawn from Northwood Institute. Seems a shame that a player of Bird's capacity wouldn't want to continue his education and ball playing. The decision was Larry's and for his sake we hope it was the right one." Just above this short piece was a narrative about Larry's brother Mark, "an ex-Valley star who scored 12 points for Oakland City College as the Oaks defeated Southern Baptist Seminary." The juxtaposition of the two narratives likely suggested the writer's true feelings.

Oddly, Larry's leaving the Northwood team drew only a speck of notice statewide with just the Franklin *Daily Journal* reporting, "Received word that Northwood won a holiday tourney last weekend, but we didn't see Indiana All-Star Larry Bird's name in the scoring summary. Maybe he's ineligible after transferring from IU or something."

Other than these two notices, Larry simply fell off the sports reporters' basketball map, leaving the intriguing question of what might have been had he stayed on with Northwood. Meanwhile, Larry's family and the community were stunned by his walking away again from playing college basketball without explanation. Biographer Lee Levine argued that when Larry quit Northwood, "he further fueled the disappointment of people in the valley and put still more pressure on himself."

Larry's own take on the event, however, suggests other-

MITCHELL
BLUEJACKETS

Larry Bird's future AAU coach, number 8, Bill "Monk" Clemons.

wise. This time Larry really did not seem to care, putting into play what his heart had been telling him to do all along—get a job and stay away from the stress of deciding about college for a while. If there was a peaceful healing time during Larry's year of being "lost," the period between late November and early February was that brief stretch. Larry happily recalled, "I went to work at my uncle's gas station on and off for a month and then I got a job in French Lick in what they called the Street Department." The crew included Beezer Carnes, one of Bird's high school friends and fellow Blackhawk player. Larry picked up trash once a week, mowed grass, painted park benches, and fixed roads. "I was working outside and loved every minute of it." Finally making his own money for the first time, Larry eventually saved up enough to buy his first car, a 1964 Chevy. "It was a piece of junk but that was all right."

Sadly, this healing time would be of short duration, and whatever strength Larry gained from it, he would need all of it and then some for what was about to happen.

On a Monday afternoon in early February 1975, Larry Bird's father took his own life. All other problems Larry faced—college, money, what he was going to do with his life—must have suddenly disappeared as he tried to come to grips with his father's passing and the way in which it had happened. Joey Bird had seemed unable to hold down a steady job for some time because of a severe drinking problem and had fallen far behind on child support payments to Larry's mother.

His father's death, though Joey had hinted at such actions, must have left Larry shocked, sad, and bewildered. Joey had been a presence in his children's lives even as he struggled to provide for them. Larry later reported he remembered little about what he did to get through the next several months after his father's death. As one might have suspected, however, basketball once more came to his rescue, but in an unexpected way.

Roughly two weeks after Joey Bird's death, the Bedford paper announced that the eight-team AAU basketball state tournament would be played in Mitchell, Indiana, twenty or so miles from Larry Bird's home in French Lick, the games to be played in the old Emerson gym. The main organizers of the 1975 state tourney, Monk Clemons and Dan Moore, coached the local Mitchell AAU team, Hancock Construction. The teams came from eight regional sites, including Terre Haute, Indianapolis, and Fort Wayne, but the Mitchell team had hosted the tourney for the last few years, having the financial support of the local Kiwanis Club and of the town's mayor, Jerry Hancock, who also owned Hancock Construction. As fate would have it, one of the members of the Hancock team was the football coach at Springs Valley High School, Chuck Akers. The Valley coach and AAU basketball were about to play a pivotal role in Larry Bird's life.

Once the state tournament drew near, AAU rosters were quickly swelled by any exceptional players a coach could talk into joining. Coach Clemons got busy and brought in Bill Perkins, who, the local paper explained, was "a 7-footer, 240-pounder, who played for Southern Illinois University and is now living in New Albany." Bill James, another Hoosier and an "All-American candidate at Marshall University," was another great addition. More under the radar was a quick guard who had played at Bellarmine College, Terry Morrison.

There were other new additions, but the most unexpected catch was brought in by Chuck Akers. It's possible the valley football coach was aware of Larry's situation, and reached out to Larry about joining the Hancock squad. At this point, Larry lacked a car for transportation, but Akers was able to drive him from French Lick to Mitchell for the two-day tournament that took place on a February weekend. Coach Moore recalled his first encounter with Bird, saying, "Larry was in turmoil at the time. He was really quiet. A nice boy and everything, but just one that was shy, a little backward."

The weekend before the games began, Larry was back in the sporting news again, the local Bedford paper carrying his senior class picture and a brief write-up about his joining the Hancock crew. Johnny Budd, a young boy at that time from Mitchell, recalled a very personal experience he had with Larry during tournament play, one that spoke to Bird's difficult situation.

Monk Clemons oversaw the tournament, and my dad was helping in some capacity. The final day of the tournament was scheduled like the old pre-class high school tourney with two games in the morning session and the championship contest at night. After the morning session, my dad and I swept the floor, picked up trash and restocked the concession stand. The gym was empty except for the two of us and Larry Bird. My dad informed me we were not going home between sessions as we had to have things ready for the championship game, so he was going to get us something to eat from a local fast-food restaurant. I asked Larry why he was still here, and he said he didn't have a car, so my dad let me stay in the gym with Larry while he went to get all three of us something to eat. I shot baskets while Larry lay on the scorers' bench resting. I remember my dad bringing back burgers and fries and sitting on the bench with Larry, having a conversation while we ate.

The Hancock team won the tournament, cutting down the

STATE AAU CHAMPS — Hancock Construction Company cagers recently won the state AAU tourney title at Mitchell. The players and coaches included: front row, l. to r., Bill 'Monk' Clemons, coach; Rick Ramey, Bill James, Charlie Akers; Dan Moore, assistant coach; back row, Jerry Hancock, Mitchell mayor, sponsor; Terry Morrison, who won the sportsmanship trophy; Larry Bird, Bill Perkins, David Terry and Jim New. Players not shown—Stan Neal, Rick Flynn, Mark Mathews and Gary McCooe.—(Photo courtesy Mitchell Tribune.)

competition like a sharp scythe advancing through tall grass. The local French Lick paper's take on the tournament results could only be described as joyful, a glimpse of their hero from his glory days, before the IU and Northwood setbacks. "Larry Bird, 6-7 forward for the Hancock team, helped his team tremendously by playing some of the best basketball anyone in Indiana would ever want to witness, which everyone was sure he was capable of doing in the first place." Larry, the report also asserted, "is one of the smoothest and most capable players in Indiana today." In the three games that gained the championship, Larry racked up thirty points in the first contest and thirty and sixteen in the last two. Terry Morrison, a New Albany native, however, took top scoring honors for Hancock Construction by posting games of thirty-two, thirty-five, and thirty-four points, and also gaining the tournament's Sportsmanship Award.

Larry had two more rounds of glory with the Hancock team, his amazing play bringing him back to the attention of coaches and to the large fan base he had built up during his high school days. The first occurrence involved the state champion Hancock team moving on to the AAU national level in regional play in Iowa in late February. Larry's team, one of eight, lost in the first round to a Detroit, Michigan, squad 113-95, but Bird still managed to knock down thirty-four points. An MVP trophy came to Larry after he played in a local Indiana independent team tournament for the Hulman All-Stars out of Terra Haute later in 1975.

Larry now began to branch out in his basketball endeavors, playing in mid-March for an independent team from his hometown in the prestigious Evansville Tri-State tournament played in the city's old armory building next to the Evansville College campus. Larry's team lost to Nashville Speedway on a last-second shot 96-94, but Bird was the top scorer for that night's contests, hitting thirty-four points. Dave Schellhase, an Evansville native and former consensus All-American basketball player at Purdue, was in the stands that evening, hoping to talk to Larry about coming to Moorhead State University in Minnesota, where Schellhase was coaching at that time. "I told the guy sitting next to me about my interest in recruiting Bird and he said, 'You're too late buddy. I hear he's going to Indiana State.'"

In truth, it's difficult to know exactly when Larry got back on Indiana State's radar. Larry himself mentioned Indiana State coaches coming to one of his games in late June, when the 1975 Indiana All-Star team played a game against the Hancock Construction team at the old Mitchell gym. One Hoosier newspaper noted about the upcoming contest, "This year's Indiana All-Star squad is the best shooting unit in the history of the series."

Larry was in high form in the heated contest, leading his team with thirty-nine points and twenty rebounds in a shocking 122-121 win over the hot-shot Indiana high school players led by the great Sam Drummer. Sam had twenty-eight points and made, according to a newspaper account, the most spectacular play of the game, a thunderous dunk shot "over the top of Bird." Drummer then finished off the effort with a foul shot for a three-point play.

The next day Bedford's *Times-Mail* headlined "Bird flying for the Hancock team," and noted that Larry was "one of the best as he proved last night." Most every other Indiana sports page carried the news of the All-Stars' defeat and of Larry Bird's part in the game. More importantly, in just seven months' time, Larry Bird had gone from fading from the sports pages to being highly sought after again by college coaches.

By July 1975, Indiana State had almost won the prize. The *Evansville Sunday Courier and Press* reported that Bird would likely soon be joining the Sycamore team. "If he does go there," the article noted, "and if it turns out to be the right place for him to be happy, he should make the school a tremendous ballplayer." An interviewee also pointed out how important Larry's AAU play and independent basketball had been for keeping Bird's skills sharp.

ISU head coach Bob King explained to one sports reporter that the hardest part of landing Larry was not convincing Bird "to play ball at Indiana State, but to come to college at all." The key to changing Bird's mind? Assistant Coach Bill Hodges. Hodges' persistence proved greater by far than any of the other coaches in pursuit of Larry. Hodges suggested Larry visit the Terre Haute campus with a friend, Tony Clark, who was already attending ISU. Clark had been on Valley's "lost season" team with Larry in the 1972–1973 high school year. That key visit took place in the spring of 1975.

Like most young adults, Larry Bird had been in bondage to the demands of family, coaches, and community. But through a series of hardships, starting with his lonely trip with his uncle Amon Kerns to IU, followed by his false start at Northwood Institute and the unexpected death of his father, Larry slowly and painfully found himself. Perhaps the redemptive moment, the ultimate magic, is how Larry Bird came to be in his beat-up Chevy with Tony Clark just seven months after escaping IU by hitchhiking part of the way back home down Highway 37. The two young men drove west one spring morning down US Route 50 with the sun to their backs, Larry's future finally in his own hands, on his way to a greatness beyond imagining.

E P I L O G U E

In 2004, in the early morning hours when there just wasn't enough caffeine to see straight, State Police Officer Wayne Flick clocked a late-model Cadillac speeding along US 31 north of Indianapolis. It had been thirty years since Wayne had played basketball for the Loogootee High School Lions. A power forward, Wayne had gone toe-to-toe with Larry Bird in a game for the Blue Chip Conference championship. In that fierce contest, Flick was the unsung hero, keeping Larry from scoring at his usual pace under the basket and helping to change the course of the game in Loogootee's favor. Flick could feel the results of those years every time he pulled himself out of his squad car. But it was more than just physical. Wayne was almost fifty now, a time in life's journey when many folks begin to wonder what they have really accomplished, what things of value beyond wealth or acclaim they have been a part of. Flick sighed and grunted and peeled out onto the highway, his red and blue lights flashing.

The Cadillac pulled over. Wayne stepped out of his car, cocking his state police hat, and walked over to the driver's-side door. The driver was wearing doctor scrubs coming off a late shift in the ER. Flick took the man's registration and driver's license and grumbled to the driver he would be right back. What he read, as he began filling out a ticket form, shocked him.

"While going over his paperwork, I realized it was Steve Land! We had not seen each other in over thirty years, not since the night I knocked him down to stop him from making that layup and we beat Springs Valley in an extremely close game."

Unbidden memories came flooding back as Flick, awake now, walked to the Cadillac to give the driver his registration and license. He handed Land a warning ticket and told him,

"I didn't have the heart to write you a ticket. Now we are even."

When Steve discovered it was Wayne Flick, he got out of the car and the two men, once adversaries, embraced. They stood next to Flick's squad car, talking and laughing as the memories poured out, as if a dam had been broken—the packed crowds at the Valley/Loogootee games; Coach Jack Butcher giving a ref an earful; the really pretty Springs Valley cheerleader; a gym crowd rising to its feet, every eye wide, when Bird gets his hands to the ball. As the two men conversed, traffic slowed down like water flowing around a rock. Drivers might've wondered what a state trooper and the guy he had pulled over were talking about so intently. Steve and Wayne were far away, conjuring ghosts all their own, from another world, remembering a time and place and a game—a world touched as if by magic. A place future generations perhaps could not understand, but the players from that golden age of basketball could not forget.

SOURCES

Because this is not an authorized biography, quotes attributed to Larry Bird and other people involved in Larry's early journey toward greatness mentioned in this work, other than the interviews, came from secondary sources. These sources comprise books, magazine and journal articles, and newspaper accounts.

Books

Numerous publications, including several books, examine Larry Bird's early life, as well as his high school years. They include *Basketball's Magnificent Bird* by Frederick Lynn Corn (New York: Random House, 1982), *From Valley Hick to Boston Celtic* by L. Virginia Smith (self-published, 1982), *Bird: The Making of an American Sports Legend* by Lee Daniel Levine (New York: McGraw-Hill, 1988), *Drive*, by Larry Bird with Bob Ryan (New York: Doubleday, 1989), *Larry Legend* by Mark Shaw (Chicago: Masters Press, 1998), *Bird Watching: On Playing and Coaching the Game I Love* by Larry Bird with Jackie MacMullan (New York: Warner Books, 1999), and *When the Game Was Ours* by Larry Bird and Earvin Johnson with Jackie MacMullan (New York: Houghton Mifflin Harcourt, 2009).

Books used for this work that presented important historic information about Indiana and regional basketball history include *The Valley Boys: The Story of the 1958 Blackhawks* by W. Timothy Wright (Lulu Publishing Services, 2018), *Hoosiers: The Fabulous Basketball Life of Indiana*, by Phillip Hoose (New York: Random House, 1986), and *Hoosier Hysteria*, by Herb Schwomeyer (Greenfield, IN: Mitchel Fleming Printing, 1970).

Magazines & Journal Articles

Important information about Larry Bird and his early world came from several articles in various magazines and journals. They include four years of *Hoopla* magazine issues (1970–

1974), a regional southern Indiana production put together by several sports enthusiasts in Jasper, Indiana; three articles in the *Spectator* magazine, a publication out of Terre Haute, Indiana— "He's Still "33," "Larry Bird: Growing up in Orange County," September 29, 1979, and "Larry," March 3, 1979, all three written by Mike McCormick; "James Naismith Didn't Sleep Here; A Re-examination of Indiana's Basketball Origins" by Chandler Lighty in *Indiana Magazine of History*, Winter, 2014; "Larry Bird's Greatest Shot Was the One He Didn't Take" by Michael Rubino in the *Indianapolis Monthly* magazine, December 24, 2015; "A Terror to the People: The Evolution of an Outlaw Gang in the Lower Midwest" by Randy Mills in the *Midwest Social Sciences Journal*, Volume 23, 2020; "The Peoples' Choice: A Classic Indiana Basketball Story" by Roxanne Mills in *Traces of Indiana and Midwestern History*, Spring, 2021; several *Sports Illustrated* articles in issues dated November 28, 1977, February 9, 1978, November 9, 1981, March 3, 1986, and March 28, 1988. Important newly discovered information about Larry's short time at Northwood Institute came from a *Northwood of Indiana 1974-1975 Basketball Press Book* book provided by Dave Early.

Sourcebooks & Shot Charts

With the help of Gary Holland, Kevin Smith, and Todd Marshall, I was able to examine Springs Valley scorebooks from both Larry's junior and senior years, as well as shot charts from several games. These sources were helpful in fine-tuning the narrative of several important basketball games discussed in this book.

Newspapers

As noted, previously unexamined Indiana newspaper accounts offered essential information for reframing the story of Larry Bird's high school basketball days. Indiana newspapers used in this work include the *Jasper Herald, Springs Valley Herald, Paoli Republican,* Bedford *Times-Mail, Evansville*

Courier, Evansville Press, Evansville Sunday Courier and Press, Indianapolis Star, Indianapolis News, Indianapolis Journal, Ferdinand News, Vincennes Sun-Commercial, Seymour Daily Tribune, Mitchell Tribune, Terre Haute Star, Noblesville Daily Ledger, Muncie Evening Press, Franklin Daily Journal, Jackson County Banner, Lafayette Courier and Journal, Kokomo Tribune, Munster Times, Washington *Times-Herald,* Linton *Daily Citizen, Loogootee Tribune* and Louisville, Kentucky's *Courier-Journal.*

It is important, too, to recognize some of the key newspaper sportswriters who helped capture the essence of Larry's high school basketball accomplishments and a deep sense of that time and place. Sports reporters mentioned in this book include Jerry Birge, Harry Moore, Arnold Bledsoe, Jim Plump, Al Brewster, Bob Williams, Tom Tuley, Pat Biggs, John Updike, Chip Draper, Jim Ballard, Bill Wright, Bob Kelley, Charles McPherson, Phil Bloom, Russ Brown, Dave Koerner, Ron Critchlow, Denny Spinner, and Jeff Bartlett.

Photo Sources

The photo of the young Bird family was taken from Virginia Smith's *From Valley Hick to Boston Celtic.* (See book sources). The lion's share of the photos and the snapshots of sports headlines used in this book came from the listed newspaper sources. High School yearbooks from Spring Valley, Paoli, and Orleans also provided important pictures for this book, as did the *Northwood Basketball Press Book.* Robin Coulter at the Melton Library connected me to the French Lick West Baden Museum and the Wayne Stalcup Photo Collection. This site had an abundance of photos taken at Springs Valley High School that did not make it into the yearbooks. Several appear in this book.

Interviews

Using interviews of those who were a part of Larry Bird's world and his basketball journey— Larry's fellow players, coaches, opponents, and fans—helped enhance the important communal aspect offered in this book, an element essential in understanding the factors that propelled Bird to greatness. Interviews for this work came from Kevin Smith, Jeryl Luegers, Mike Luegers, Mike McClintic, Tim Eubank, Dave Smith, Steve Land, Wayne Flick, Terry Tucker, Tom Berger, Tom Roach, Logan Carnes, Gary Holland, Jim Jones, Brad Bledsoe, Johnny Budd, Jeremy Collins, Larry Hembree, David Small, Dave Schellhase, Ron Prosser, Larry Bledsoe, Jerry Birge, Jim Plump, David Early, and Todd Marshall.

A C K N O W L E D G E M E N T S

In this book, I stress how Indiana high school basketball was fundamentally a communal effort, no matter how great one particular player might have been on a team, even Larry. So too, was the writing of this book. I now wish to acknowledge the many people who helped me in putting this story together, the list roughly following chronological order. First and foremost, my wife and early copy editor, Roxanne Hill Mills. Her suggestions always turned out to be right, and this book is much a better story because of her thoughtful ideas.

Then there were the many folks who, early on, helped make this book come to life. Joe Betz, who said to write it. Kevin Smith provided me with scorebooks and shot charts from Larry's junior and senior years, information that proved essential to this work and served as a springboard to my writing. Kevin was also an excellent go-to guy to talk with whenever my writing efforts bogged down. Jeryl Luegers helped put together and hosted an early meeting I had with several of Larry's high school opponents. Jeryl also served as an excellent sounding board regarding where I needed to go with the book. Mike McClintic was also an important part of helping find players to interview in the early part of this work.

Thanks to Jim Jones and Gary Holland for graciously hosting me at their homes and sharing stories, photos, score books, and other important artifacts pertaining to Larry's early sports endeavors.

Early on, several Oakland City University folks were instrumental in supporting the work on this book. Todd Mosby, vice president for development, marketing, and communications at the university, helped secure a writer-in-residence position and an office at Oakland City University for my work and offered much encouragement. Also, Professor Steve Custer and Professor Kevin Smith were always available to discuss writing issues in their offices.

Many thanks to the people, more than I can remember, who helped me track down old photos and assisted me by giving context to the pictures. God bless, too, librarians such as Denise Pinnick, retired director of the Oakland City University Library, for her help (and patience) in finding early books about Larry Bird in the library's collection, and for guiding me in my archive searches for information about Mark Bird, who attended Oakland City College. Also, Joan Knies at the Dubois County Library, Ferdinand, Indiana, branch, for making space for me to do research and writing, showing me the library's important collection of *Hoopla* magazines, providing the use of the microfilm machine, and helping me give my first public presentation about Larry Bird's high school basketball days. Then there were Robin Coulter and Trista Rue at the Melton Library in French Lick, Indiana. They gave super help in guiding me through their newspapers, high school yearbooks, and other materials pertaining to Larry's childhood and school days at Springs Valley High School, essential resources for the book. Jill Watson and Jordan Schuetter at the Dubois County Library, Jasper, Indiana, branch helped me give an early and well-attended presentation, with lots of engagement from the audience, on Larry Bird's high school basketball days. Also, Christi Morgan at the Orleans, Indiana, Public Library for helping me find important material used in the book about one of Springs Valley's toughest rivals, the Orleans High School Bulldogs. Vicki Gross, a reporter at the *Orleans Progress Examiner,* also provided access to valuable newspaper issues about Orleans' "glory days."

A special thanks also to Steve Land, "the forgotten Blackhawk," for giving me several interviews, helping me find and contact some of Larry's basketball companions, and allowing me to contact him numerous times to fact-check the timing of key events in the book. Steve's help was invaluable, as has been his friendship.

There are many others I must thank. Todd Marshall gave Roxanne and me the grand tour of the Springs Valley High School gymnasium, helped me find photos used in this book, discussed some important Valley games and players, and loaned out old scorebooks. Andrea Turner at Oakland